FRANK LLOYD WRIGHT

BETWEEN PRINCIPLE AND FORM

FRANK LLOYD WRIGHT

BETWEEN PRINCIPLE AND FORM

PAUL LASEAU ■ **JAMES TICE**

VNR VAN NOSTRAND REINHOLD
New York

Copyright © 1992 by Van Nostrand Reinhold

Library of Congress Catalog Card Number 90-27775

ISBN 0-442-23478-3

Printed in the United States of America.

Van Nostrand Reinhold
115 Fifth Avenue
New York, New York 10003

Chapman and Hall
2-6 Boundary Row
London, SE1 8HN, England

Thomas Nelson Australia
102 Dodds Street
South Melbourne 3205
Victoria, Australia

Nelson Canada
1120 Birchmount Road
Scarborough, Ontario MIK 5G4, Canada

16 15 14 13 12 11 10 9 8 7 6 5 4 3

Library of Congress Cataloging-in-Publication Data

Laseau, Paul, 1937-
Tice, James, 1945-

        Frank Lloyd Wright: between principle and form / by Paul Laseau and
James Tice.

                p.   cm.
        Includes Index.

        ISBN 0-442-23478-3
        1. Wright, Frank Lloyd, 1867-1959 — Criticism and interpretation.
2. Architecture — Philosophy. I. Tice, James. Title.
NA737.W7L37 1991
720'.92—dc20   90-27775
                            CIP

Contents

Foreword

There are many ways to look at architecture, and certainly the works of Frank Lloyd Wright have been subjected to them all. It would seem, therefore, that our understanding of his architecture should be especially profound. For most of us, however, an understanding of Wright's architecture is clouded by details of his life, his clients, the times in which he worked, his own misleading rhetoric, and by an elaborate taxonomy of his stylistic inventions and their subsequent influences on later architects and architecture. This is not to say that the setting for his practice or the influence of his architecture is irrelevant or even unimportant, but, if it is the timeless and universal qualities of his architecture that we are after, its more temporal circumstances inevitably deflect our attention. Therefore, it is gratifying to see such a focused research into Wright's architecture as the one conducted here by James Tice and Paul Laseau.

Although this study is limited to the architecture of Frank Lloyd Wright, its real significance lies not in what it tells us about his works so much as what it reveals about architecture itself. By distilling and comparing Wright's buildings, and stripping away the extraneous and peripheral circumstances of their creation, we are shown universal principles involved in design of buildings, and their universality invites comparison to other buildings far removed in time and place. Through the application of a particularly incisive set of analytical tools, we are given an excellent example of a means to architectural analysis, one which may be used with equal facility to better understand any work of architecture that is rich enough to sustain a concentrated inquiry. So we begin with a focused look at the works of one architect and we discover in the process a kind of cosmology for the art of architecture.

Because this study goes beyond the immediate problem of Wright's architecture to address what are seen as the universalities it embodies, its usefulness will likely be as significant outside the study of Wright's work as within it. Most studies aimed at articulating fundamental architectural principles do so by employing a broad range of diverse examples of varied authorship selected from all of historical time, rather than by concentrating upon the works of a single architect. Indeed, several current studies, including careful works by Thiis-Evensen and by Rob Krier, do explore principles of architecture through sets of diverse examples, each example selected to illustrate a particular quality or important architectonic principle. And there were popular 19th-century works, such as those by Auguste Choisy, J.N.L. Durand, and Julien Guadet, which did the same things, each in its own way. But the work of a single architect, Frank Lloyd Wright, compared and analyzed as it has been here, provides us with a glimpse into the active process of designing, a process involving thought and experimentation developed over a long and prolific career. The book reveals that Wright's creativity, and by extension all high-level creative processes, are founded upon first principles, the result of "a patient search", to use Le Corbusier's term.

A further word ought also to be said about the graphic techniques applied here to the problem of architectural analysis. The drawings demonstrate, I believe, how visual information techniques can be as eloquent as written and spoken language in communicating complex and subtle ideas. Most literature on architecture presents us with a variety of photographic views and drawings reproduced from unrelated sources and at unrelated scales. So it is indeed refreshing when we are presented with a consistency in graphic expression, drawings created specifically to facilitate comparative evaluation and to describe succinctly the particular theoretical principle which the authors intend for us to see. It is perhaps in the role of analysis that computer graphics, as were employed here, will come of age as a useful aid to architectural publication and, consequently, to architectural understanding.

Analysis, of course, can be a dangerous thing. It dissects to understand and thereby tends to discourage a more holistic view. But if analysis is seen as only half of a quest of understanding, with the other half as its opposite, then the quest can come full circle. Taking Wright's ingenious architecture apart, then putting it back together again, provides us with insights into the range of possibilities for richness inherent in architecture everywhere.

N. Crowe

Preface

To provide a fresh look at the rich heritage of ideas that Frank Lloyd Wright contributed to the theory and practice of architecture, this book brings together our research and that of several scholars. We put special emphasis on the interaction of principle and form and on the role of formal order in architectural experience.

Most writing about Wright's architectural design suffers from preoccupation with his personality, and understanding of his design methodology is often blurred by his own writing. In contrast, this book attempts to convey an understanding of Wright's contributions through a direct analysis of his designs. This alternative view of Wright's work is undertaken in a search for its broader implications for architectural design.

Analytical illustrations are used extensively to reveal the conceptual and experiential order of the architecture, and the book is organized and written to provide easy access for readers. We emphasize a close tie between verbal and visual communication.

Excellence in architectural design, as exemplified in the designs of Wright, integrates the designer's intuitive and intellectual grasp of architecture. Too often, critical discourse sets emotion and intellect in opposition to each other. With some promotion by Wright himself, his designs are largely accepted on an emotional level that avoids the scrutiny of their intellectual roots. Students and architects need to become more aware of the sound, rational, and coherent basis of his architecture and the symbiotic relationship with its emotional, qualitative reality.

The book should be useful and appealing to students, educators, and professionals. It should also attract the general reading public, which exhibits an increasing appetite for an understanding of architecture and architects as well as a curiosity about creativity. This book presents an extensively illustrated analysis of selected works of architecture by Frank Lloyd Wright. It is intended to provide a clearer understanding of his designs as well as architecture in general.

We have attempted to provide architectural practitioners with a fresh look at the best known and least understood of American architects. We hope that students will gain an understanding of the conceptual power of Wright's work independent of its stylistic qualities and that researchers and educators will be encouraged to undertake alternative approaches to the study of the work of Wright and other architects. We also hope that due to Wright's prominence as an architect this book will promote a deeper public understanding of architecture. We see this effort as a complement to the current resurgence of interest in Frank Lloyd Wright as a person and an architect. The perspective of almost thirty years and the profusion of theoretical studies in recent years provide an opportunity to gain new insights into Wright's contributions to architectural design.

Acknowledgments

This book is the result of our association of almost twenty years during which we have shared our interests in design research and architectural theory. The three years of writing and illustrating this book have been challenging and enriching due to the complementary nature of our respective careers. In dedicating this book each of us has a number of people to thank for providing background that is essential for a book of this scope:

My interest in Wright began as a student at Cornell where my teachers, Lee Hodgedon, Werner Seligman, Colin Rowe, and Bernhard Hoesli opened my eyes to his work in the studio. Thanks to a grant from the Graham Foundation, I was able to tour the United States in 1965, which further nurtured my interest through the direct experience of his work. Over the years I have had the good fortune to share insights about Wright's architecture with colleagues and students. I have exchanged ideas about Wright's theories and work with Leonard Eaton, Charles Calvo, Narcisco Menocal, and Jeffrey Chusit who have generously offered critiques of my intuitions and have helped give form to my thoughts. I am also indebted to Ohio University, the University of Southern California, Columbia University, and the University of Oregon for providing support and a setting for my courses which either focused on Wright's architecture or included his work as a major component. The emphasis of all these classes was formal analysis founded on the premise that an understanding of principles is a primary means of understanding architectural intentions and is essential for a deep meaning of the work. I am particularly grateful to my students, whose keen visual thinking, expressed through insightful analytical drawings, acted as a direct inspiration for this book. J. T.

My appreciation of the role of architectural theory began with the innovative graduate architectural program at the State University of New York at Buffalo which was led by John Eberhard and Michael Brill. Through Forrest Wilson's example and encouragement at Ohio University, I developed an interest in writing about research and theory so as to make it useful to architectural students and practitioners. My understanding of both theory and writing has grown in large part through exchanges with a diverse group of researchers, teachers, and practitioners; I am especially indebted to David Stieglitz, Kirby Lockard, Steve Oles, Frank Ching, Rob Woodbury, Tony Costello, and Bruce Meyer. I am grateful to Ball State University and particularly to the College of Architecture and Planning for the environment and encouragement that make my research and writing possible. Finally, my thanks go to the many students who have inspired and challenged me to clarify ideas we have shared about architecture. P. L.

For the realization of this book we are grateful to Everett Smethurst, former senior editor at Van Nostrand/Reinhold, for his enthusiastic promotion of the project, and Wendy Lochner, Ken Allen, and Monika Keano of Van Nostrand for their patient support. We wish to thank Janet Parks, curator of drawings at the Avery Library, for providing access to its Frank Lloyd Wright collection, Wayne Meyer and Barbara Ballinger of the Ball State University Architectural Library for their advice and assistance and Becky Amato for her help with the text production. We are grateful to Mike Bartlein, a graduate research student at the University of Oregon, for his tireless assistance and many thoughtful drawings, and to Paul Lew, Xuan Fu, Julia Maciel, Bill Brown, Somsri Kraiwattanapong, Don Rife, and Andrew Alphonse, students at Ball State University, for their help in producing on computer an extensive array of original drawings that are included in this book.

FRANK LLOYD WRIGHT

BETWEEN PRINCIPLE AND FORM

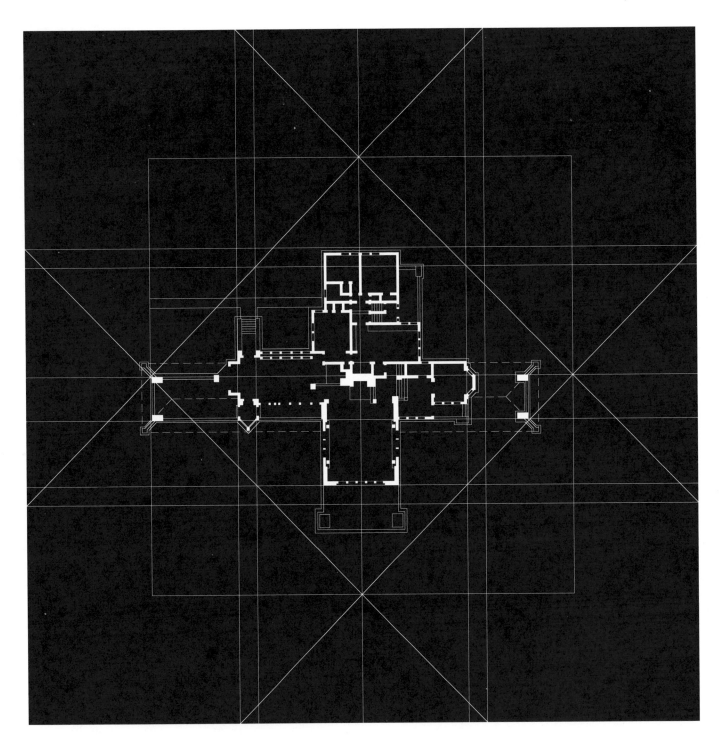

1-1 Formal analysis of the Willitts house
plan

Seeking an Understanding of Wright's Architecture   1

"Do not try to teach design. Teach principles."[1]

"Wright's output was so varied over the years that to try to define any underlying principle would be presumptuous." [2]

Frank Lloyd Wright said that architecture should be taught by its principles, yet discerning the principles underlying his diverse work has been difficult. How can education proceed if it depends on understanding principles that cannot be defined? We believe that the study of Wright's work must begin with the premise that knowledge is attainable, important to the practice of architecture, and not, in itself, the enemy of creativity and quality.

Our purpose in this book is to derive a practical understanding of Wright's architecture through observing and analyzing his buildings. We believe the cause of architecture is better served by going beyond Wrightian mythologies that may prolong the inaccessibility of his work. Focusing on the glamour of individual creativity has tended to downplay the important role of a collective body of architectural knowledge. To draw a parallel, the scientific revolution has perhaps diminished our appreciation of the traditional skills of the craftsman, but few of us would suggest abandoning modern manufacturing; although the feats of individual scientists provide high drama, the foundation of the "miracle" of science has been the collection of individual insights into a shared body of knowledge.

During his long career, Frank Lloyd Wright displayed a passion for a highly developed and personal architectural vocabulary. This world of form was not to be concerned with superficial effect, as Wright often reminded us, but was to be animated by principle. This belief suggests a profound attachment to values that were beyond question. For Wright these principles transcended the particulars of program, client, materials, and even site. He rather elusively described those truths as "democratic" and "organic." The challenge for students of his work seems to have been to reveal the underlying "democratic" and "organic" forces in a Fallingwater or a Guggenheim Museum. Consequently, the emphasis has been on the symbolic meaning of his architecture rather than on an understanding of its intrinsic formal structure.[3] The assumed split between idea and form, with the higher valuation usually given to the former, has made achieving the necessary connection between the two more difficult.

To address the important issue of the relationship between principle and form, this book introduces an alternative to a stylistic or symbolic approach to Wright's work, one focusing on the structure of form. We may posit that the world of form is not arbitrary but displays an internal logic that has the capacity to convey meaning. We believe Wright to be a supreme example of the artist who understands the principles of form and is able to imbue his creations with profound meaning precisely because of that critical mastery.

1-2 Collection of seashells

Although recognizing that any analysis of works of architecture risks losing touch with some of its integrative forces, we feel the resulting extension of our understanding justifies the effort. Creativity is enhanced by a deeper, more articulated comprehension of design that provides multiple views of architectural phenomena. The challenge is to go beyond a romantic view that stresses the individuality and isolated action of the heroic architect, a view that tends to discourage research and communication as important supports for design.

FORM AND MEANING

Perhaps the clearest and most charming explanation of the relationship between principle and form advocated by Wright is found in a transcript of his conversation with students at Taliesin.

Look carefully at these hundreds of beautiful, infinitely varied little houses [a tray of seashells]. Here you see housing on a lower level, it is true, but isn't this humble instance a marvelous manifestation of life? Now where in all this bewildering variety of form is the idea? Is there not just one idea or principle here? But where is the limitation to variety? There is none... There is no reason why our buildings and the housing of human beings, which we so stupidly perpetuate all alike as two peas in a pod, shouldn't be quite as fertile and imaginative a resource as these little shells.[4]

The higher value given to underlying cause over superficial effect is a persistent theme for Wright. Although it may have first surfaced as an indictment of academic eclecticism during his Oak Park years, it remained as a test of architectural and artistic integrity throughout his career. He admonished would-be followers to "emulate rather

than imitate." The message was simple but elusive: those who understand his principles need not worry about generating appropriate architectural forms. In a slightly different context he defined architecture as a "fine spirit" and not a collection of "objects, soon to decay." This statement focuses on the contrast between continuity and change: animating principles never change even though their physical manifestation must necessarily change to reflect the changing temporal conditions in which it is created. The connection between principle and form is reaffirmed, but the means of achieving it remain elusive. We are implored to discover universals, but we are required to remain relatively ignorant about the means of expressing them. Our studies depart from traditional analyses of Wright's work particularly in our examination of the origins of his assertions of a dichotomy between underlying principle (spirit) and superficial effect (form) and its impact on the study of his architecture. Our purpose is not to explore in depth the origins of his theories, which indeed form a tangled web, but to speak about them only insofar as they have consequences for our study of Wright's formal and spatial ideas as demonstrated by his works.

Wright's posture seems to be derived from the traditions of Platonic thought and Christian belief. Plato's description of the tangible world as the "mere shadow" of reality establishes a distinction between the ideal and material worlds and affirms the superiority of the former. The New Testament message that "the spirit is willing but the flesh is weak" echoes this opposition theme and introduces a moral imperative as well. In this case the transcendent ideal is contrasted to a transient, corruptible physical state. As adopted by Wright, Platonism and Christianity have conspired to value intangible spirit over material form. A style of criticism that focuses on this duality to describe Wright's architecture tends to avoid study of the specific intrinsic qualities of his forms and their meanings in favor of a general discussion of motivations and beliefs; it treats form as an effect rather than as a cause. Our premise is that form and principle are integral in Wright's architecture and that both are fully understandable only in light of their interactions.

APPROACHES TO WRIGHT AND HIS WORK

Following Wright's lead, past studies of his work seem to share a set of biases. Emphasis has been placed on a narrow view of principles, the architect, the chronology of his works, and his concept of "organic architecture." These approaches have relegated Wright's actual designs to a kind of shadow of some higher essence; they have not speculated upon his design methodology, perhaps on the assumption that it was ultimately too mysterious to unravel or too personal to be of any relevance. The "spirit" —a timeless, transcendent value—is thereby contrasted with the "flesh" —a transient, corruptible state. This interpretation appeals to our curiosity about Wright's colorful and sometimes tragic life and sheds light on his cultural heritage, which was profoundly influenced by the thought of Whitman, Thoreau, and Jefferson. Although this approach reveals a strong sense of Wright's motivations, it relegates the physical manifestation of his ideas to a secondary status. Architectural forms have meaning only when seen in the light of a higher theoretical order. The direct appreciation of his form, and the meaning thereby derived, is of less import. This mind-set overlooks the possibility that form may precede meaning and even shape its content. We contend that Wright developed his architectural concepts through exercises in visual form and pattern, subsequently integrating meaning with those forms. Principle may have grown out of practice, inherent in the form-generating systems that Wright had adopted.

A number of historians have wondered why so few architects have consciously emulated Wright's architecture, whereas the architectural works and theories of Mies van der Rohe, Le Corbusier, and Alvar Aalto have received broad following. Although the influence of Wright can be seen in many works of modern architecture, leading architects more frequently acknowledge the influence or inspiration of other twentieth-century masters. This condition may be partially attributable to a respect for Wright's well-known distaste for academia and its methods; some architects may believe that to follow Wright's example would be to destroy the very principles of individual creativity he stood for. However, we believe the strongest cause of the absence of an informed Wrightian following is the impact of the prevailing means of exposure to Wright, the literature. Not only has the majority of the traditional literature about Wright illuminated the man more than the work, but also it has tended to insert the personality of Wright between the reader and the work. Wright's remarks seem to spring to mind as readily as the specific images of his architecture. Some may even admire and seek to adhere to Wright's principles without recognizing the significance of their architectural consequences.

Much of the discussion of Wright's work relies heavily upon a chronological explanation that treats his forms as evolutionary, as if the buildings were fruit on a simplistic genealogical tree. However, human behavior is not necessarily analogous to biological evolution. As Geoffrey Scott demonstrated, early Renaissance architecture was not necessarily immature, high Renaissance not always refined, and architecture in the twilight of the Renaissance not predictably feeble or decadent.[5] Wright's career also defies simple explanations or the application of ready-made patterns. Who could have predicted the sudden appearance of the fully developed Prairie House at the turn of the century? What were the chances of Wright's masterpiece, Fallingwater, appearing when the architect was close to seventy years old?

There is a tendency to seek a dogmatic interpretation of Wright and his work. Words such as *organic* become so much a part of the vocabulary that we may cease to wonder if they are truly descriptive and, if so, descriptive of precisely what. Over time these words may have become more like mantras than illuminating vocabulary. Rather than building a bridge of understanding between us and the architecture, they appear as a form of "newspeak."

In 1939 Wright stressed the "organic" or "natural" role of his theoretical basis for design by stating, "organic architecture is a natural architecture, the architecture of nature, for nature." Not "cherishing any preconceived form... exalting the simple laws of common sense... independence from all imposition from without..." and "resolute independence of any academic aesthetic."[6]

Organic (or intrinsic) architecture is the free architecture of ideal democracy.[7]

The word organic refers to entity; perhaps integral or intrinsic would therefore be a better word to use. As originally used in architecture, organic means part-to-whole-as whole-is-to-part. So entity as integral is what is really meant by the word organic.[8]

I am trying to present that architecture here in words as architecture "organic": the living expression of living human spirit.[9]

Even as expressed by Wright, the term *organic* has so many definitions that it becomes the equivalent of "good" architecture. In an attempt to be all-encompassing, organic sacrifices specific definition. We find in these statements by Wright a search for the dimensions of architecture and not the absolutes that will assure success.

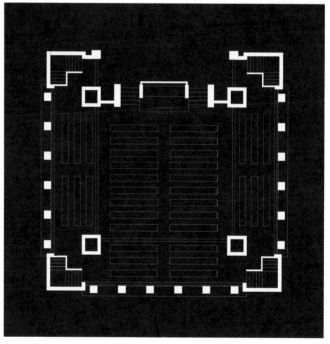

1-3 Frank Lloyd Wright portrait
1-4 Unity Temple, central worship hall

Formal Analysis as an Approach to Wright's Architecture

We undertake a formal analysis of Wright's architecture with the belief that neither academicism nor self-reliance is the hero or the villain; they are interdependent and as good or bad as the uses to which we put them. The fruit of academicism is theory. Theory becomes tyranny when it degenerates into unquestioned dogma of the type that Wright detested. However, theory can also be used as a powerful force for growth and understanding if it is seen as principle, a path to ideas, rather than as a solution that dismisses further question and exploration.

The loose association of the themes of cause and effect, idea and matter, and change and continuity seems to have formed the basis for Wright's architectural theories. The sophistication of Wright's architecture evidently extends well beyond his ability to elucidate its theoretical constructs with the written or spoken word. Therefore, we look directly to his work for a broader understanding of what and how he designed. His work is our primary text.

The emphasis of our approach is on the interaction of form and principle: the architecture rather than the architect, typological rather than chronological relationships, and the search for design knowledge rather than dogmas. The most helpful analytical approach to the study of architecture seems to us to emphasize the relationship between form and principle rather than their distinctions. The division of the spiritual or transcendental from the concrete or tangible is a theme that has dominated the development of philosophical thought. In recent times philosophical stances such as phenomenology and systems theory have challenged these traditions by asserting the importance of the interaction or communication between distinct categories of experience, including that between the spiritual and physical worlds. In this view

principles and form are seen as a dynamic, interactive unity rather than as separate mechanisms in a cause-and-effect relationship. Just as designed form responds to underlying principles, it is also the prime means by which the existence of these principles is revealed.

If in Wright's terms principles are the servants of function (the principles of growth and the form of the seashell are responses to internal and external needs or functions), then his conclusion that "form and function are one" must imply that form and principle are one as well. Wright claimed a kinship between his concept of organic architecture and the Taoist philosophy.

It was Lao-Tze...who...first declared that the reality of the building consisted not in the four walls but inhered in the space within, the space to be lived in.[10]

Taoism also calls for a balance between the world of spirit and the world of substance, an interdependence rather than the dominance of one over the other.

Formal analysis also has roots in the tradition of artistic criticism that employs observation of the artifact rather than the intentions of the artist as the basis of its search for understanding.[11] This tradition, which holds that the purpose of criticism is insight, starts with the observation of artifacts followed by formal analysis. Following this method, buildings are treated as found objects whose special qualities we wish to explore.

Typology Formal analysis of architecture treats form much as early biologists such as Darwin treated animals and plants, first describing their forms and then categorizing them according to the formal distinctions. D'Arcy Thompson, a twentieth-century biologist, undertook a comparative analysis of the forms of a broad range of natural forms.[12] Typical of his approach, his descriptions of seashells went beyond Wright's obser-

vations of a typology of seashells to describe the geometric variables of angles of spiral, envelopment, and retardation. His descriptions take us beyond a general wonder at natural variety to a more precise understanding of the formal variables involved that enabled speculation about how and why that variety is achieved. We approach the typological study of Wright's work with similar objectives.

The study of architectural form types accepts observable phenomena and, at its best, avoids dogmatic simplifications for the sake of making a point. The typology diagram comparing the plan compositions of several of Wright's buildings provides an understanding of some of the variables that he employed in search of variety and individuality. Through typology we can often see beyond the particular unique forms of buildings such as the David Wright and Lloyd Lewis houses to the formal understanding of underlying principles of design.

Search In the spirit of research, formal analysis is focused on the pursuit of questions rather than the packaging of answers. It welcomes complexity and the aberration instead of ignoring them. In the hands of the researcher, typology is a framework for understanding and communicating; in the hands of the designer, typology can be the framework for invention. French cuisine provides an excellent model. The initial description and structure of the French meal has led to the development of subtypes of everything from appetizers to desserts, distinguishing hundreds of wines, and inventing more than four hundred types of goat cheese. Typological categorization was not the conclusion of French cuisine but the doorway to limitless invention.

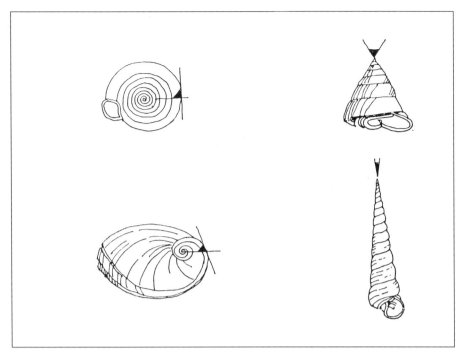

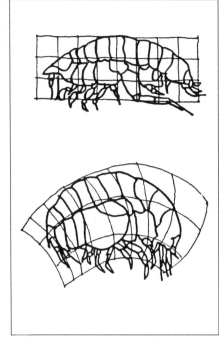

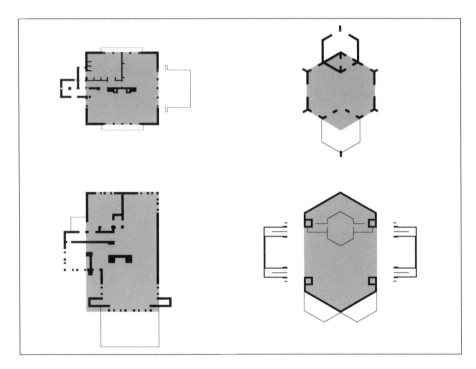

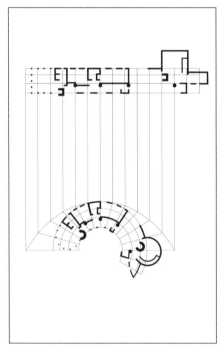

1-5 Comparison of seashell types and transformations
from D'Arcy Thompson

1-7 Comparison of F.L. Wright building plans and transformation

1-6 Grid transformation showing
relationship between crustacean types;
from D'Arcy Thompson

1-8 Grid transformation showing
relationship between circular and
in-line Usonian house plans

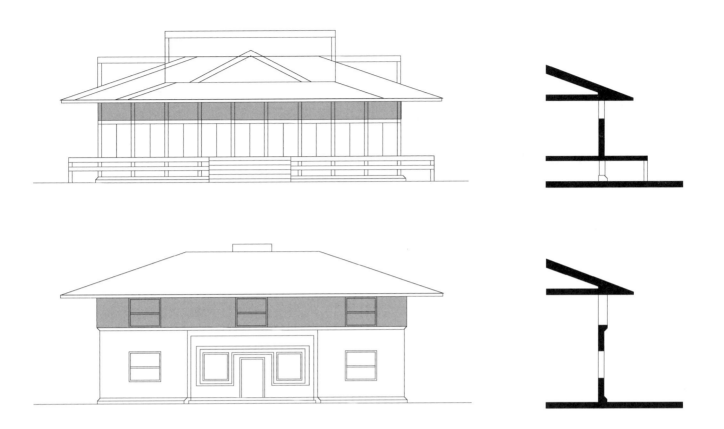

1-9 Comparative elevations of the Ho-o-den Shrine at the Columbian Exposition and the Winslow house

1-10 Wall profiles of the Ho-o-den Shrine and the Winslow house

The Typological Approach

The principal form of research employed in the preparation of this book is typological analysis. Insofar as they are involved with problem solving, architectural or other types of design are attempts to create a fit between need, context, and form where such a fit is lacking[13]. In the process of design, architects experiment, through drawings, with several variations of form to arrive at a fit with need and context. The study of types is pursued to provide designers with an understanding of the scope and nature of the variations in form evidenced in built architecture and to provide a framework for further exploration. The study of typology attempts to distinguish between the inherent, consistent characteristics of forms and those that are superficial or circumstantial.[14]

The basic underlying method of typological studies is comparison. These comparisons can range from the simplest verbal or graphic descriptions to geometrical, topographical, or mathematical descriptions of increasing complexity. The process involves observation and speculation throughout, often affecting the direction in which the typological study will proceed.

The basic objective of the study of form is insight. Even the simplest of techniques, graphic description, can reveal important insights. To demonstrate this assertion, let us consider the Winslow House, whose three-part vertical composition can be considered to be derived from the Japanese Pavilion at the 1893 Chicago World's Fair. At first view, the middle horizontal window band would seem to imitate the horizontal void between the roof and the exterior screens of the Japanese Pavilion. However, drawing (graphically describing) the profile of the exterior of the Winslow house reveals that the window

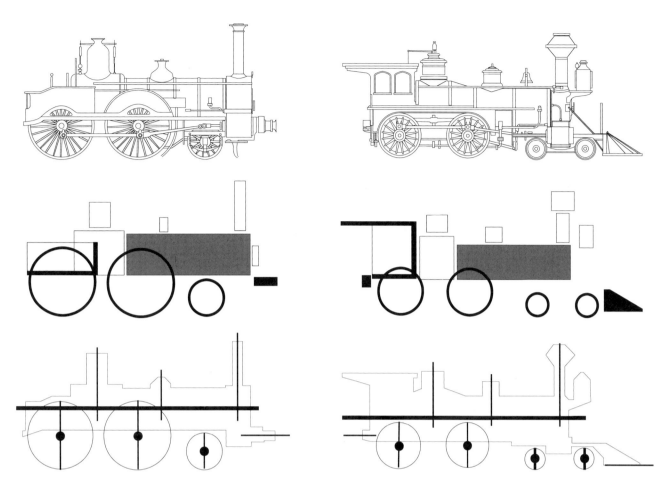

1-11 Comparative analysis of nineteenth century British and American railway engines

band protrudes rather than recedes from the face of the lower wall. Closer inspection indicates that the dark sections between the windows are relief-sculpted friezes that were probably originally a light color to help reveal their patterns. The attempt at graphic description has led to new insights and questions. Was the three-part vertical organization of the facade initially inspired by classical precedent, only to be transformed later by an emerging perception inspired by an exotic, nonclassical source?

Careful comparative graphic description can also uncover or sharpen perceptions about a range of familiar forms. Consider the study of railway engines. The typological study begins with comparable, representative views of the engines. For purposes of facilitating comparisons, some variables—color, level of detail, and scale—are held constant. In subsequent steps, composition of elements and proportions are graphically emphasized. At each of these steps, attention is drawn to parallel features of the two engines, and insights are provided into the contexts within which the engines were designed.

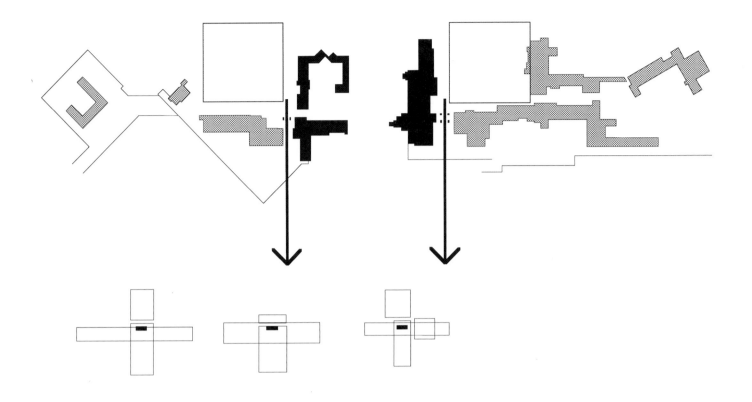

1-12 Comparative plan diagrams of
Taliesin West and Taliesin East
1-13 Cruciform plan diagrams of three Prarie houses

IMPLICATIONS

Assembling Wright's work for comparative analysis has enhanced our understanding of it. The complete array of Wright's architecture overwhelms us by its quantity, diversity, and quality. Confronted with this awe-inspiring production of one man, we are tempted simply to admire his genius. Both the whole body of his work and the unique, nonrepeating examples seem to defy analysis.

Yet if we subject a complete set of his architectural work to even a cursory examination, we can find some striking similarities. Some family resemblances are well known, such as the cruciform plan of the Prairie years. Others are more subtle and require a bit of detective work. Taliesins East and West, upon closer scrutiny, exhibit similar plans and identical planning strategies, although one is a mirrored image of the other, making them appear to be quite different on paper. The formal characteristics these examples hold in common establish groupings that define a type. Obviously, we have no absolute measure by which to determine type in this manner, for it is a matter of interpretation rather than mathematical precision. Upon sustained investigation, however, plan composition and patterns emerge with rather startling clarity to provide a taxonomy of his work.

These observed phenomena provide a basis for further investigation and speculation about the meaning of his work. In some cases plan groupings consist of buildings separated in time and place (for example, the Larkin Building and Guggenheim Museum) and do not necessarily share a common program in the narrow sense of that word. In other examples buildings that appear superficially dissimilar in external expression have similar plans (such as the Freeman House and Fallingwater). The comparative analysis of these juxtapositions provokes questions about Wright's architectural ideas and his creative methods. The intention then is to speculate upon the nature and meaning of these groupings. The fruits of this exercise constitute the substance of our exploration.

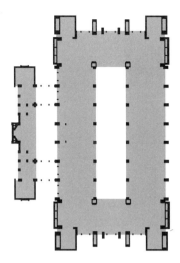

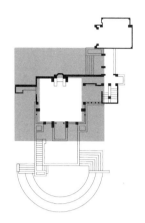

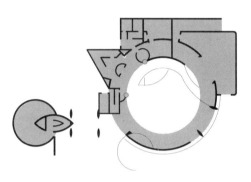

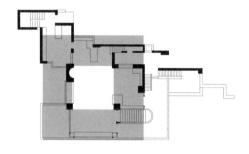

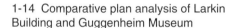

1-14 Comparative plan analysis of Larkin Building and Guggenheim Museum

1-15 Comparative analysis of Freeman house and Fallingwater

Two objects that at first seem dissimilar, as in the previous case, may share upon closer examination a deeper, less obvious relationship. Through formal analysis we can discover transformations, formal changes from one state to another. This ability to see connections between apparently dissimilar phenomena is one of the key traits of creative insight. Wright's work demonstrates a proclivity for transformational rather than radical change, which demonstrates his allegiance to the type; ultimately his work unfolds as variations on a theme. Outlining these themes can provide a richer set of perceptions about his architecture. The implications of formal analysis for the architectural designer relate directly to the usual pattern of design study. The design process normally includes the consideration of many variations of form, only a few of which will reside in the final design. This sifting would be a loss if the discarded ideas were never put to use, but master architects such as Wright tend to carry a residue of these ideas forward to other projects over many years, often in the form of themes that they might pursue for the rest of their careers.

ORGANIZATION OF THE BOOK

Our approach will be to focus on Wright's architectural form as a basis for our speculations. His work, not the man, will serve as our primary source. In a sense, we intend to interpret his architecture as a landscape containing a marvelous collection of "found objects" whose meaning can unfold from a direct analysis of those objects and their context. By replacing chronology as the chief critical framework with the notion of typology, we hope to provide a fresh look at his work through a set of studied comparative analyses, the focus of which is the meaning and structure of form.

In our research we have relied heavily on the study of plan drawings. Wright often drew a distinction between the architectural plan and its expression. For him the one precedes the other and is the generator of the architectural idea. The plan is the "seed," the origin of the structure that could, in the hands of a master, develop into a three-dimensional reality. Wright seems to have been saying that the chain of creation is from idea to plan to expression. Although all three are inextricably intertwined, clearly Wright places a higher value on the plan form than on its possible picturesque expression and a higher value on the plan than on perspective, which he claimed could be proof of, but could never nurture, the plan. This interpretation of cause and effect suggests a high valuation of form

insofar as it concerns the plan and not merely the superficial aspects of style. If this notion of plan form as underlying cause is valid, then a formal analysis based on plan is an examination of a central aspect of his architecture.

Through this method we hope to provide insights into Wright's work and pose questions that will contribute to a better understanding of his architecture. Using the visual logic of the thinking eye, we separate his buildings into their constituent elements. In the process, unifying ideas and principles emerge with astonishing clarity. The nature of the analytical enterprise is to be sustained and rigorous but also speculative and intuitive; in short, the method of study is scientific. The process recognizes the capacity of building to embody cultural ideals through sign and symbol, whose reality is no less crucial than the substance of brick and stone. This work sees architecture as something more than a lockstep technological process or an inconsequential exercise in scenography. Instead, it reveals the unfolding complexity and richness of architecture and can serve as a challenge and inspiration for the future.

We see this book as one alternative way of understanding Wright's work. It is an attempt to add other dimensions to the explanation of Wright's architecture. We also hope that our approach will suggest alternative ways of seeking an understanding of architecture in general.

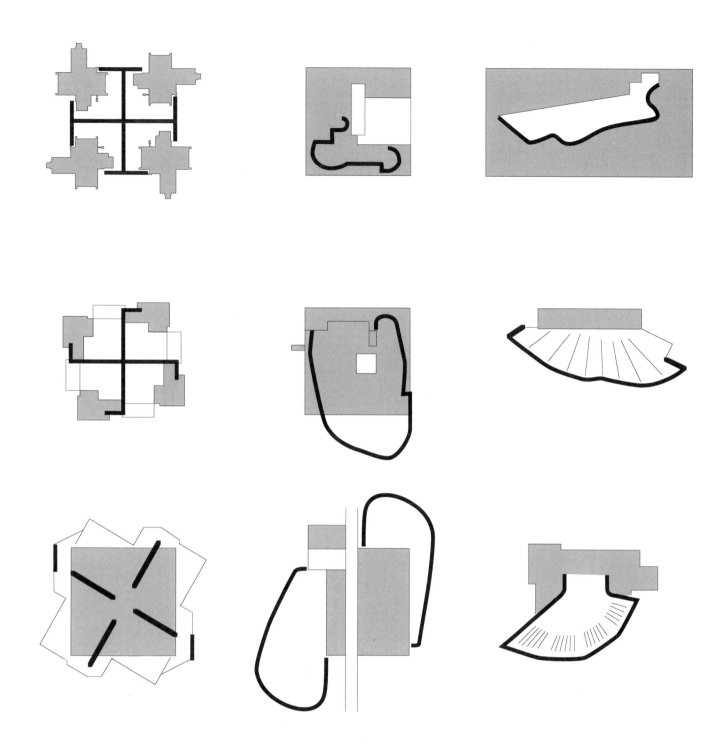

1-16 Comparative display of typical plan themes by
Frank Lloyd Wright, Le Corbusier, and Alvar Aalto

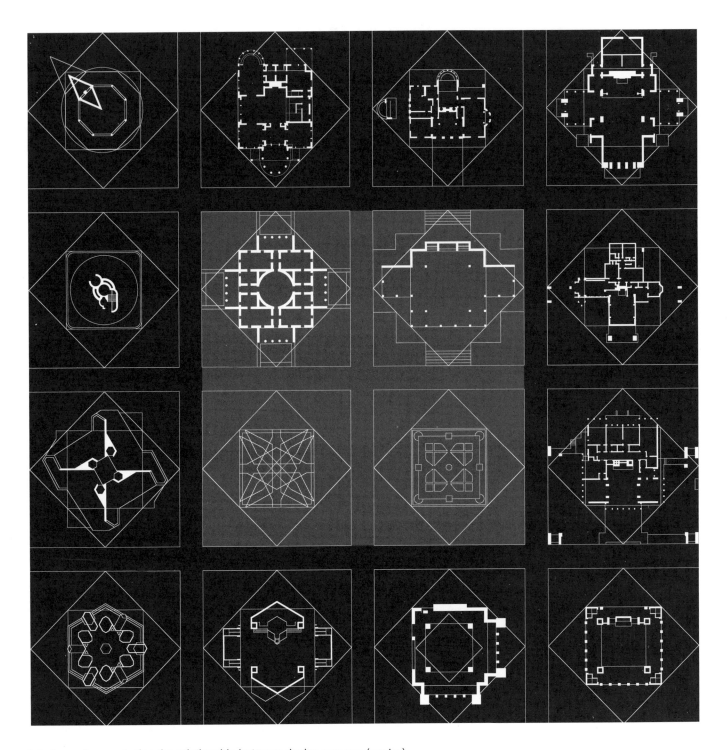

2-1 Array demonstrating the relationship between design sources (center)
and Wright's building plans (perimeter):

Romeo and Juliet Windmill, Blossom house, Winslow house, Coonley playhouse,
Johnson Research Tower, Villa Rotunda, Ho-o-den Shrine, Willits house,
St. Mark's Tower, Islamic tile pattern, Louis Sullivan tile design, Cheney house,
Steel Cathedral, Pfeiffer Chapel, Hillside Home School, Unity Temple

The Sources
and Influences

Had he designed and built nothing else after 1924, Frank Lloyd Wright would still rank as one of the greatest architects in history.

Alone and unaided, he had created organic architecture, that profound and yet simple concept that buildings must develop naturally out of their environment, reflect their central purpose, and use building materials best suited to those two factors.[1] (italics ours)

Like Howard Roark in Ayn Rand's *The Fountainhead*, one of Wright's principal virtues, as portrayed by many writers including himself, is absolute originality achieved in complete isolation from others.[2] Not surprisingly, this perception of Wright's work as completely original has tended to make more difficult relating it to other important architecture. We believe his work will become more accessible by emphasizing that Wright and other architects have shared common values and the means for expressing them. Our task is to remove barriers that would separate his work from the culture from which it springs.

Although Wright may have portrayed himself as a heroic loner at odds with the world around him, he was not a cultural hermit, isolated from that world and its history. Wright was a keen observer of the natural and cultural landscapes of his time. He was a disciplined artist who had an extraordinary ability to understand both the goals of architectural design and the means by which they could be addressed. His unique synthesis of architectural design is built upon sources to which he was

exposed and that he actively sought out. His intuition was developed as a critical response to his environment, not in spite of it.

We reject the notion that Wright's unique talents flowed exclusively from a mysterious, unfathomable inner core of his being. He certainly had a unique sensitivity to environment and peoples' needs and a special interest in finding a fresh and appropriate architecture. However, we believe his talents were wrought from a long struggle with the questions of design. To categorize Wright as a natural genius and to hitch that genius to independence from the world fails to give him credit for the determination and hard work by which he achieved his successes. In a rare, unguarded moment, Wright spoke of his design of the community hall for Unity Temple:

To vex the architect, this minor element becomes a major problem. How many schemes have I thrown away because some minor feature would not come true to form. Thirty-four studies were necessary to arrive at this as it is now seen.[3]

These are not the observations of a spontaneous genius!

As Vincent Scully has pointed out:

Wright's work was directly and indirectly influenced by all the architectures mentioned above [Cretan, Japanese, Mayan, Greek, and Roman], but, unlike LeCorbusier with his own influences, Wright consistently refused to acknowledge the fact. His refusal to do so was partly based upon his own tragic need,

2-2 Froebel table grid with typical two-dimensional design variations

2-3 Froebel block constructions

which was to keep the romantic myth of the artist as isolated creator and superman alive in himself.[4]

The recognition of diverse influences in Wright's work should in no way diminish the significance of his architecture or our admiration of his accomplishments. These same sources were available to other architects who lacked his capacity to assimilate them into a personal vision through concentrated labor. An understanding of these influences helps us to better appreciate Wright's virtuosity in building upon them an architecture of extraordinary depth and variety.

RESEARCH INTO THE STRUCTURE OF FORM

Froebel Games

Wright wrote about the profound influence of his early childhood experiences with Froebel games:

For several years I sat at the little kindergarten tabletop ruled by lines about four inches apart each way making four-inch squares; and, among other things, played upon these "unit-lines"with the square (cube), the circle (sphere) and the triangle (tetrahedron or tripod)—these were smooth maple-wood blocks. Scarlet cardboard triangle (60 degrees–30 degrees) two inches on the short

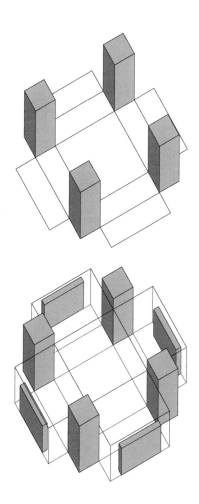

2-4 Froebel blocks as generators
of architectural form

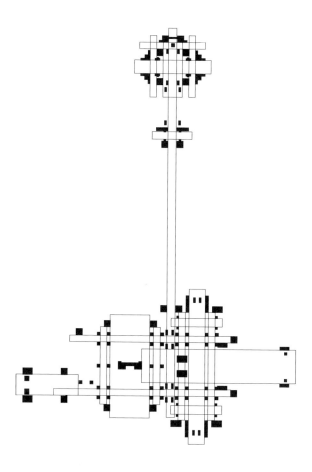

2-5 Froebel weaving pattern exhibited in
an abstraction of the Martin house plan

side, and one side white, were smooth triangular sections with which to come by pattern—design—by my own imagination.

Eventually I was to construct designs in other mediums. But the smooth cardboard triangles and maple-wood blocks were most important. All are in my fingers to this day.[5]

The Froebel games were one of the inventions of Friedrich Froebel that grew out of his development of a revolutionary method of kindergarten education in which play was designed to expose children to concepts underlying nature and human endeavor. This experience was important to Wright for it helped instill (1) an awareness of geometrical systems and their design properties(2) sensitivity to three-dimensional solids and voids, (3) an appreciation of the compositional possibilities of diverse elements, (4) fascination with the "weaving" of complex two-dimensional patterns and three-dimensional spatial volumes, (5) ability to visualize the three-dimensional implications of patterns inscribed on the two-dimensional surface of his drawing board.

The influence of the volumetric qualities of the Froebel games on Wright's architecture is readily discernible, particularly in the Unity Temple, the Larkin Building, and other designs of that era. Moreover, the Froebel influence extends even deeper, beyond design output, to his processes of design and visualization. The underlying organizational patterns, such as the "unit system" or grid, seem to be forever present, regardless of the geometry or composition employed in a particular design. Looking to Wright's building plans, we can also see the influence of the Froebel weaving exercises in the complex integration of space and structure as a unified fabric. These methods of design helped inform every scale of his work right down to furniture, tile, and textile designs.

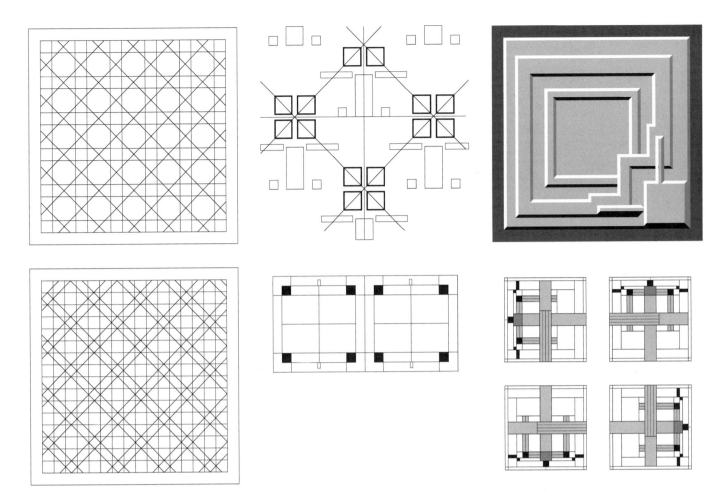

2-6 Two Tartan grids that are, according to Owen Jones, the basis for all Moorish ornamental design

2-7 Ornamental designs by Wright exhibiting Owen Jones' principles

Owen Jones

The Grammar of Ornament, by Owen Jones, first published in 1865, provided a rich source of visual ideas for Wright. In commenting upon this nineteenth-century standard text, Wright said, "I ...traced the multi-fold design, I traced evenings and Sunday mornings until the packet of one hundred sheets was gone and I needed exercise to straighten up from this application."[6] As we will discuss in more detail later, Wright seems to have been particularly fascinated with two pattern systems about which Jones had written:

The number of patterns that can be produced by these two systems would appear to be infinite; and it will be seen… that the variety may be still further increased by the mode of coloring the ground or the surface lines. Any one of these patterns which we have engraved might be made to change its aspect, by bringing into prominence different chains or other general masses.[7]

Jones had revealed a different way to look at ornament: as ordering system rather than caprice, as process rather than mere artifact. The discovery that an infinite variety of shapes and patterns might be developed within the context of a single underlying order must have

reinforced Wright's belief that underlying principles could generate a wealth of specific expressions. Throughout his architecture the influence of 45, 30 and 60 degree angles can be detected either as an ordering datum or as a defining edge, producing a variety of plan forms including octagons, diamonds, and lozenges. It is also probable that the potential for generating different scaled shapes within these pattern systems inspired Wright's adoption of the "tartan" planning grid in much of his work, especially during his Oak Park years.

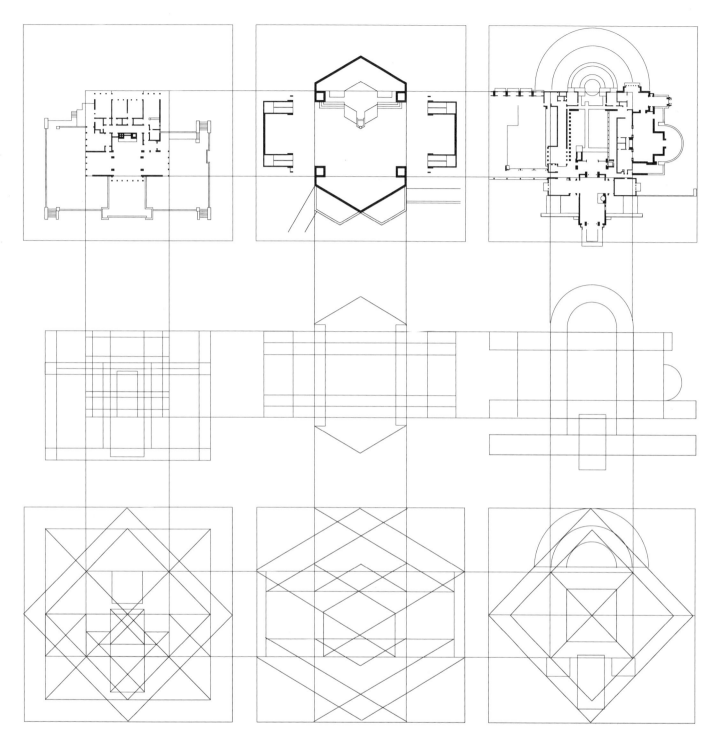

2-8 Comparative plan analysis showing underlying grid
in the Cheney house, Pfeiffer Chapel, and Hollyhock house

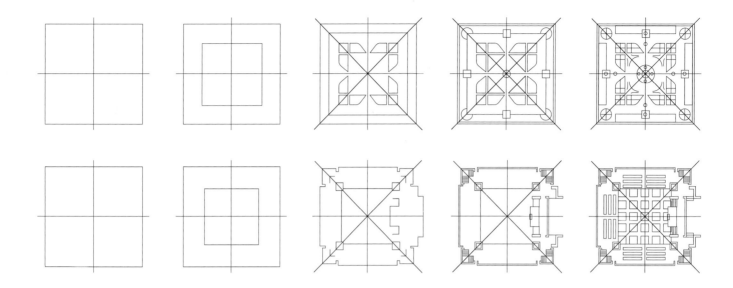

2-9 Comparative diagrams showing Louis Sullivan's design process for an ornamental tile and a hypothetical development of the plan for Unity Temple suggested by Thomas Beeby

Louis Sullivan

Of all the influences that Louis Sullivan had on Wright, one seems particularly prominent. Sullivan's explorations of ornamental schemes demonstrated the capacity for invention inherent in basic geometries. Exercises such as his "development of a blank block through a series of mechanical manipulations" support the validity of approaching design by way of explorations of form. At first, this may seem in conflict with his often-quoted dictum that "form follows function," but Sullivan never intended the narrow interpretation of this statement, namely, that form is to be largely derived from building program. "Func-

tion" for Sullivan could include physical, social, psychological, and even political needs as well as the programmatic needs.

As Thomas Beeby convincingly illustrated in *The Grammar of Ornament/Ornament as Grammar*, "The process of design in Wright's Unity Temple and in Sullivan's development of ornament are clearly analogous."[8] Wright continued to use similar techniques to develop his designs at all levels of scale while maintaining their aesthetic unity. We are convinced that Wright conceived and developed his architecture principally through the exploration of form and that he employed geometrically based planning systems that provided the

necessary flexibility to accommodate and enrich the "functions" of his buildings. The quality of his architecture is derived from the depth and complexity of his understanding of both form and function.

WESTERN ARCHITECTURAL INFLUENCES

H. H. Richardson: Space and Composition

The architecture of Henry Hobson Richardson was another important source for Wright. Richardson typically captured his flowing, volumetric forms within an informal, Romanesque vocabulary; his plans were derived from an understanding of residential English

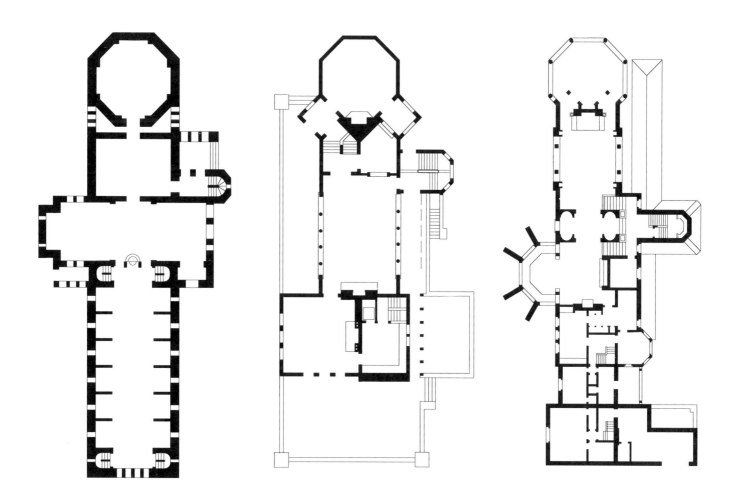

2-10 Comparative plans of the Winn Library by H. H. Richardson and the McAfee and Husser houses

planning on the one hand and formal French academic planning for large public buildings on the other. He anticipated the freedom with which Wright was later to juxtapose abstract symmetries and natural, organic rhythms. In the Winn Library at Woburn, Richardson explored the interpenetration of interior volumes and their expression in the exterior shell of the building. The juxtaposition of vertical and horizontal volumes was employed in a more compact way in Richardson's Glessner House in Chicago. The Winn Library and this house seem clearly to have influenced Wright's designs for the McAfee and Husser houses. Although subsequent Wright buildings were not so obviously derived from Richardson's design, properties such as extended space, asymmetrical three-dimensional composition, local axes, strong horizontal elevations punctuated by repetitive vertical elements, and a strong articulation of volume profoundly influenced Wright's architecture throughout his career.

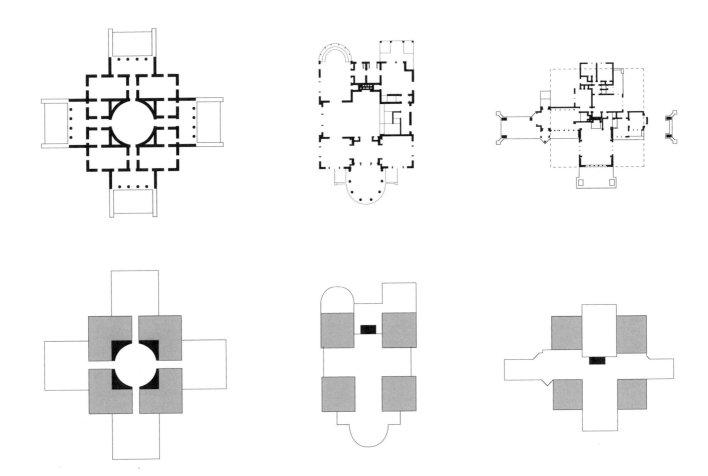

2-11 Comparative plan analysis of Villa Rotunda by Palladio and the Blossom and Willitts houses showing differing emphasis on square and cruciform themes

The Academic Tradition

Our review of the plan compositions of Wright's buildings reveals convincing evidence that Wright was aware of and influenced by examples of architecture developed within the classical Beaux Arts tradition. Although he decisively rejected the classical vocabulary of the "orders" after 1893, he assimilated classical composition.

Viollet-le-Duc's prescription for the architectural design process needs little alteration to serve as a description of Wright's approach to design:

The true architect does not allow his mind to be preoccupied by these monuments of the past. His plan settled upon, his elevations are a part and expression of them; he sees how he should construct them, and the dominating idea of the plan becomes the principal feature of the facades.[9]

Referring to his own building plans, Wright wrote that

No man ever built a building worthy of the name architecture who fashioned it in a perspective sketch to his taste and then fudged the plan to suit…. A perspective may be proof but it is no nurture.[10]

Henry-Russell Hitchcock and other scholars have cited the Blossom House as Colonial Palladian revival. We can see in this rather conventional design the early stirrings of Wright's trademark spatial extensions, interlocking spaces, and asymmetrical composition. Equally important, we can also trace the impact of the Palladian footprint in many of Wright's subsequent building designs, such as the Willitts House. As we will see in detail later, the centering, stabilizing power of the square became a dominant feature of his plans. Classical, academic traditions also are present in the plan for Midway Gardens, which is as accomplished a work as any of the Prix de Rome projects of the period. [11]

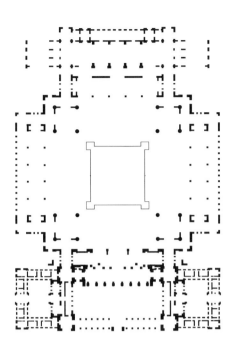

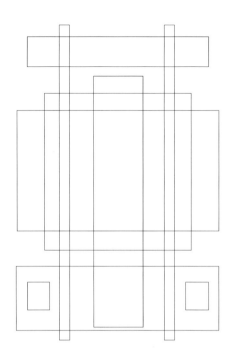

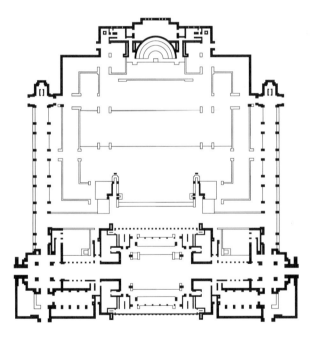

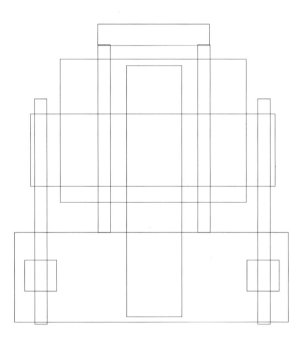

2-12 Plan and diagram of the Prix de Rome
Project by Tony Garnier

2-13 Plan and diagram of Midway Gardens

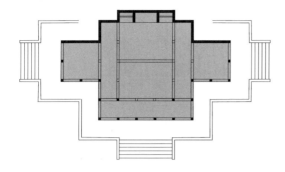

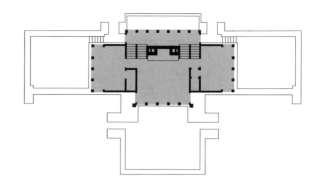

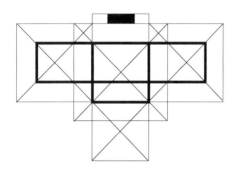

2-14 Plan analysis of Ho-o-den Shrine

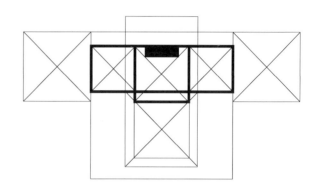

2-15 Plan analysis of the Hardy house

NON-WESTERN TRADITIONS

In *Frank Lloyd Wright to 1910*, Grant Manson provides us with ample reason to believe that early in his career Wright was fully aware of Japanese architecture. Manson specifically points out that while working on Louis Sullivan's Transportation Building at the Chicago Columbian Exposition of 1893, Wright became aware of the Ho-o-den Shrine at the imperial Japanese exhibit. While recognizing possible influences of form, including the large overhang roofs and the dissolution of the exterior walls, we are particularly struck by the compositional features of the plan of the shrine in light of the house plans Wright developed over the following decades. First is the cruciform aspect of the plan, with the central hall forming one axis and the two tea rooms forming the cross axis. Second is the repeated use of the square as a basis for the proportions of the spaces. Finally the anchoring element, the shrine altar, is preceded by a central space that reaches out to the exterior. Many of Wright's building designs suggest that he sustained an interest in oriental architecture throughout his life. Without asserting any direct connection, we can observe a similarity of intention between other Wright works and Japanese buildings. His tower projects such as St. Mark's could refer to the Japanese pagoda by serving similarly as a vertical marker in the landscape. Wright's Fallingwater house of 1937 and the Katsura Palace in Kyoto provide another instance for comparison. In these latter examples, abstract form is juxtaposed with natural form to achieve a dynamic balance in the Taoist tradition of yin and yang.

2-16 Site plan comparison of the Katsura Palace and Fallingwater

2-17 Entry sequence comparison of the Kompira temple and Martin house

Other important Eastern influences can be found in the consistent way in which Wright emphasizes the extension of space from building interior to exterior and how he organizes the entry sequence to his houses. The skillful way in which he redirects movement, slows the pace, and prepares one for the climactic experience of arrival at the central space of the house is reminiscent of both the Japanese garden and the entry sequence to a Japanese temple.

As intriguing as we may find the life of Wright as lone creator, we are more fascinated by the way Wright skillfully incorporated and synthesized concepts of form from a variety of sources. These special processes of incorporation and synthesis are what we seek to understand in looking more closely at his work.

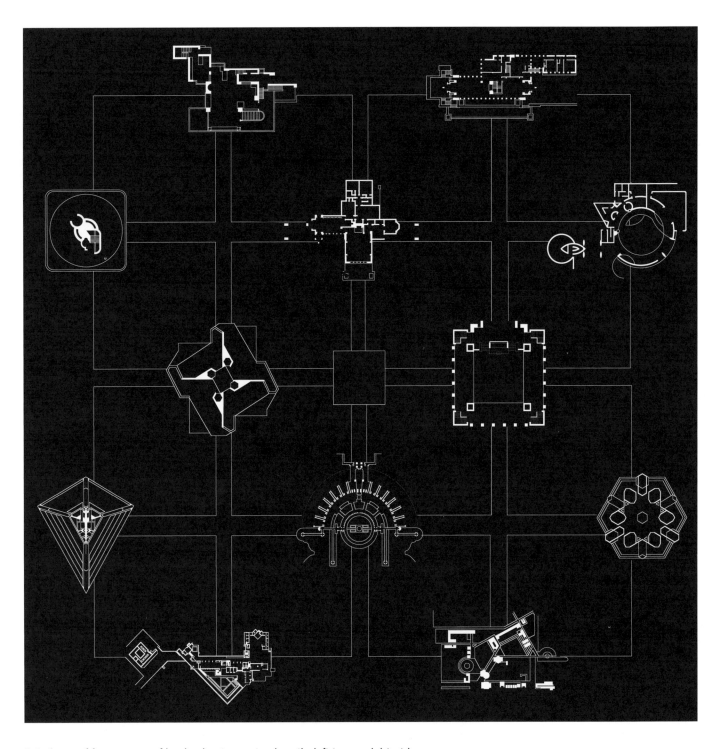

3-1 Array of four groups of basic plan types: top-hearth, left-tower, right-atrium, bottom-site patterns

Fallingwater, Robie house,
Johnson Research Tower, Willitts house, Guggenheim Museum
St. Mark's Tower, Unity Temple,
Mile-High Skyscraper, Wolf Lake Park, Steel Cathedral
Taliesin West, Florida Southern Campus

Wright's Work Typologically Considered

During Frank Lloyd Wright's long career he produced more than four hundred completed works and at least as many unexecuted projects.[1] Almost all of his works have an irreducible essence that distinguishes them as unique, non-repeatable works of art. Indeed the rich array of Wright's architecture seems to defy categories. It embodies a bias toward approaching each work as a unique, free-standing manifestation—albeit an expression of a constant principle.

Yet this approach has limits. It tends to emphasize what is formally unique over what is formally shared. By establishing the specificity of each work over the general body of work, it tends to deny the evolutionary nature of Wright's architecture and makes difficult connecting work that may spring from the same source but superficially appears to be different. This view encourages us to believe that Wright arrived at form in a purely empirical, inductive way and changed his approach with each new problem. Seeing each work in isolation obscures another aspect of his methodology, that suggests a strong deductive approach to form, emanating from favored form types, a repertoire Wright referred to as his "portfolio." The unique objet d'art approach generally avoids plan analysis and instead concentrates on details and stylistic expression through a study of evocative photographs and perspective drawings. This tendency overlooks what could be the strongest form determinant in Frank Lloyd Wright's architecture: the plan.

Our contention is that formal groups do exist and that they are inextricably woven into the very essence of Wright's approach to architecture. Strong evidence suggests that even in his early work Wright began his architectural investigations in light of known form types that evolved from his own radical exploration of form and his knowledge of architectural and artistic precedents.

However, these form types guided and did not dictate the final solution. Although the designs may have remained within defined boundaries, they were also in a constant state of transformation. Given Wright's probable working method, we think that establishing a typology based on the formal structure of his work is a particularly appropriate critical device. In this manner comparisons can be made and the unique and shared characteristics of each design can be better understood. This method of critical inquiry attempts to analyze architectural form systematically and then derive meaning from an understanding of that form in both its architectural and cultural contexts. The development of definitions, a taxonomy of types, formal comparisons, and attention to transformations (structured change) constitute the backbone of this methodology.

A TYPOLOGICAL OVERVIEW

To guide us through our studies of Wright's work, we have assembled a map of the territory we plan to cover in the form of the accompanying typological chart of his building plans. Obviously, each architectural plan cannot convey the complete three-dimensional complexity of an entire building. Yet, if the plan is the generator of architectural form, as Wright claims,[2] then perhaps the plan can represent the essence of each building in abstract terms. The chart displays over one hundred plans of both executed and projected buildings, beginning with Wright's Oak Park home in 1889 and ending with the Marin County Civic Center designed two years before his death in 1959. We believe the buildings chosen include Wright's most accomplished efforts and therefore are representative of his highest creative powers. The matrix follows a simple organization with a horizontal axis representing time and a vertical axis representing formal spatial groupings that we have termed hearth, atrium, and tower.

27

FRANK LLOYD WRIGHT ARCHITECTURAL PLANS A TYPOLOGICAL CHART

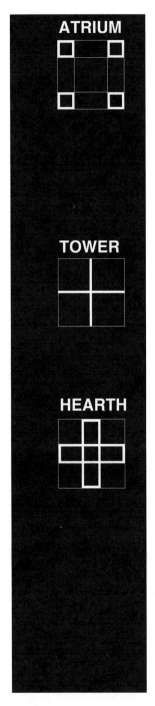

ATRIUM

The Atrium embodies an idea of community and shared purpose. It is typically an introverted, centralized space filled with light from above.

The Atrium type is divided into two sub-tracks: the upper consisting of plans based on a simple geometric shape such as a square or circle; the lower including plans based on a cruciform with a more horizontal extension of space and light.

TOWER

The Tower embodies an idea of place making within the larger natural or urban landscape typically marking the horizon with a vertical axis and outwardly oriented to the four compass points. Tower programs include housing, offices and laboratories. It shares the hearth type's central core, extending it vertically and anchoring to the earth with a structural "tap root"

HEARTH

The Hearth embodies an idea of domestic life with its central core rooted to the earth. It also embodies the idea of personal identity and freedom with its outward extensions into the landscape.

The Hearth type is divided into four sub-tracks: the upper consisting of compacted plans, the second including cruciform "L" and "T" plans, the third tending toward a pinwheel plan, and the lower track consisting of plans with a linear composition.

1889

Site Pattern: urban and civic themes

Wolf Lake 1895

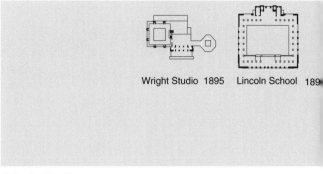

Wright Studio 1895   Lincoln School 189

Collective Dwelling: courtyard type

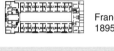

Francisco Terrace 1895

Romeo and Juliet 1896

Collective Dwelling: cross-wall type

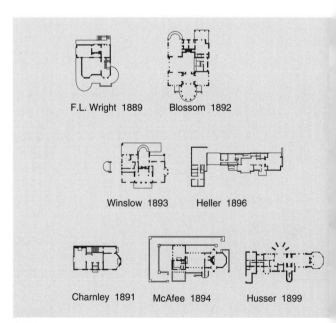

F.L. Wright 1889   Blossom 1892

Winslow 1893   Heller 1896

Charnley 1891   McAfee 1894   Husser 1899

Site Pattern: domestic themes

1889

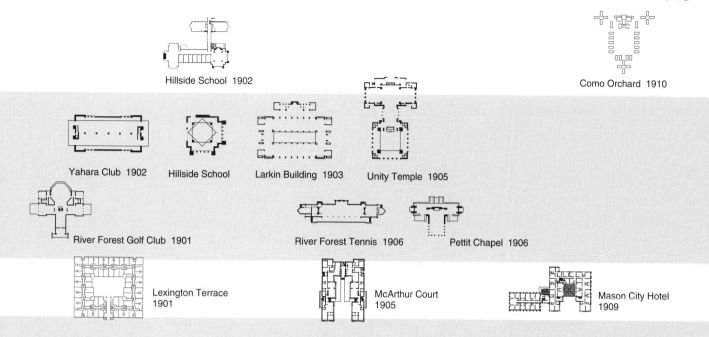

Hillside School 1902

Como Orchard 1910

Yahara Club 1902   Hillside School   Larkin Building 1903   Unity Temple 1905

River Forest Golf Club 1901   River Forest Tennis 1906   Pettit Chapel 1906

Lexington Terrace 1901   McArthur Court 1905   Mason City Hotel 1909

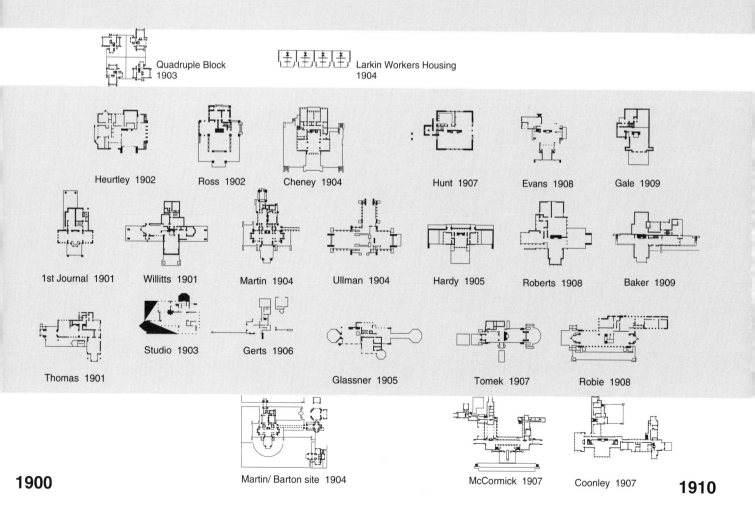

Quadruple Block 1903   Larkin Workers Housing 1904

Heurtley 1902   Ross 1902   Cheney 1904   Hunt 1907   Evans 1908   Gale 1909

1st Journal 1901   Willitts 1901   Martin 1904   Ullman 1904   Hardy 1905   Roberts 1908   Baker 1909

Studio 1903   Gerts 1906   Glassner 1905   Tomek 1907   Robie 1908

Thomas 1901

Martin/ Barton site 1904   McCormick 1907   Coonley 1907

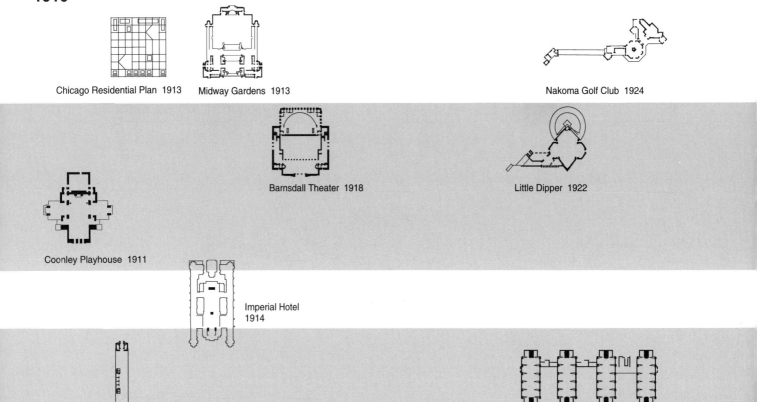

Chicago Residential Plan 1913   Midway Gardens 1913

Nakoma Golf Club 1924

Barnsdall Theater 1918

Little Dipper 1922

Coonley Playhouse 1911

Imperial Hotel 1914

San Franciso Press 1912

National Life Insurance 1924

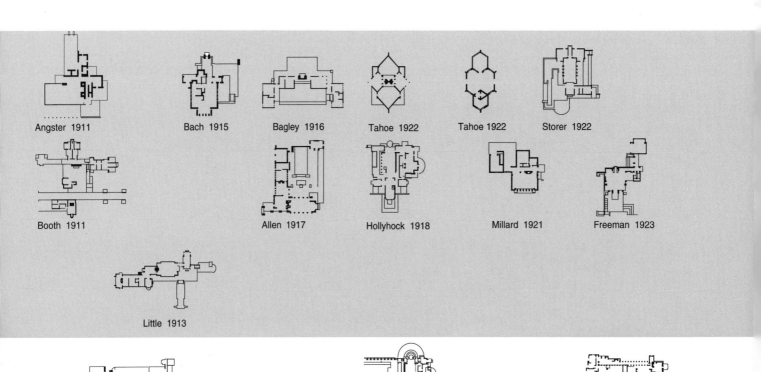

Angster 1911   Bach 1915   Bagley 1916   Tahoe 1922   Tahoe 1922   Storer 1922

Booth 1911   Allen 1917   Hollyhock 1918   Millard 1921   Freeman 1923

Little 1913

1910   Taliesin East 1911

Hollyhock Site 1918

Ennis 1924

Broadacre City 1934

Florida Southern Campus 1938

Auto Objective 1924

Steel Cathedral 1925

Gas Station 1928

Johnson Wax 1936

Florida Southern Chapel 1938

San Marcos 1928

Noble Apartments 1929

Capitol Journal 1931

St. Mark's Tower 1929

Chicago Towers 1930

Crystal Heights 1939

Chicago Tower Group 1930

Cudney 1927

Young 1928

Schwartz

Fallingwater 1935

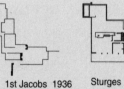
1st Jacobs 1936   Sturges 1939

Rosenbaum 1939

1st Willey 1932

2nd Willey 1934   Hanna 1936

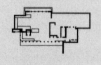
Goetsch 1939

Ocotillo 1928

Lloyd Jones 1929   Mesa 1931

Johnson 1937

Taliesin West 1938

Monona Terrace 1935-55

Pittsburgh Point 1947

Madison Unitarian 1949

Marin County Civic Center 1957

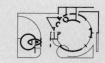

Kansas City Church 1940   Guggenheim Museum 1943   Morris Gift Shop 1948

Beth Shalom 1954   Greek Orthodox 1956

Rogers Lacy site 1946

Price Tower site 1952

Johnson Tower 1944   Rogers Lacy Hotel 1946

Price Tower 1952

Mile High 1956-9

Suntop Homes 1940

Pittsfield Housing 1942

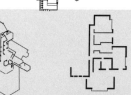
Wall 1941   Brauner 1943

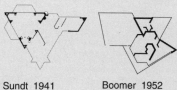
Sundt 1941   Boomer 1952

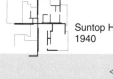
Jester 1940

Pope 1940

Pew 1940

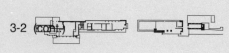
3-2   Lloyd Lewis 1940   Pauson 1940

2nd Jacobs 1942

David Wright 1950

Price 1954

The straightforward organization of the typology chart is intended to act as a basic structure for a more detailed understanding of the formal-spatial groupings and their subgroups. Collectively the plans provide an opportunity to compare Wright's work over time and to cross reference this chronological development with themes that deal with other aspects of his architecture. Considerations of program, composition, and spatial and formal properties are just some of the issues that emerge with their own substructure. The interrelationship of all these factors creates a shifting pattern that reveals the complexity of Wright's work. For example, if we focus on the formal structure of the plan, then the chart can reveal the affinity between two of Wright's buildings separated by more than half a century, namely, his studio of 1895 and the Guggenheim Museum, completed in 1959. Similarly, a closer inspection based on plan alone uncovers some remarkable similarities between the Martin House of 1904 and the contemporary Larkin Building that suggest an overlap in formal devices independent of program. Ultimately the process by which we view—and construct—such a chart is an interpretive one and open to multiple readings. Nevertheless, the exercise will prove itself effective if such observations can assist speculations about his architectural ideas and his method of creation. In this chapter we provide an overview of Wright's architecture by first defining his major spatial archetypes—hearth, atrium, and tower—and then introducing several subthemes that contribute to the variety of Wright's formal types.

THREE ARCHETYPES: THE HEARTH, THE ATRIUM AND THE TOWER

The bulk of Wright's architecture can be seen as derivative of three archetypes based on consistent relationships between program and form types: residential/hearth, communal/atrium, and landmark/tower.

Mircea Eliade has observed in *The Sacred & the Profane* that religious man feels compelled to create a sacred place by making it observable.[3] This sacred place may be accomplished by marking a point, bounding a space, or erecting a vertical *axis mundi*. We might see Wright's architecture as an affirmation of such primordial place making. The Prairie House, which embodies perfectly the notion of the hearth type, centers its energy around the most sacred place in the house, namely, the hearth, which fixes it in space and anchors the house to the earth. The atrium or bounded space of Unity Temple shuts out the profane world from an inner court of tranquil harmony filled with light from above. The tower, whether it be the diminutive Romeo and Juliet Windmill or the gigantic Mile-high Skyscraper, marks a place on the horizon and with its vertical axis establishes a connection between heaven and earth. All three provide orientation within the physical and psychic landscape of man.

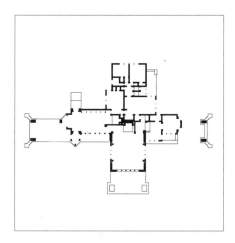
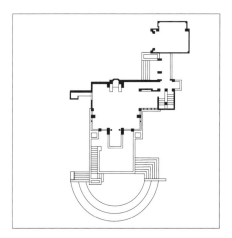
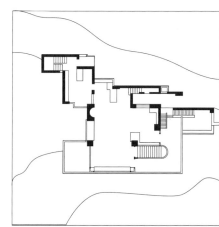
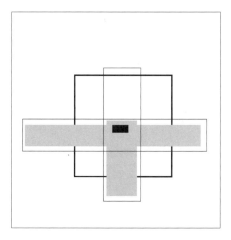
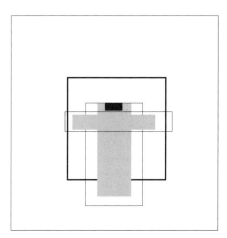
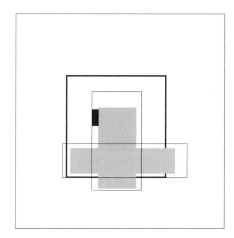

3-3 Examples of the Hearth type: Willitts, Freeman, and Fallingwater houses

The Hearth Type

The first and largest form type, the hearth, includes virtually all of Wright's residential designs. The ideal realization of the hearth type can be represented by a square and an overlapping, extended cruciform emanating from and anchored to its center by a solid. Although the hearth type is reserved for the everyday needs of the individual and the family, its dimensions include the ritualized aspects of family life symbolized by the hearth itself. It is private in nature and extraurban in its setting. Its compositional characteristics are usually asymmetrical, qualified by important areas of local symmetry that tend to stabilize the otherwise informal composition. It exhibits a dual tendency toward horizontal, centrifugal extension in the

form of porches and terraces and a pyramidal buildup at its core, which is invariably anchored by the hearth. The actual fireplace core is offset from the exact geometric center to allow for the space directly in front of the fireplace (usually an inglenook or alcove) to occupy the most sacred place. The connection to the earth and the ground plane is its most important site attribute.

The idealized cruciform type makes its first significant appearance in the Willitts House of 1902. Its geometric and spatial themes continued to inspire Wright throughout his career. Once the type had been articulated, the strategy seemed to be to transform the ideal rather than dispensing with it altogether. The succession of plans based on the cruciform is a virtuoso display of

variations on a theme paralleled by few architects in history. The hearth type and the cruciform, as well as many variations, are discussed in chapters 4 and 5.

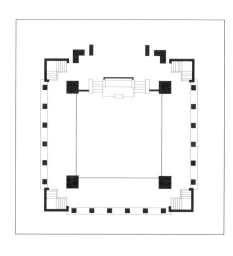
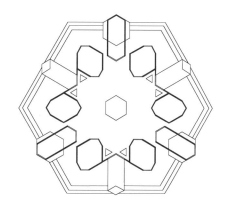
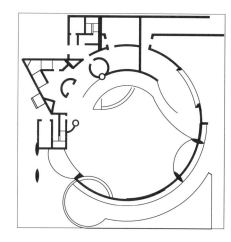
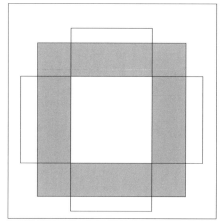
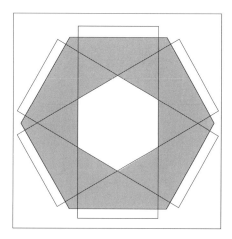
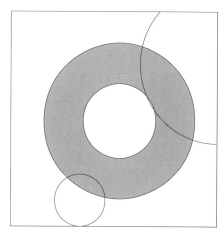

3-4 Examples of the Atrium type: Unity Temple, Steel Cathedral, Guggenheim Museum

The Atrium Type

The atrium form type is defined by buildings in which a sense of collectivity was extracted from (or imposed upon) the program. They include projects dedicated to public communal gatherings, whether religious or secular in nature. This category can be described by a square inscribed by a cruciform yielding, in its ideal form, a classic nine-square organization with a void at the center. The atrium type further embodies a notion of compacted centrality rather than peripheral extension.

The idealization of the atrium type becomes apparent in the Unity Temple of 1906, although the Larkin Building of two years earlier is very similar in parti. It is public in nature and urban in its setting. Its compositional characteristics are centralized and symmetrical about one or more axes. The type usually—but not always—divides into a binuclear parti of major and minor volumes with entry in between. The type exhibits a tendency toward inward centripetal movement that culminates in a major central volume with an upward orientation to a skylight or clerestory. Unlike the hearth type, the sacred space is to be found at its center, which is always left open, by implication, to the sky. The atrium type is discussed at more length in chapter 6.

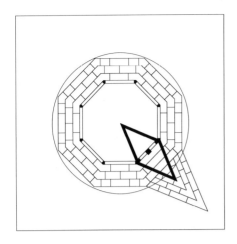
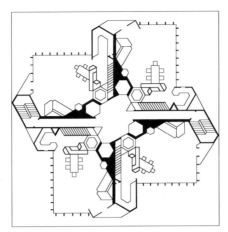
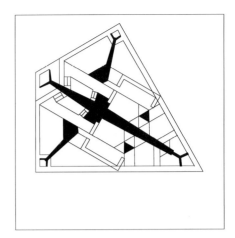
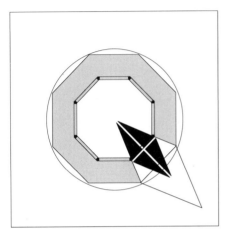
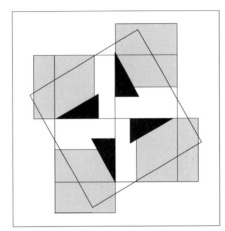
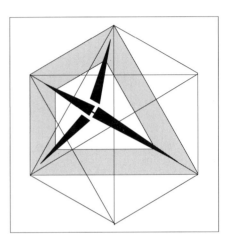

3-5 Examples of the Tower type: Romeo and Juliet Windmill, St. Mark's Tower, Mile-High Skyscraper

The Tower Type

The third grouping, the tower, includes housing and a variety of other programs. The high-rise structure acts as a landmark within the natural or urban landscape, similar to the campanile in the medieval city or perhaps a Japanese pagoda.

Compared to the two previous examples, this type presents a different but related notion of form and space. Its abstraction yields a square and an inscribed cross, resulting in a quadrant or four-square organization with vertical extension implied. This grouping is usually expressed as the high-rise structure, which acts as an orienting point on the horizon.

The tower or spire form has a more ambivalent programmatic meaning than the other two types, but it is often used for dwelling units stacked and isolated from one another about a central core. The office space finds an application here, as well as the laboratory. In the last analysis, however, the "purpose" of the tower may be its role as symbol or orientation for the surrounding landscape rather than its response to a specific program. The tower is both public and private, its public aspect contrasting with a private prospect. Its composition is centralized; it is stabilized both compositionally and structurally by its central mast, which subdivides each floor into quadrants in its residential

applications. In these instances, it further acquires a pinwheel composition that has a disorienting effect. The outward spin appears to dematerialize the edges into the atmosphere. The vertical extension of its spirelike massing contrasts to the rhythmic enclosures at its sides, which project like ribs. If the hearth type is earthbound, following the horizon, then the tower type is clearly skybound, in opposition to the horizon. The tower type and its variations are discussed in chapter 7.

3-6 Examples of site plans: Pittsburgh Civic Center, Rogers-Lacy Hotel, Hillside Home School

When confronted by large-scale projects and the development of housing, Wright often created hybrids of the three principal archetypes, always in such a way that the primary type and its meaning were left intact. Wright explored the combination of his form types to address the issues of site planning and urban design in projects such as the East and West Taliesins and Broadacre City and to address the issues of collective form in multiple housing (including the hotel).

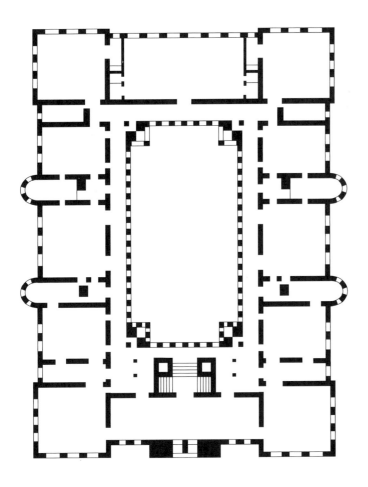

3-7 Plan of the Allegheny Courthouse, by H.H. Richardson

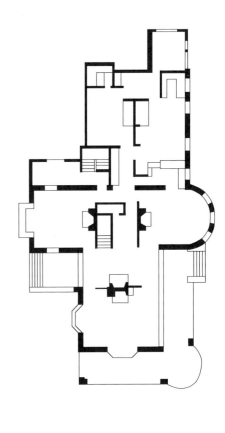

3-8 Coolidge house, by Howard Walker

FORMAL AND PROGRAMMATIC THEMES

Although much of the variety of Wright's architecture can be traced to his specific responses to the peculiarities of building sites or programs, variations are also the result of his continuing exploration of several themes.

Formal and Informal

Norris Kelly Smith has pointed out an important link between generic program and formal-geometric type in Wright's work from 1892 to 1909:

At one extreme we find a formal and geometrical mode of relatedness which the architect associates with the city and with institutional order, with stability and with the submission of parts to a clearly defined whole; and at the other, a casual and irregular mode which connotes personal freedom and the repudiation of institutional conformity. While his public buildings all lie at the formal end of the scale, his private homes are distributed from one end of the scale to the other, with respect to the whole design and to the ordering of individual rooms and lesser details.[4]

The pattern of public-formal, private-informal is not unlike that demonstrated in the work of Wright's nineteenth-century predecessors. The origins of this approach derive from the notion of decorum that required a building's demeanor to be appropriately suited for its intended use. As Colin Rowe has pointed out in his discussion of nineteenth-century criticism, *composition*

was a value associated with the academic establishment. It resulted in symmetrical, axially planned buildings, usually in a classical mode, light in color, and refined in texture. In contrast, *character* was a term that grew out of a romantic notion of building. Formally it translated into a freer, picturesque arrangement of darker values and rustic finishes that celebrated rather than denied the nature of materials.[5] H. H. Richardson, whom Wright greatly admired, generally conformed to this formula, as his public and private buildings prove, although his rugged use of materials and picturesque composition tended to invade the public sphere as well as the private.

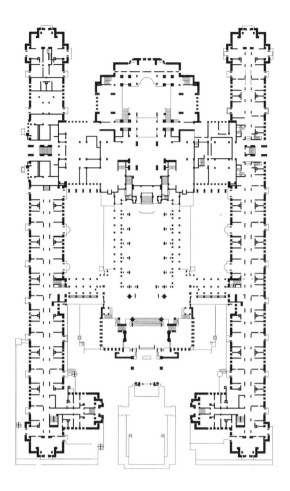

3-9 Plan of the Imperial Hotel

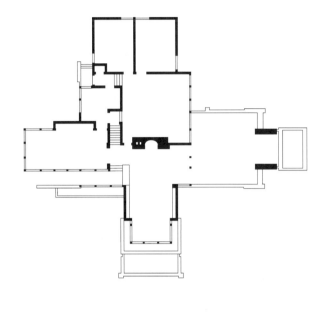

3-10 Plan of the Isabel Roberts house

In a like manner, Wright's work operates between these two poles of formality and informality. We can easily demonstrate that this principle guides his work to a large extent. For example, the Imperial Hotel exhibits the formal values of "composition;" the Coonley House might be said to demonstrate the informal virtues of "character." The reasons for this polarity seem to be that the public world requires an order and hierarchy that would be oppressive or inappropriate in the more intimate milieu of the individual and the family.

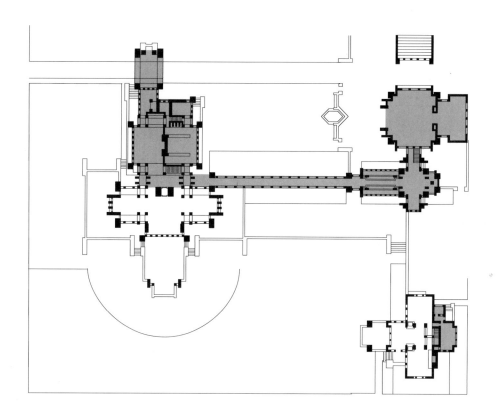

3-11 Site plan of the Martin/Barton houses
showing symmetrical living zones

SYMMETRY AND ASYMMETRY

Wright employs two basic strategies to
create a dynamic but balanced plan
organization. The first is to create an
overall asymmetry that is stabilized by
one or more local symmetries. The
Martin House is an example of this
principle. Wright carefully chose a
hierarchically significant space for his
compositional "stabilizer," which is
typically the living-dining areas but
frequently includes bedroom suites at
terminal projections. Wright tends to
dispense with axial symmetry in his late
houses, but in his nondomestic work it
makes a regular and even exaggerated
appearance. Given Wright's polemical
position against composition and the
academy, his debt to its principles of
axial planning and symmetrical design is
astonishing.

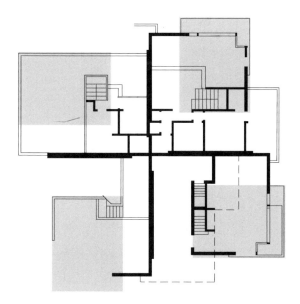

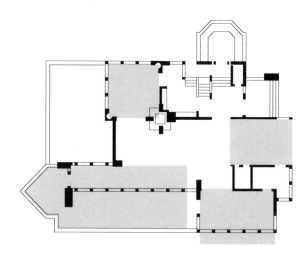

3-12 Plan of Suntop Homes showing rotational symmetry

3-13 Plan of F.L. Wright Studio house showing inflected rotational symmetry

Another means of creating a dynamic relationship among plan elements is to employ rotational symmetry, frequently producing a pinwheel effect. Wright seems to have found this dynamic shift particularly appealing, judging from his early architectural and ornamental designs. As Thomas Beeby has pointed out, the lessons of composition gleaned from Owen Jones's *Grammar of Ornament* could have been the source of inspiration for this compositional strategy. The pinwheel occurs in pure form in the Quadruple Block project of 1900 and the Suntop Homes of 1939 and in a modified form accommodates site or programmatic requirements into a more subtle arrangement. His studio house project of 1903 and the Walter Gerts House of three years later are beautiful examples of the latter.

Wright did not openly acknowledge his debt to academic planning, even though he mastered its principles as early as 1893. He mentioned composition only in disparaging terms.[6] When Wright employed biaxial symmetry in his compositions, his presentation of the plan is frequently quartered or halved (see, for example, the published plans of Unity Temple), ostensibly to show more floors in a single drawing. However, It also has the effect of disguising the biaxial symmetry of the composition. Wright may have chosen this graphic device to downplay his dependence on formal academic composition. Yet the academic planning principles of major and minor axes, carefully devised proportional systems, and a developed sense of hierarchy are clearly evident in his work.

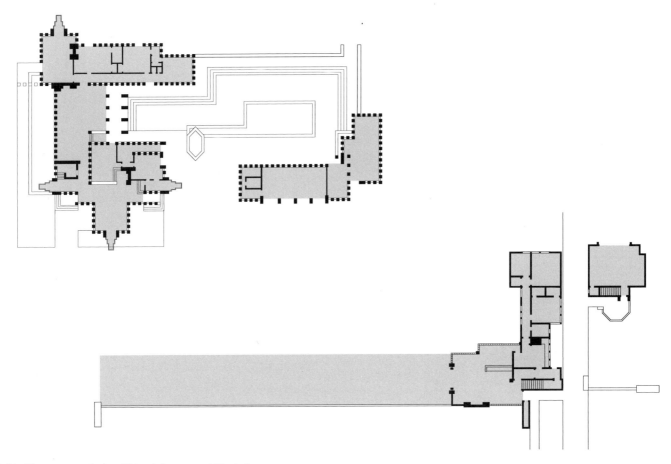

3-14 Plan comparison of Lloyd Jones and Gerts houses
showing embracing and extending site strategies

EMBRACING AND EXTENDING

Some of Wright's buildings are distinctive for the way they embrace the
landscape in a manner similar to Italian
or French country estates. Buildings
such as the Midway Gardens, the
Coonley House, and the Lloyd Jones
House claim and stabilize a portion of
the landscape. In contrast, buildings
such as the Marin County Civic Center
and the Martin and Barton houses act
more like a series of epicenters with
extended linkages.

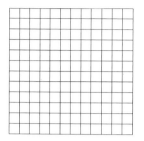 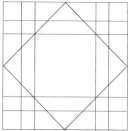 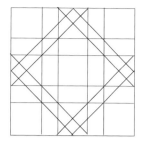 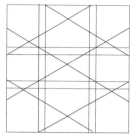 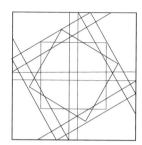

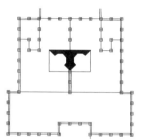 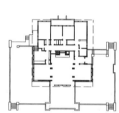  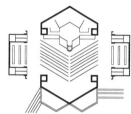 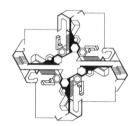

3-15 Comparison of organizing grids:

Square- Gerts summer cottage;
Tartan-Cheney house;
Overlap and shifted at 45 degree-Taliesin West;
Overlap and shifted at 30 and 60 degrees with Tartan-Pfeiffer Chapel;
Overlap and shifted at 45, 30, and 60 degrees with tartan- St. Mark's Tower

The Unit System

Besides his treatment of various forms of symmetry, Wright used the grid or "unit system," as he preferred to call it. This simple device provided a structure to unify the parts into a larger whole. The reasons for Wright's fascination with this ordering device may stem from his exposure to the "unit line" system of Froebel blocks. According to Wright, his early Froebel experience gave him an aesthetic appreciation of simple primary shapes such as the square, circle, and triangle. These shapes form the basic triad of "units" for his designs with a tendency for the stricter limitations of the square being replaced by the diamond, triangle, and circle in his later work.

Interestingly, the Froebel unit module was four inches on a side, and Wright's favorite planning module was four feet, with four 12-inch and three 16-inch subdivisions possible. Throughout his career he was preoccupied with this module. For example, his textile block system adhered to the sixteen-inch unit measurement, and his Usonian homes were usually planned on a four-foot module. These measurements had the virtue of conforming to the American construction system of four-foot and sixteen-inch wood and masonry units.

The relative simplicity or complexity of the grid could vary as the occasion warranted. By overlapping or shifting grids, new relationships could be achieved. As the discussion of Owen Jones has shown, the alternation of narrow and wide patterned grids (the tartan plaid) could sort out structure and movement and otherwise qualify and enrich the neutrality of the square grid. The rotated grid could increase the complexity of the geometry as in the thirty-and sixty-degree shifts in the St. Mark's Tower project of 1929 and the forty-five-degree shifts in Taliesin West a few years later. The geometric virtuosity Wright exhibits in this particular mode is nothing short of awe-inspiring.

Wright's early preference for oblique views, in both plan and section, and his penchant for the octagon and diamond demonstrate a deep, abiding affinity for the diagonal. As Neil Levine has pointed out, the virtual oblique becomes a literal oblique in his later work with a plethora of hexagonal designs initiated by the Hanna House of 1939.[7]

TRANSFORMATION STRATEGIES: STRUCTURED CHANGE

True to his philosophy, Wright did not settle for mere imitation of the ornamental design heritage from Owen Jones and Louis Sullivan. In these systems of ornamental design he saw strategies for structured change that could be applied to architectural forms at every scale, from furnishings to an entire building site. These strategies include form repetition, shifting, rotation, and scaling.

Finally we return to the central questions raised at the beginning of this book. Is seeking further definition of the underlying principles of Wright's output presumptuous? Does great artistic work defy analysis? The insights scholars developed into the complexity and variety of the music of Bach and Mozart give us hope that a similar understanding can be developed for the architecture of Frank Lloyd Wright. Our enthusiasm for seeking such an understanding is fueled by the observation that study of the art of Bach and Mozart has enhanced rather than diminished our appreciation of their music while in no way obscuring its beauty. We hope that through the discussions in the remainder of this book we can share the bases of our enthusiasm.

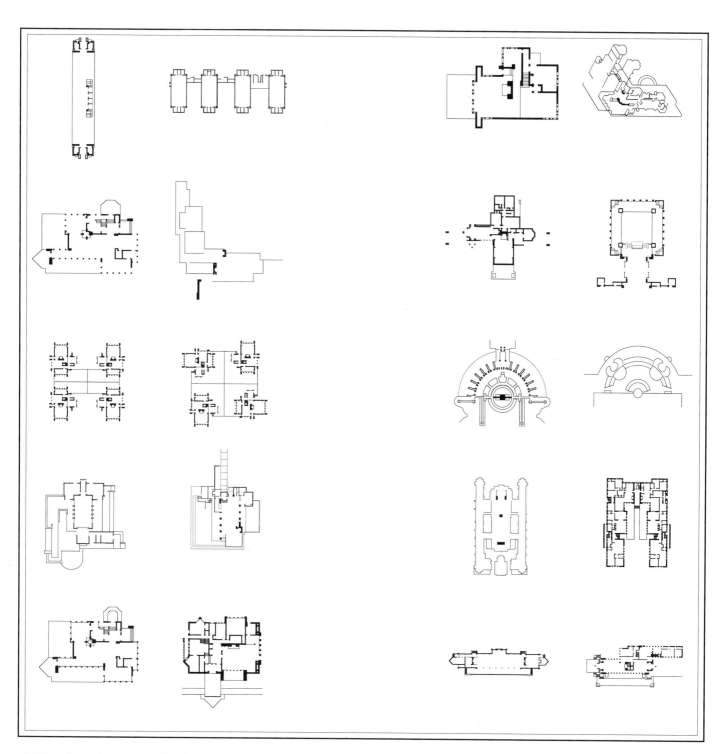

3-16   Operations generating form transformation:

Repetition - San Francisco Press Building to National Life Insurance Building; Reflection- Studio house to Jacobs house; Rotation- Quadruple Block Housing, version one to version two; Asymmetric Distortion- Storer house to Life house; Contraction- Studio house to Heurtly house

Oblique Distortion- Gale house to Hanna house; Spatial inversion- Willitts house to Unity Temple; Figure-Ground reversal- Wolf Lake Park to Monona Civic Center; Subtraction- Imperial Hotel to McArthur Apartment Building; Addition- River Forest Tennis Club to Robie house

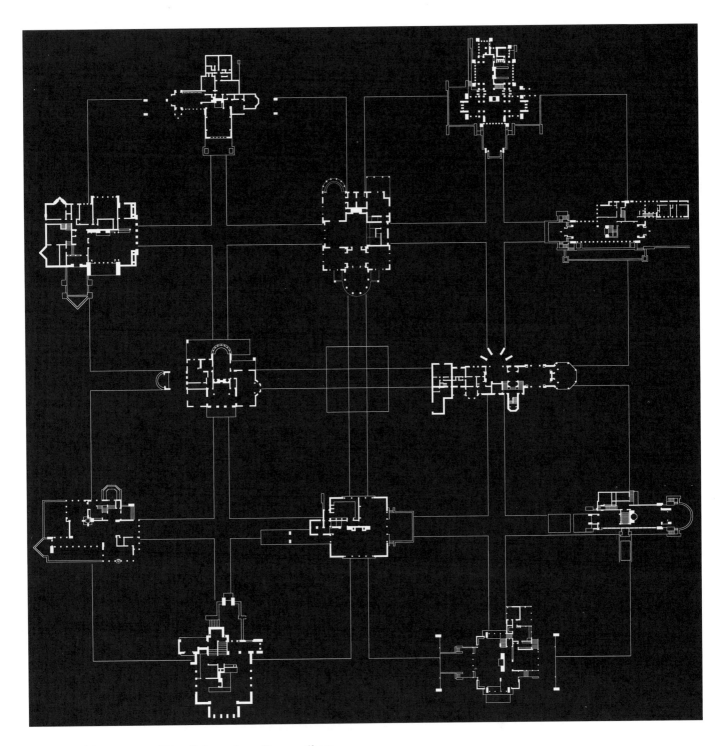

4-1 Array of four groups of Hearth type plans: Top-cruciform,
left-pinwheel, right-in-line, bottom-compact

Willitts house, Martin house,
Heurtley house, Blossom house, Robie house
Winslow house, Husser house,
F.L. Wright Studio house, Fireproof house, Tomek house,
Bach house, Evans house

The Hearth Type

Frank Lloyd Wright's contribution to twentieth-century residential architecture is acknowledged by even his severest critics. Scale, proportion, the tactile qualities of material and light, the relationship to the natural environment, and his masterful handling of space distinguish Wright's work as the most appreciated residential architecture of his era. In general, modern architecture has been concerned with universals and emphasized the need to come to terms with mass society. Its tendency has been to see the house as only part of the larger issue of housing—an attitude that dominated every aspect of design. The house was seen as an endlessly repetitive unit whose identity was sacrificed to the whole. That the house was mass-produced was not enough; it had to look mass produced. This approach was antithetical to Wright's belief in the supremacy of the individual. Although Wright was preoccupied with the problem of the house in society and saw it as a vehicle toward social amelioration, as did European moderns, with Wright this concept took a radically different form.

His first concern for the house as a prototypic solution dates back to his *Ladies Home Journal* projects at the turn of the century. Both versions were architectural achievements toward that exploration of space and planning that characterized his Prairie houses for the next ten years. In addition to the architectural design, however, Wright was also concerned with the sociology of the house, its cost, and its place within a larger context, albeit a suburban one. The Usonian House—efficient, low cost, and modeled on a simple life-style—was a new vehicle for exploring older problems that Wright had studied at the turn of the century.

Postdepression America needed this vision, so Wright felt, of a new, uncomplicated way to live and build. They needed to escape from the city to the country, rediscover their roots in the good earth, and thereby develop the innate democratic values of self-reliance. The Usonian House, set in the dispersed, agrarian-based community of Broadacre City, was a solution Wright believed would simultaneously liberate the individual economically, politically, socially, and morally. In this sense the house—and specifically the Usonian House—was the most important building block in his projected scheme for a better American future.

Although he designed important housing projects, Wright focused on the individual dwelling and sought to express the transcendent values of the home. He consistently denied the hegemony of the collective and the anonymity that it implies. In the process Wright has been accused of retreating to nineteenth-century values. This accusation may be true, but in his houses he was able to embody enduring human values that make his works as vital today as the day they were built.

THE IMAGE OF THE HOUSE

There should be as many kinds of houses as there are kinds of people and as many differentiations as there are different individuals.[2]

In confronting Wright's house designs, we are overwhelmed by the variety and quantity of work. Yet we have a sense of Wright's hand in all—like that of a portrait painter whose work identifies the artist as much as it does his subjects.

Then, if the architect is what he ought to be, with his ready technique he conscientiously works for the client, idealizes his client's character and his tastes and makes him feel that the building is his as it really is to such an extent that he can truly say that he would rather have his own house than any he has seen. Is a portrait, say by Sargent, any less a revelation of the character of the subject because it bears his stamp and is easily recognized as a Sargent?[3]

Like the good portrait artist, Wright attempted to represent his subject faithfully and capture his ineffable character. Like all great artists, he was even more concerned with the manifestation of an ideal that would transcend the individual and hold true for all people. "To believe that what is true for you in your own heart is true for all men—that is genius"[4] sums up his attitude and illuminates an otherwise paradoxical concern for himself as an individual seeking expression for other individuals. Was Wright a great portrait artist, or was he in some sense a great self-portrait artist? Do we have a succession of carefully rendered clients' houses, or do we have different views of the same house inhabited by Wright himself?

If we imagine Wright as a great portrait architect, effectively rendering his clients' characters and wishes with brick and stone, we should recognize that this achievement is only part of his agenda. Even more important to him was rendering the universals embodying the ideal house, a house that would be capable of transcending the particular.

OVERVIEW OF RESIDENTIAL WORK

With the design of the Winslow House in 1893, Wright's career as an independent architect began. For the next sixty-six years he was to design many different kinds of buildings, but the house occupied most of his creative energy, and he always seemed to return to it for inspiration. The house is Wright's chief vehicle for his most important architectural ideas and as such deserves our closest attention. Wright's residential designs include such memorable episodes as his Prairie houses, the concrete textile block houses and other regional experiments during the twenties, and his later Usonian houses of the thirties, forties, and fifties for suburban America.

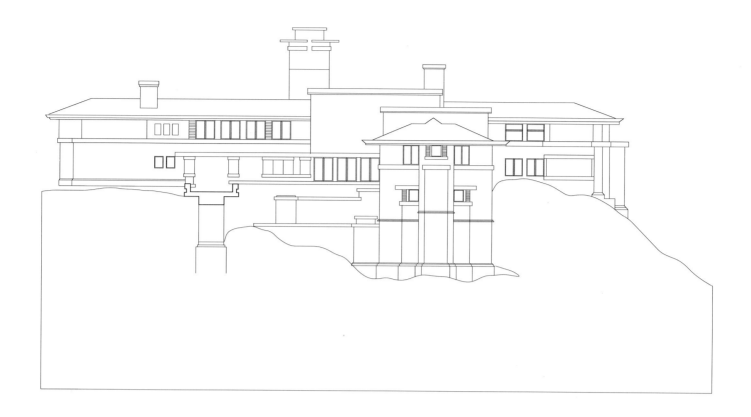

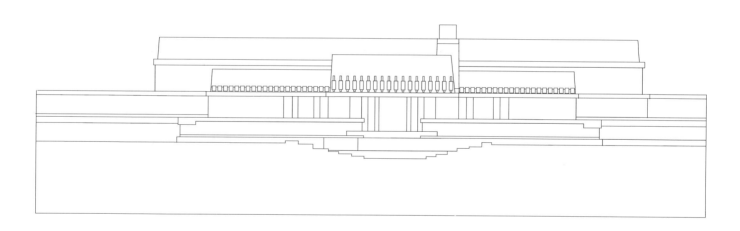

4-2 Elevation of Booth house

4-3 Elevation of the Hollyhock house

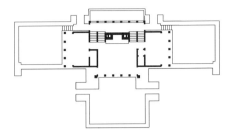

The Midwest Prairie House (1900–1917)

The Prairie House—predominantly cruciform in plan with classically informed axes but open in composition and to the site—pivots horizontally about its hearth, which anchors it to the earth and symbolically enshrines domestic values. The cruciform might be symmetrically disposed (Willitts and Hardy houses), asymmetrical (the McAfee and Robie houses), or part of more complex compositions (the Martin and Coonley houses).

The Wilderness House (1917–1936)

The desert, mountain, and forest houses of Wright's middle period, the "wilderness houses,"[5] show a simultaneous reliance on past work, particularly in the Hollyhock House, and a search for new possibilities in planning, materials, and expression. The California venture looks to Mesoamerican precedents and new building technology for inspiration. The Arizona desert houses especially explore the diagonal—both literal and phenomenal—with increased intensity. This emphasis may express itself in planning ideas (Cudney House, Lake Tahoe Cabins) or in the "diagonal" of the sloping site itself (the Freeman, Storer, and Doheny Ranch houses). The open horizontal extension of the Prairie House is exchanged in the desert houses for a more introverted, oasislike quality that filters the harsh environment through its semipermeable skin. The desert plan results in a higher degree of containment, and the expression is cubic rather than planar. The forest houses at Lake Tahoe explore the power of the roof form as a distinctive feature in the landscape and forge links to Native American architecture.

The Suburban Usonian House (1936–1959)

The Usonian House—modest in size, efficiently planned, and economically constructed (for example the Jacobs House)—displays a degree of informality only implied in Wright's earlier houses. Their "meaning" was to be understood in the larger economic, political, and moral context of post-Depression America; they carry an implicit polemic for individuality, self-reliance, and escape from the evils of the city and a society profoundly out of line with human needs. More deluxe versions that inspire or capitalize upon this work display an increasing drama in their use of form and space (Fallingwater) with a concomitant interest in diagonal and circular planning (the Hanna and David Wright houses).

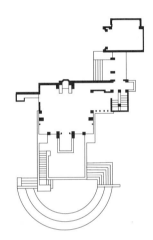

Although Wright's work with houses thus categorized gives some idea of breadth and scope, it does not necessarily provide the only valid grouping or yield insights into the subtleties of his domestic designs. The breakdown by period also has the effect of disconnecting his work from one phase to the next, although in many ways the most revealing or at least interesting aspects of the work are not the obvious differences but the more subtle continuities. Our premise is that the hidden themes of Wright's work, like the brush strokes, color palette, and compositional preferences of the portrait painter, can reveal the artist's intentions even more than the objective likeness to his subject.

4-4 Plans of Hardy, Freeman, and first Jacobs houses

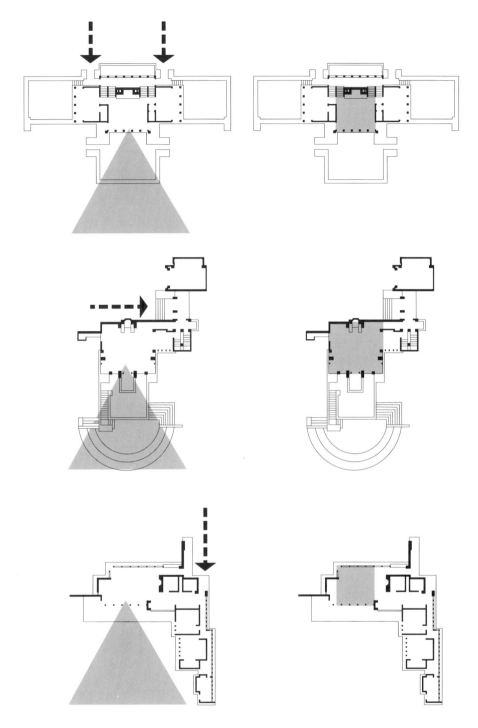

4-5 Comparative plan analysis showing continuities
in entry, view and major living area themes

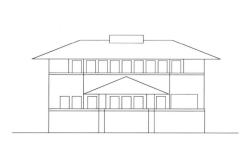

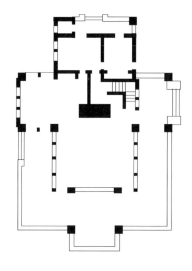
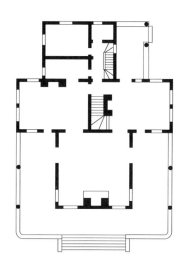

4-6 Ross House   4-7 Kent House, by Bruce Price

THE ORIGINS OF THE CRUCIFORM HEARTH PLAN

The cruciform plan and its transformations serve to inform almost all of Frank Lloyd Wright's domestic work from the Prairie years to the Usonian House. The first accomplished building using this schema is the Willitts House of 1902. Its seemingly sudden appearance may obscure its many precedents, both external and internal, to Wright's work, which gave it birth.

One of the sources of the cruciform in domestic planning can be specifically traced to American vernacular housing. Cottage builders and Shingle Style architects based many of their plans on a cross shape with a high degree of open planning. The Kent House at Tuxedo Park of 1885–86 by Bruce Price is a prime example of the type. Its openness, ability to capture the sun through ideal exposure, and suggested extension of space to the outside via an oversized porch made it particularly attractive and inviting in natural contexts. As we have seen, Richardson's Romanesque planning, both domestic and public, influenced Wright's development of the cross plan.

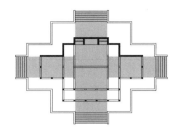

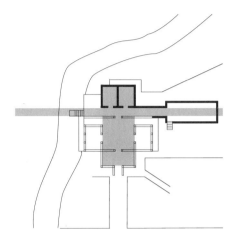

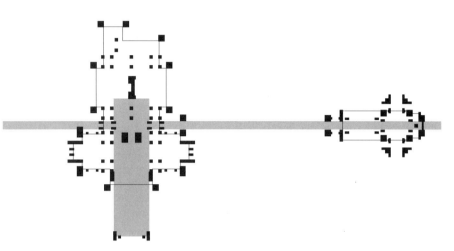

4-8 Plan of Ho-o-den Shrine showing cruciform theme

4-9 Comparative plan analysis of "Chinese Hut" illustration by Violet-le-Duc and the Martin house

Another source of the cruciform plan is Japanese design, specifically as expressed in the Ho-o-den Shrine at the Chicago World's Fair of 1893.[6] Its simple cross shape, with two interpenetrating volumes, articulated structure, and shrine on axis, is perhaps the most important precedent with which Wright was directly familiar. The lightness of the structure, its overhanging eaves, clarity of form, and absence of historical reference, particularly the classical orders, must have been a compelling model for Wright. Another possible non-Western influence, coming by way of Europe, is a small Chinese hut illustrated in Viollet-le-Duc's *Habitations*.[7] The hut is cruciform with a stepped pyramidal roof at the crossing and is connected to outbuildings in a manner that directly foreshadows the Martin-Barton Complex of 1904.

THE EVOLUTION OF THE CRUCIFORM

To fully understand the development of the cruciform plan at Wright's hand, we need to look at a third source. Although Palladianism was anathema to Wright, his design for the Blossom House of 1892 shows a clear Palladian influence. In this unlikely setting we can already see the stirrings of a major revolution in the way Wright conceived his houses. The influence of Palladio comes through the filter of late nineteenth-century colonial revival houses, such as the Taylor House by McKim, Mead, and White. This episode of Palladianism in American architecture was viewed as a return to cultural roots perhaps best expressed by Jefferson's Monticello, which in turn was based on Palladio's Villa Rotunda as seen through the eyes of English architects.

Writers such as Vincent Scully have emphasized the differences between Palladio and Wright while drawing connections to Jefferson.[8] A comparison of all these structures might reveal Wright's degree of indebtedness to both Palladio and Jefferson. A remarkable similarity between Palladio and Wright that stylistic analysis alone cannot reveal is apparent in certain plan abstractions. A comparison of the Villa Rotunda, Blossom House, Monticello, and the Willitts House demonstrates that Wright was aware of his culture to an extraordinary degree and that he had the ability to synthesize seemingly diametrically opposed tendencies into a new whole. A more extended comparison can serve to acknowledge more fully Wright's debt to the classical tradition in America.

The plans of the Villa Rotunda and the Blossom House reveal a simple geometry of a square inscribed by a cruciform. However, the absolute bilateral symmetry of the Rotunda and its strong, centralized dome contrast with the Blossom's inflected plan, which nonetheless is ordered about two centralizing axes. The extensions to the Rotunda's square plan occur in the form of four identical, axially disposed porches that continue the transparency of the inscribed cruciform. The porches dematerialize the building wall and make a transition to the landscape beyond. It has a consistent theme of concentric energy that is concentrated at the center and dissipated at the edges along its two axes. Energies are stable and axially balanced.

In the Blossom House the absence of a dome as a central stabilizing force releases a peripheral outward movement. It has a single semicircular entry porch on its exterior axis that is countered by the semicircular conservatory placed in an opposing and non-axial position, causing a rotational movement in the plan. The indentation in the living room is countered with a small terrace that is pushed forward from the main block. Both the fireplace and stair define the central crossing without occupying it, and their asymmetric relationship further enforces the secondary dynamic theme of rotational energy. Also important, however, is the stabilizing effect of the four corner blocks, which are articulated to suggest four discrete volumes. The major reading of the Rotunda is as a cube with four discrete porch projections. The Blossom's major reading is ambivalent. The initial reading of a single cubic volume has a very strong secondary reading of a cruciform contained within four corner pavilions.

The latent cruciform in the Rotunda, which became more apparent in the Blossom House and emerged as a more explicit feature in Jefferson's Monticello, finally reveals itself with unequivocal clarity in Wright's Willitts House.

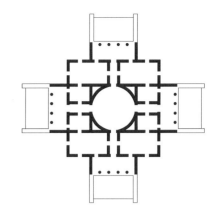

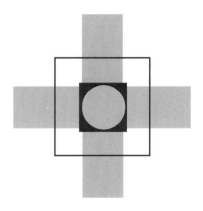

4-10 Comparative analysis of Villa Rotunda, the Blossom house, Monticello (by Thomas Jefferson), and the Willitts house showing differing relationships between square and cruciform

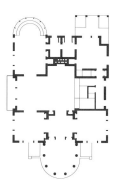
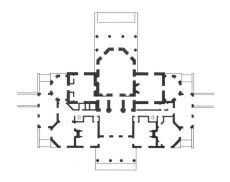
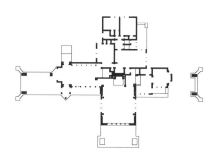

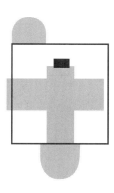
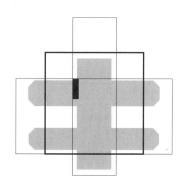
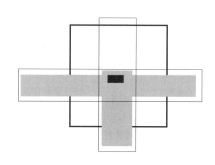

Interpreting the geometry of Palladio's Villa Rotunda in a new cultural context, Monticello describes an idea of the house in the landscape that Wright was to explore as a key theme in many of his residences. At Monticello we can see precursors of Wright's work in the embryonic cruciform, the asymmetrical distribution of the core, the hierarchical expression of the extending wings, and the exaggerated extension of spaces into the landscape. Extended porches and split octagonal bays distend the cubic, compact Palladian plan into two cross volumes that mark a center that significantly lacks the domed centralizing space of Palladio's model. Wright's

Willitts House can be seen as a further logical development of this theme of extended periphery and concomitant de-centering at the crossing. In the Willitts, the corner volumes of the Blossom that acted to buttress the internal space have been removed like form work to reveal cruciform volumes they have molded. The plan abstractions of the four buildings reveal a remarkable similarity, suggesting a transformation (changed emphasis) from one to the next rather than any radical reformulation. Although the cruciform has found complete expression in the Willitts House, the cubic volume is now implied rather than explicit. It is described by the outer

edges of the living, dining, and reception rooms (excluding their prowlike bay windows) and the inner edge of the paired maids' rooms, which are articulated with a step back in the building line. The centralized dome space of the Rotunda, de-emphasized as a mere intersection in the Blossom House, is replaced by the insertion of a fireplace at the center of the Willitts House. Like the Rotunda, Willitts has a strong concentric organization, but it is that of a solid that disintegrates with centrifugal force toward the four outstretched arms of the cruciform rather than the centripetal force that climaxes upward into the centralized dome.

An analysis of the four building elevations reveals similar themes. The
underlying cruciform organization yields
a tripartite composition on all four
facades. The emphasis on the central
bay is clear for each, as is a lateral
extension. The cross plan has an
equivalent and complementary elevation. Moving from Rotunda to Blossom
to Monticello to Willitts, we can observe
the cross becoming a more dominant
theme until it seems to completely deny
any bounding cubic volume. The
relationship between plan and elevation,
interior space and exterior form is
complete and unambiguous. The perfect
synthesis or "plasticity" that Wright
strove for has been achieved.

Wright's use of the cruciform suggests
first and foremost a preference for a
peculiar spatial "weaving" and a
compositional preference for additive
rather than subtractive plastic form. The
cross-axial plan releases energy to the
four compass points and simultaneously
anchors the composition to the earth at
one point. The cruciform house has both
fluid movement and stability, change
and continuity wrapped up in a form that
enshrines the hearth, symbol of the
family, and the four open arms that
extend outward toward the landscape
and toward freedom for the individual.
The plasticity was achieved by unifying
and expressing the interior volume with
exterior form.

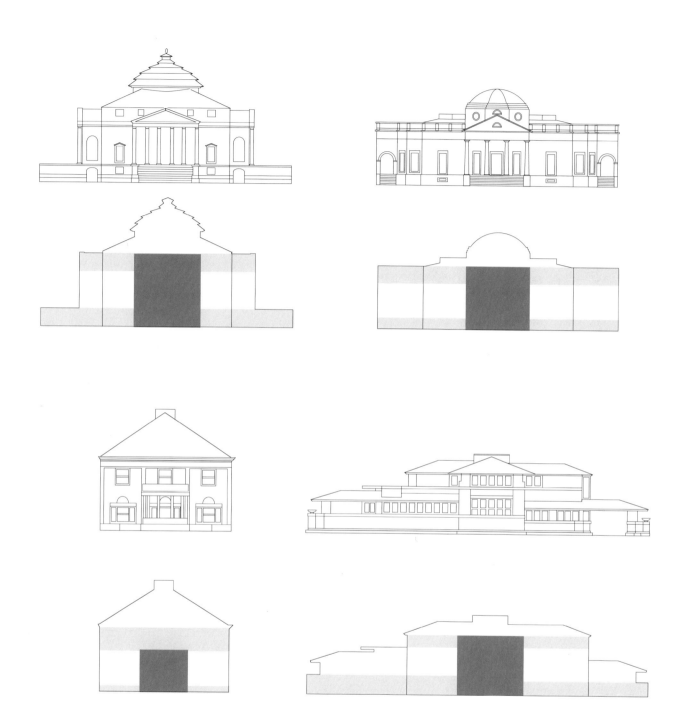

4-11 Comparative elevation analysis of Villa Rotunda, Blossom house, Monticello, and Willitts house showing similiar tripartite organization

The Cruciform Plan

In 1900 and 1901 Wright published two projects for the *Ladies Home Journal*. The first was called "A Home in a Prairie Town," the second, "A Small House with 'Lots of Room in It.'" These unbuilt projects were the first "unveiling of the Prairie House"[9] and were to establish two distinct types of cruciform plan: formal frontality with a T-shaped arrangement of major living spaces and informal asymmetry with an L-shaped arrangement of these same spaces. Wright's work for the next ten years developed different versions of these two basic cruciform types, and traces of them can be found in later residential designs through and beyond the Usonian houses.

The first of the *Journal* houses to be published was the more deluxe version. It has a plan configuration that resembles an airplane: a linear body, two symmetrical wings, and a tail. The hearth occupies the cockpit location, along with a stair and a passageway that link the front and tail portions. The front end consists of a formal T-shaped suite of rooms, the central living room flanked by the dining room and library in symmetrical wings. The tail end has a less formal arrangement of spaces, including a porte cochere, reception area, kitchen, and service area. Bedrooms are located on the second level above the living and dining rooms and the library. In the published version of this type, Wright proposed two variations of this second level. One included a pair of bedrooms over the living room; the other shows them removed, creating a grand living space with mezzanine above.

Siting, approach, and entry sequence to the house are important considerations for Wright. The house is oriented with its main axis parallel to the street; a dynamic effect is introduced through the overall asymmetry of the street facade in tension with the localized symmetry of each of the forward wings. The approach by car is also asymmetric and on the periphery; likewise, by foot a person moves off center and is required to turn no fewer than six times to arrive at the living room space facing the hearth. The movement pattern and entry is clearly a foil to a more structured architectural composition that can be described in terms of major and minor axes with secondary shifts. Houses incorporating this formal type include the Cheney, Hardy, Martin, and Hollyhock.

The second cruciform plan, more modest in size, incorporates more asymmetries, increasing the spatial dynamics. The overall composition is again organized by cross-axes that intersect at the fireplace core. However, there is no overall symmetrical grouping of wings, although each of the four wings show traces of local symmetry. The axes of the living room and dining room are resolved within the hearth core. The axis of the entry, suggested by a small octagonal reception space, is shifted slightly off the axis of the roof and its support piers, which constitute the port cochere. The kitchen axis, expressed in the exterior windows, is also shifted from the axis of the "tail" of the house. Among the houses based on this informal type are the Willitts, Roberts, Coonley, and Usonian first Jacobs.

With these two types of the cruciform plan in mind, we will now examine four major groups of houses that represent major variations in Wright's residential designs: the classic cruciform house, the hillside house, the in-line house and the pinwheel house. We chose these groups for more detailed study to facilitate both an overview of the transformations of concepts and the comparative analysis of specific designs.

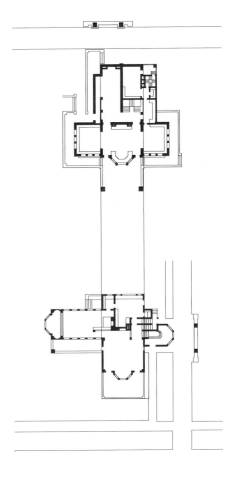

4-12 Plan of First Ladies Home Journal house

4-13 Plan of Second Ladies Home Journal house

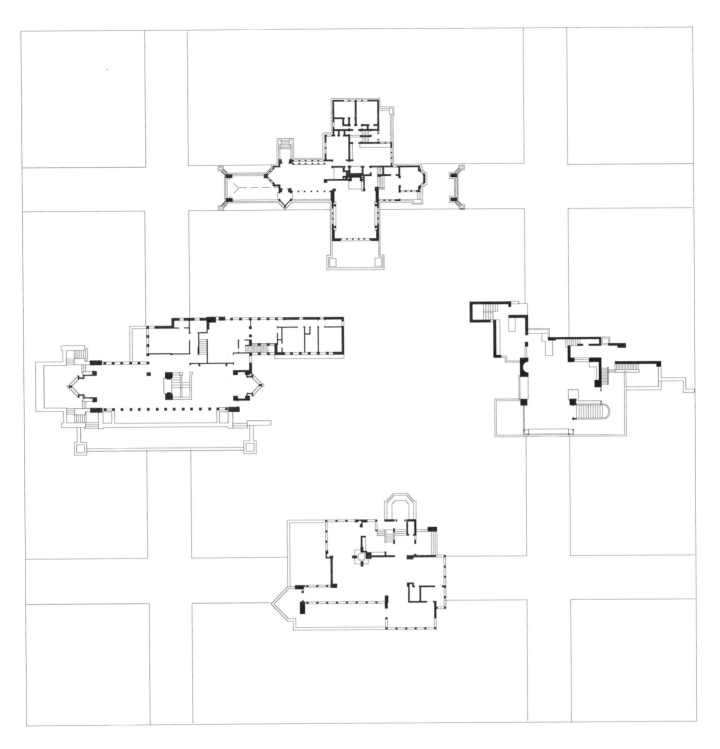

4-14 Plan array showing variations of the Hearth type:

Willitts house;
Robie house; Fallingwater;
F.L. Wright Studio house

THE CLASSIC CRUCIFORM HOUSES

The Willitts House

Built in 1902, the Willitts House is the first clear, comprehensive embodiment of the cruciform Prairie residence. The two major intersecting spatial volumes are clearly expressed in the exterior massing of the building. The continuity and extension of spaces are emphasized by the horizontal lines of the large overhanging roofs and the low parapet walls. The hierarchy of spaces and overall stability of the three-dimensional composition of volumes are supported by the symmetry of the facade of the forward living wing and the nearly symmetrical disposition of wings extending to either side. In this house Wright converts the average program of a house of that time into a formal composition of tremendous visual impact, in the tradition of the Palladian-style English manor house or the nineteenth-century French château.

The Willitts House was enclosed with a simple, controlled skin of wood frame and stucco that clearly reveals the distinct volumes of the house. Articulation consisted of the large overhanging roofs and the arrangement of windows. By the time he designed the Martin House, Wright had experimented with expressing the extension of space through exterior walls while maintaining a strong sense of enclosure in a number of ways, including parapets and piers.

The Martin House

The Martin House of 1904 is the earliest example of a deluxe Prairie house in which budget was no constraint. It provides the most extensive and refined example of the development of his ideas about the Prairie type. This house incorporated a sophisticated orchestration of solids and voids, animating in an unprecedented way the exterior and interior of the house. The availability of expert furniture carpenters in Buffalo enabled Wright to extend the vocabulary established in these plans to a complete set of details for the woodwork.

The Coonley House

The Avery Coonley House of 1908 was built the year before the Robie House. The most lavish of the Prairie houses ever to be executed, it was a favorite of the architect. Its site is a large parcel of flat land next to the Des Plaines River. The house presents a more informal, less imposing exterior that blends into the natural landscape, almost as if hiding its size. The concern for simple aesthetic unity shown in the Willitts design gives way to variety, experimentation, and idiosyncrasies at Coonley, and the architecture is enriched by extensive ornamental design.

The Hollyhock House

The Hollyhock design recalls some of the feeling of Willitts. It returns to the imposing, symmetrical expression reminiscent of Beaux Arts compositions. The rather simplistic rendition of stripped-down Mayan style on the outside shell hides a more subtle, animated, but serene set of encircled spaces, including the garden court. Possibly because of the limitations of poured-in-place concrete, as Wright saw them, ornament seems more applied than integral to the architecture. Soon after this project he addressed this problem with his California "textile" concrete block house designs, including the Millard, Storer, Ennis, and Freeman houses.

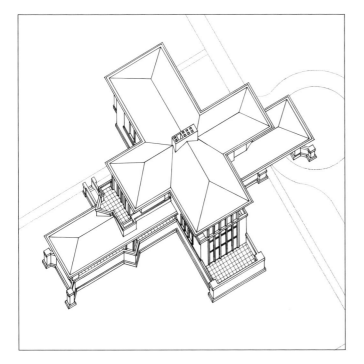

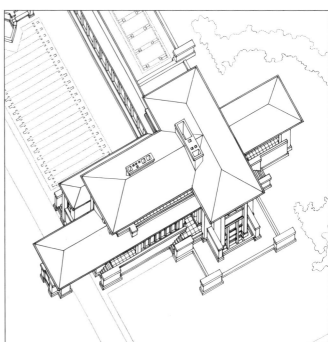

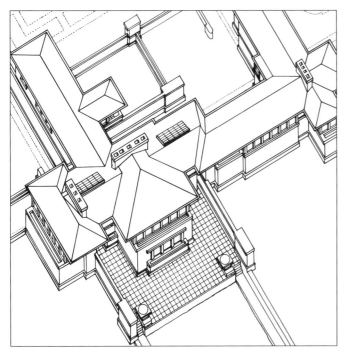

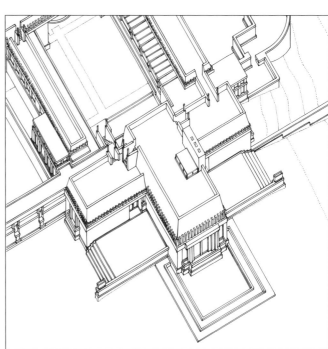

4-15 Plan projection of Willitts house

4-16 Plan projection of Martin house

4-17 Plan projection of Coonley house

4-18 Plan projection of Hollyhock house

In the plan of the Willitts House, the long volume parallel to the street and the shorter perpendicular volume intersect to form four wings. Although the exterior expression of the wings appears balanced and formal, the distribution of interior functions is informal, based on the L-shaped plan of the *Ladies Home Journal* "Little House." Principal functions, the living and dining rooms, are placed in two of the front wings, a porte cochere, entry, and reception occupy the other front wing, and the service functions are placed in the back wing behind the central volume of the hearth. The house is approached on foot or by car from the front, although the visitor spirals into the entry off the axis in a more dynamic apprehension of the building's composition. The entry to the house seems purposely de-emphasized in order to preserve the balance of the facade composition.

Located on a corner site, the Martin House derives its layout from the more formal type of cruciform house that was first revealed in the *Ladies Home Journal*. The T-shaped suite of principal living areas faces one street, and entry from the other street is inserted in a slot between the living suite and a less symmetrical grouping of support spaces. This slot of space is extended as a pergola that acts as an organizing spine for a complex of structures, including the smaller Barton House, a garage, and a conservatory. The organization of the volumes of the Martin House are more formal than the Willitts, and the exterior expression emphasizes this quality.

The composition of the Coonley House is a looser version of the informal cruciform type, with a nucleus that consists of a living room core lifted above a playroom, formal terrace, and reflecting pool. The dining room wing extends to one side, with the bedroom wing opposite. The service wing, containing kitchen and servant quarters, extends to the back behind the hearth. Structures at the Martin House were composed to punctuate rather than explicitly define exterior space. The Coonley House captures and dominates exterior space by its composition of forms, including the U-shaped residence proper, guest house, gardener's house, garage, and other outbuildings that form a compound. The drive and approach are not frontal to the formal cross-axis of living room but perpendicular to it behind and under the kitchen wing that serves as a porte cochere.

In closely associating the cruciform plan with Wright's Prairie houses, we could miss its strong role in buildings of a different time or style. The Hollyhock House is a brilliant extension and transformation of the formal version of the cruciform plan as found in the Martin House. In one of his clearest expressions of extended, interlocking space, Wright moves the hearth off axis and splits the back wing to create a strong linear exterior space that in effect becomes the fourth leg of the cruciform. Because the hearth as core and anchor was the theme of most of Wright's houses, this departure at Hollyhock had to have a compelling reason. Perhaps it is a recognition of the unifying role of the central court tradition in the warm climates of southern California and the Mediterranean. It may also derive from his exposure to enclosed exterior spaces in the Orient. In any case, the creation of an "oasis" protected by fortresslike walls seems to make a lot of sense on this exposed hill site in the desert setting of Los Angeles.

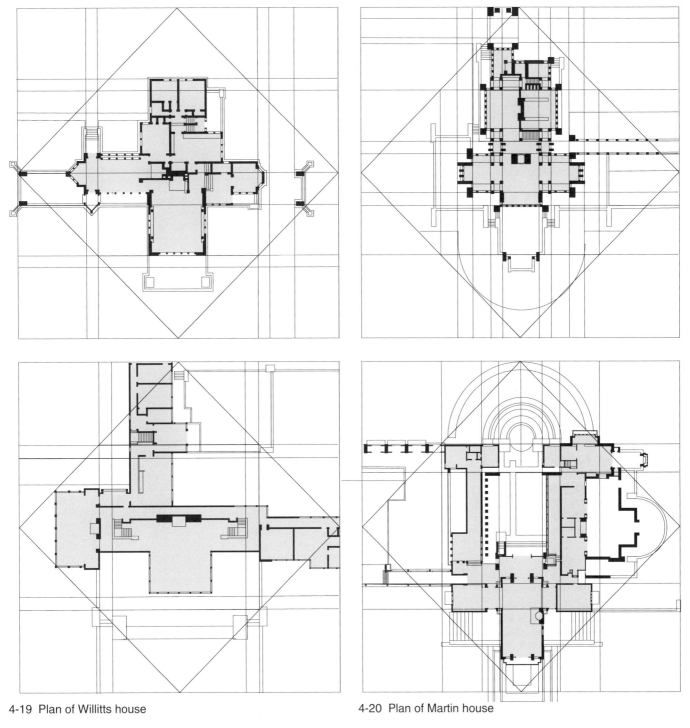

4-19 Plan of Willitts house

4-21 Plan of Coonley house

4-20 Plan of Martin house

4-22 Plan of Hollyhock house

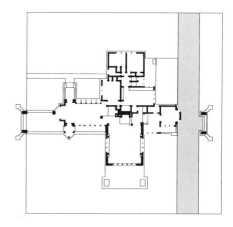

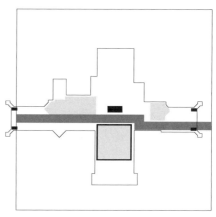

Analysis of the Willitts House plan reveals that its dynamism is counterbalanced by the clear expression of several local symmetries, the most important being the projecting living room wing. Interior spaces are organized around axes implied by the octagonal protrusion in the reception area, diamond protrusions in the dining area, and the five-part composition of the principal fenestration of the living room. Additional symmetries are expressed in pairings of exterior piers at the porch and porte cochere and other landscape features. At the Martin House a complex interweaving of local symmetries is achieved through an extensive set of clustered piers, mullions, and planters. The result is a strong sense of spatial definition and richness throughout the house. Although local symmetry is strongly reinforced in some areas of the Coonley House, particularly the living room nucleus, which includes the lower terrace and reflecting pool, it is generally employed in a looser, incidental manner overall. Internal generation of spaces seems tempered by the concern for

definition of exterior spaces. At Hollyhock local symmetries again appear to be integrated with the major axial composition of the house even more emphatically than at the Martin House. The effect is one of a more controlled, unified plan, and it is perhaps one of Wright's most classicized later designs.

The persistence of compositional themes underlying the exploitation of form and context in these four houses suggests a parallel continuity of design approach. In approaching each new design, Wright seemed to build upon previous plan concepts that embodied his fundamental concerns: sense of the hearth, zoning, hierarchy of spaces, relationship to site, and sequence of entry. In the Prairie houses, Wright fine-tuned the role of the cruciform configuration of spaces. Upon this experience he built a career of continuing discovery in which the cruciform would be stretched, shifted, and otherwise distorted without losing its power to act as a solid formal means to order and identity.

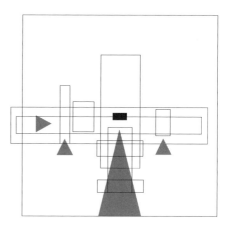

4-23 Comparative plan analysis of Willitts, Coonley, Martin, and Hollyhock houses:
Access;
Circulation armature and spatial hierarchy;
Spatial weave and view orientation

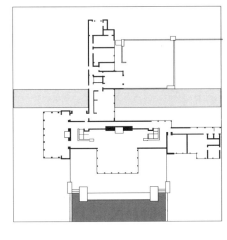
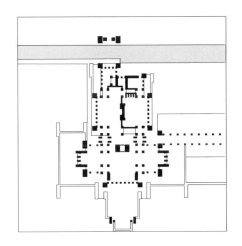
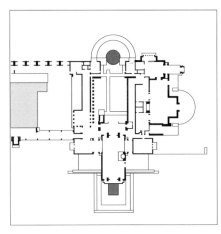
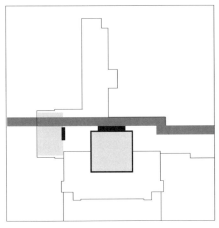
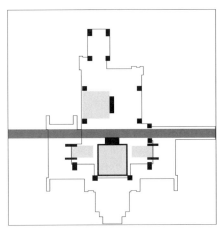
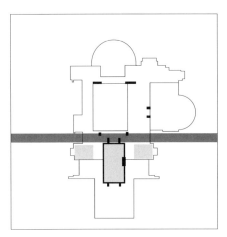
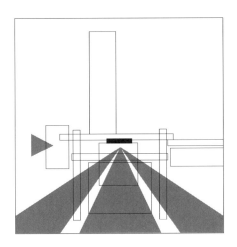
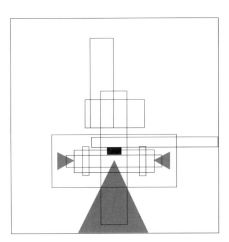
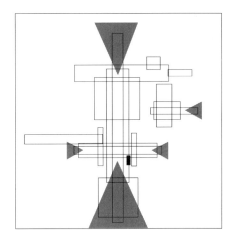

THE HILLSIDE HOUSES

This structure might serve to indicate that the sense of shelter—the sense of space where used with sound structural sense—has no limitations as to form except the materials used and the methods by which they are employed for what purpose. The ideas involved here are in no way changed from those of early work. The materials and methods of construction come through them, here, as they may and will always come through everywhere. That is all. The effects you see in this house are not superficial effects.[10]

That each of Wright's buildings is unique and without precedent within architecture in general or within Wright's own work is often asserted. However, we have seen his debt to the architecture of H. H. Richardson and Japan, among others. Likewise, we realize that this contention does not account for the many themes Wright developed in his early years that remained immensely important to him throughout his career. No greater error could be made in the study of Wright's work than to believe that he had no "memory" of his previously executed designs. Like the Heraclitian metaphor of the constantly changing stream that is always the same, Wright worked within an evolving set of principles; even if their outward manifestation changed, the principles followed a defined course.

This phenomenon becomes more readily apparent when we compare Wright's architectural response to similar sites. Our task will be to recognize the variations while trying to understand the shared intentions and organizational ideas underlying each work. We will focus on the plan and section and their three-dimensional realization in form and space. We will then attempt to demonstrate the interrelatedness between each pair of houses, to show how certain ideas become developed and elaborated, others are transformed, and still others disappear only to recur. An examination of these four houses provides a good example of Wright's working methodology, demonstrating not only his tenacious hold on organizational ideas but also his ability to transform those principles into a new and creative work.

FROM THE HARDY HOUSE TO FALLINGWATER

The Hardy House from 1905 seems unrelated to Fallingwater, which was designed thirty years later. The symmetrical plan and rather monumental aspect of the first contrasts strongly with the asymmetrical, seemingly casual organization of the second. The three-dimensional massing and use of materials makes these differences even more apparent. The stepped-earth terraces of the Hardy House contrast with Fallingwater's cantilevered concrete balconies, which seem to float above the land. One accepts gravity; the other defies it. The stucco and wood structure of the Hardy House is expressed on the exterior in simple, unadorned volumes, revealing in the glazed sections a species of "half-timbering." The only cantilevered element is the low hip roof that hovers above like a canopy. Fallingwater's smooth concrete trays in tension and the massive stone walls in compression express an "appropriate" use of materials and develop a poetic sensibility in accordance with Wright's idea of the nature of materials and their structural potential.

During the early twenties, Wright built two works in southern California that can help establish a link between the Hardy House and Fallingwater. Along with the other three houses from this region, La Miniatura of 1921 and the Freeman House of 1923 are buildings that usually claim an independence from Wright's larger output. Both projects employ a vaguely Mesoamerican style and use precast concrete textile blocks designed by Wright. The romantic response that each house evokes springs from the remarkable degree to which it acknowledges a cultural and landscape context. These characteristics suggest a clear break with the Prairie houses and seem to predate but not envisage the streamlined modernity of his late work. Yet comparing the characteristic relationship to the larger landscape issues of site and topography and studying the architectural plan and sectional development enable us to see all four works as a series of variations on a theme.

Both the Hardy House and Fallingwater are situated on a dramatic sloping site overlooking a water element (the Hardy House overlooks Lake Michigan, Fallingwater a mountain stream). Wright's favored renderings of each building—perspective views taken from downhill—reveal his desire to exploit the drama of the setting. These views, oblique both in plan and section, are not easily experienced by the visitor; taken from off the beaten path, they are not an integral part of the entry sequence experience. The perspective view of the Hardy House (rendered by Marion Mahoney) places the structure in an exaggerated position near the top of the vertically elongated picture frame. A carefully rendered dogwood blossom is in the right foreground, and a distant tree is silhouetted in the upper left corner. Faint diagonal lines indicating the sloping bluff move in an opposing direction from upper right to lower left. The dynamic tension thus created between images near and low and high and far are the reverse of the accustomed experience in Western landscape painting. The composition is based on Japanese prints and lends a shifting, dynamic frame of reference that belies the symmetrical order of the structure itself. Whereas the means of presentation of the Hardy House is dynamic, the building itself is static; with Fallingwater, both the means of presentation and the object itself are consistently dynamic compositions. The Hardy House rendering is a graphic premonition of an idea that was to be fulfilled by the architecture of Fallingwater.

Like the Hardy House, published views of the La Miniatura emphasize its setting, featuring both a water element and a downward cascade of terraces. The Freeman House lacks an immediate water element such as La Miniatura, but perhaps the Pacific Ocean itself fills this role, for the house is directed toward a magnificent vista of the ocean to the south. The hillside site is no less dramatic than the others; quite predictably the preferred perspective and photographic views are from an oblique angle from below.

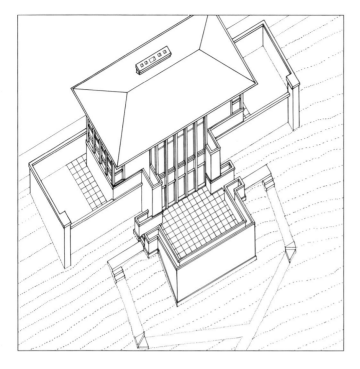

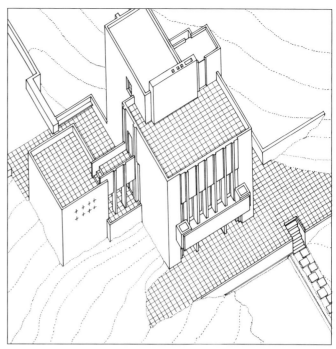

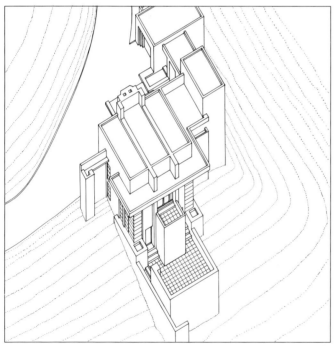

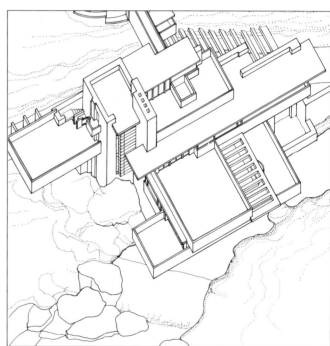

4-24 Plan projection of Hardy house

4-25 Plan projection of La Miniatura

4-26 Plan projection of Freeman house

4-27 Plan projection of Fallingwater

In addition to adopting a strong point of view about the dramatic possibilities of their sites, Wright imbues these four houses with a consistent approach to the scale and hierarchy of their spaces. Here again, as with his other buildings, Wright has employed a grid as the vehicle for translating principle into a course of action that governs his approach to creating and refining spaces. Our analysis of the plans of the four houses shows the influence of the tartan grid. At the most general level the broad zones of the grid define spaces for congregation or rest, and the narrow zones define spaces for circulation. Furthermore, the broad zones define exterior extensions of space, and the narrow zones define residual or transitional spaces, such as storage or roof eaves, that is, transitions between inside and outside space. Although the tartan grid appears to provide a strong foundation for generating designs, Wright doe not allow his plans to become slaves of the grid. The ordering potential of the grid is always balanced by the search for dynamic experiences of space in harmony with the site.

Our first view of the footprints of these houses reveals how the site conditions play an important role in varying the interpretations of the grid to create distinctive buildings out of a common base. The major axis of the Hardy House is described by the living room at the top of the bluff and the lake at the bottom. The looser organization of La Miniatura and the Freeman House reflect a more irregular topography further tensioned by conflicting demands for entry and view; however, each establishes a major axis between living and water. The footprint of Fallingwater creates a dynamic tension through the juxtaposition of the grid and a strong diagonal edge of the natural site that approximates a thirty-degree angle.[11]

The T-shaped configuration of Hardy is contrasted to a more compact cubelike volume of La Miniatura, with a smaller garage volume pulled away to form a kind of porte cochere in the connecting link. The resultant L-building footprint might be seen as a distortion of the more Platonic Hardy plan. We could also see the symmetrical "saddlebags" on either side of the living room–dining room space of the Hardy House pivoted to a back position in La Miniatura to transform the plan into a casual, site-specific structure. The Freeman House footprint is similar to La Miniatura and has a version of its porte cochere garage arrangement. The house portion, although based on a square, is less enclosed as a cubic volume and more expressed as an open composition of intersecting planes above and rather massive volumes below, with stepped terraces in the manner of the Hardy House.

The Fallingwater footprint exhibits a modified cruciform plan not unlike the earlier houses of the Prairie school. The overall configuration is obviously not regular and, unlike the more simplified arrangements of Millard and Freeman, has a fractured, stepping system of walls and volumes that roughly follow the line of the rock ledge to the rear. The porte cochere makes its required appearance, but it is attached to the rear ledge of rock, which acts formally and spatially in a similar manner to both Millard and Freeman. The interweave of space and form precisely at the point of entry creates an explosive release that recalls the same theme in the earlier houses.

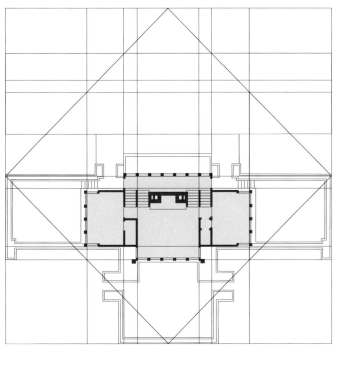

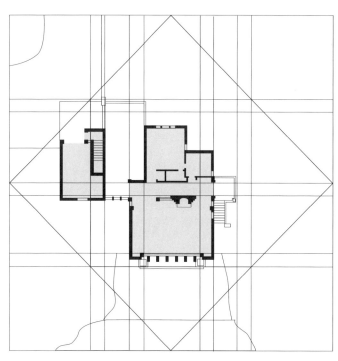

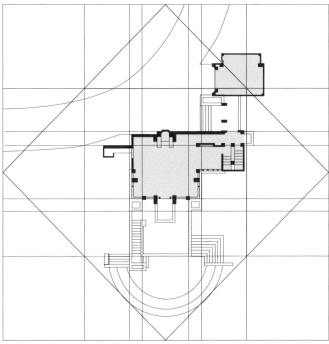

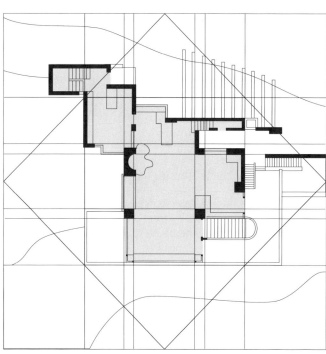

4-28 Plan of Hardy house

4-29 Plan of La Miniatura

4-30 Plan of Freeman house

4-31 Plan of Fallingwater

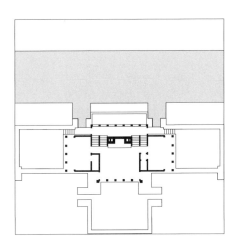

A cursory examination of the plan of La Miniatura reveals an important link to that of the Hardy House. Despite the overall asymmetry of La Miniatura, it possesses a strong local symmetry about the main living room volume that projects down the curved, sloping site and approximately at right angles to it in the manner of Hardy. Furthermore, the fireplace and stair elements retain their dominant position as core elements within the structure and serve to stabilize the structure with an articulated inner core.

The Freeman House displays similar themes. The symmetrical living room, with a downhill view perpendicular to the slope and axially opposed hearth, recalls a similar motif found in both Hardy and La Miniatura. The kitchen and stair are wrenched asymmetrically to one side to accommodate entry and a secondary view along the site's corner position. On the lower level a symmetrical pair of bedrooms occurs directly below the living room, thereby enforcing this axis, and opens onto the lower terrace. The "pouches" of storage that frame the Hardy and La Miniatura living rooms are now joined together along the central axis on the lower level. This coupling into a single volume stops at the living level to provide an axial terrace. The resultant dissolution of the corners suggests a more dynamic and oblique aspect than the bracketed condition of Hardy and Millard. The oblique view thus afforded capitalizes on the panoramic setting and is more

consistent with Wright's preference for the diagonal. The overall composition and disposition of the functional elements have changed radically from the previous examples, and yet the local symmetry of the living room provides the key to the transformations that have taken place.

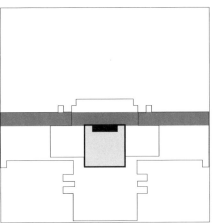

The plan of Fallingwater, despite its seeming inexhaustible movement and overwhelming dynamism, contains symmetrical volumes that provide stabilizing elements similar to the earlier houses. The main living room space, for example, is nearly symmetrical, with the most symmetrically disposed portion toward the front and dissolving into a more casual arrangement toward the rear and sides. It is emphasized by the carefully designed glazing, built-in seating, and recessed ceiling cove and lighting, all of which align perfectly with the main living room axis. The sides are allowed more freedom, as the fireplace on one side opposite the entry, water stair, and study demonstrate. Despite the overall asymmetry, the localized symmetry acts as a counterpoint to define a hierarchy of spaces and stabilize the composition. The bedrooms, study, and kitchen have been disposed in an asymmetrical manner, complementing and expressing the diagonal rock ledge to the rear. The overall effect is informal and "natural" and results in a mastery of dynamic building elements that disguises their carefully disciplined order.

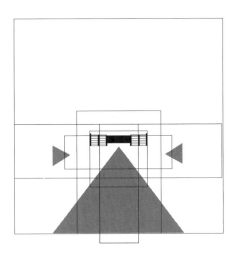

4-32 Comparative plan analysis of Hardy, La Miniatura, Freeman, and Fallingwater houses:

Access;
Circulation armature and spatial hierarchy;
Spatial weave and view orientation

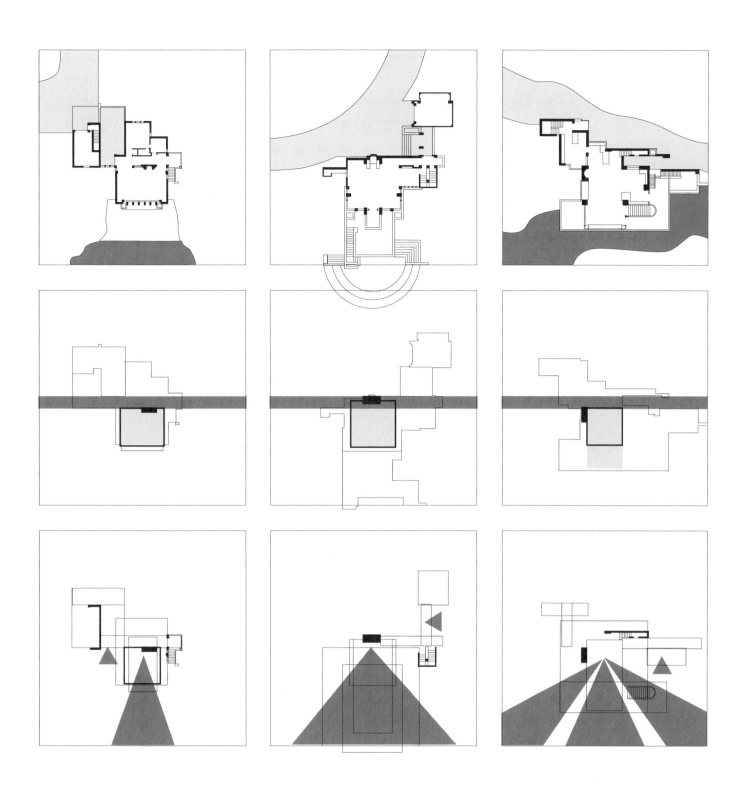

71

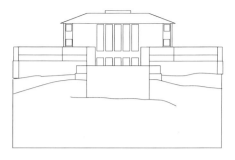

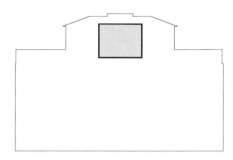

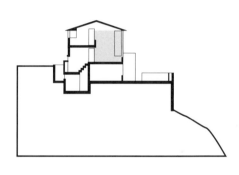

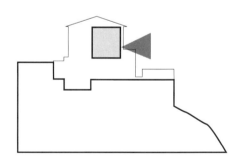

A comparison of the sectional disposition of these four houses is particularly revealing. In the Hardy House and La Miniatura the same double-volume living room exists, each with upper balcony connecting to sleeping quarters. The lowest level, directly below the living room, is reserved for the dining room; similar connections exist between its relationship to the kitchen area and, more important, to its terrace.

All of these similarities, despite the obvious superficial differences, suggest that Wright was enlisting his known earlier work to formulate a solution to a new situation. Although changes that respond to materials, to regional imperatives and perhaps even to a changing, more casual temperament are apparent, the parti has remained essentially the same.

Fallingwater stands apart from these earlier examples in its use of concrete-reinforced terraces that dramatically hover over the waterfall that gives it its name. Several houses among Wright's earlier work could provide plausible

prototypes for Fallingwater, and our intention is not to suggest that only one source or linear development of its genesis is possible. The early Charnley House uses a modest, although distinctive, balcony over the front entrance that establishes Wright's predisposition toward a vocabulary of interpenetrating and sliding volumes. A more striking example would be the Gale House, dated 1909 (but perhaps designed as early as 1905). Wright specifically cites this house as a premonition of Fallingwater. Its oblique perspective in the Wasmuth portfolio features a prescient series of balconies and terraces stabilized by a vertical chimney mass placed in a shifted asymmetrical arrangement that produces a strong rotating movement and sense of dynamism. Given this dynamic view, we are surprised to discover the strict symmetry of the forward portion, which includes the typical living room and terrace and symmetrically paired bedrooms and balcony above in a manner to be followed by the Freeman House, but with the levels simply inverted.

4-33 Comparative elevation and section of Hardy, La Miniatura, Freeman, and Fallingwater houses

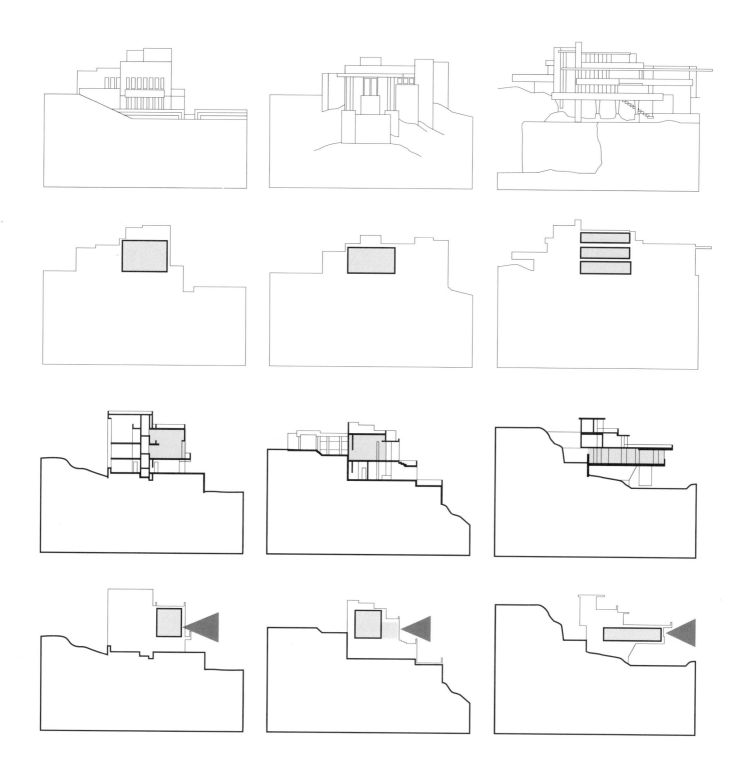

THE IN-LINE HOUSE

The in-line house, as Wright sometimes referred to it, is a variation on the cruciform theme and one of his most important residential plan types. The plan of the in-line house is established by a baseline. This horizontal axis determines the disposition of a primary longitudinal volume and serves as a foil for one or more secondary cross-axes. It initiates the design and becomes an organizational armature for its development.

The relationship between building form and land form, always a prime concern for Wright, is an especially important aspect of this house type. The nature of the landscape helps to define two versions of the in-line house. The flat site variant, exemplified in the Husser House of 1897, elevates the main living area above grade on a high podium of secondary spaces to create a kind of piano nobile. The hillside or hillcrest variant, illustrated by the Francis Little House of 1913, develops the house and its site in response to a more varied landscape that offers an opportunity to elevate the house naturally. In either case the main living level is raised to enjoy a privileged position from which to view the landscape, which unfolds on one or more sides. The reason for the extreme proportions of the type can be found in the building's relationship to the site, but they also seem to be generated by Wright's formal and spatial predilection for horizontal lines and levitating volumes, which climax in the the Robie House of 1909.

Many examples of the in-line type appear consistently throughout his career. Besides the Husser and Robie houses, some of the more significant instances of the raised living room variety include the Tomek House of 1907, the Lloyd Lewis House of 1940, and the David Wright House of 1950. The last example is a member of this family, even though it appears in an unsuspecting circular guise. Its plan and curved ramp of a "tail" can best be understood as a raised in-line house that curls around itself like an armadillo. In addition to the Little House, the hillside and hillcrest in-line house type appears in important buildings such as the diminutive Usonian Goetsch-Winkler House of 1939 and the commanding Rose Pauson House of 1940. Both the flat and hill landscape variations display similar planning themes, and both can serve to illuminate different aspects of Wright's architectural principles.

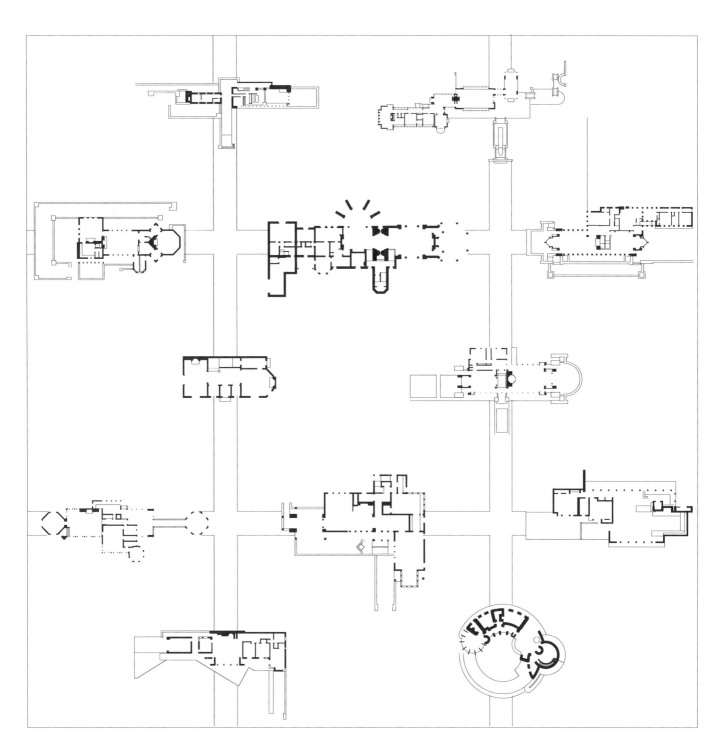

4-34 Plan array showing variations of
the In-Line Hearth type

The Development of the In-Line House

The first example of the in-line type is the unexecuted McAfee House of 1894. The site was to be a narrow flat strip on the shore of Lake Michigan. The elongated plan responds to this site constraint but in such a manner as to attempt to make a virtue of the extreme proportions. The house is raised on a shallow terrace plinth with living level below and bedrooms above. The interiors of the house are strangely unrelated to this lavish treatment at the base. A dense wall opens only occasionally to relieve its massive surface. The octagonal library and porte cochere fall in line with and articulate one end of the volume; at the other a blocklike kitchen and dining room is turned ninety degrees to the main axis. The contrast in treatment implies a dynamic movement from one end to the other, but whether the closed-to-open movement is dictated by the view and proximity to the lake (the published perspective suggests that the denser block and not the octagonal end actually enjoys the preferred view) or by some less site-inspired compositional motive is not clear. In any event it lacks the logic and assured expression that was to become apparent in the Husser House five years later. The entry is not integrated into the plan with conviction, as it occurs in a difficult knot of contrived diagonal spaces. Despite these shortcomings, the McAfee House sets the stage for the Husser House. Its similar elongated plan but raised living level demonstrates Wright's ability to critique his former work and to synthesize and edit ideas with a growing assurance. The Heller House is a critical transitional work between these two that helps to clarify planning themes.

The Isidor Heller House of 1897 represents another stage in the development of the type. This building on a narrow site might be seen as a more inflected, stretched version of the tripartite Charnley House turned ninety degrees to the street. The Heller House is sited on a slight rise and approached by a generous stepped terrace that runs perpendicular to the street and parallel to the main axis of the house. The entry occurs off this terrace at ninety degrees to the body of the house and intersects it at a midway point. The resulting tripartite arrangement is not unlike the Charnley House. The living area is situated on one side and the dining and service area on the other, with a stair hall in between. The hall acts as a universal joint that connects the fore and aft portions of the house, and the stair provides a reciprocating vertical connection through the house, that weaves the movement pattern three-dimensionally. The elongated building form articulated with a symmetrical and hierarchical living room terminus, an entry approached off the primary axis and to one side, and an internal tripartite division are themes Wright continued to develop for the next several decades in the context of the in-line house.

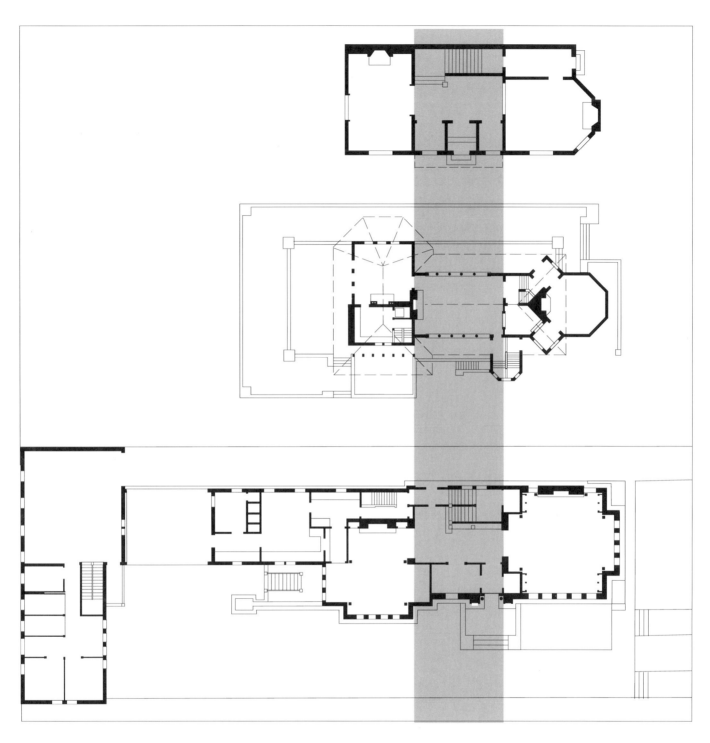

4-35 Comparative plan analysis of Charnley, McAfee, and Heller houses showing the evolution of the In-Line Hearth type

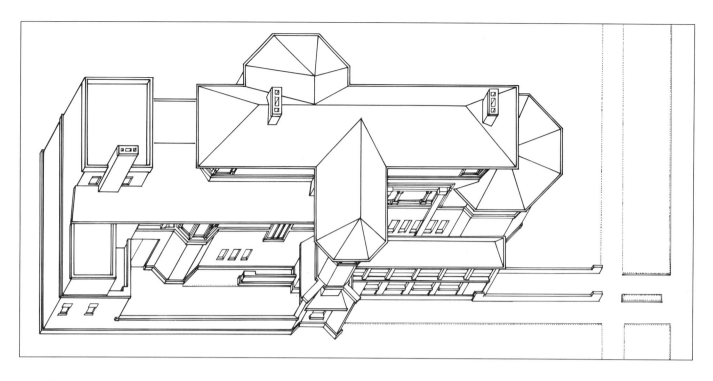

4-36 Plan projection of Husser house

From Husser House to Robie House

The Husser House is an extension of ideas first articulated in the McAfee House, which in turn was closely modeled on H. H. Richardson's plan for the Winn Memorial Library of 1877–78. Wright's Husser House was built on the shores of Lake Michigan, and its raised living level was designed to capitalize on the view that such an elevated position could afford. Its extreme longitudinal plan and its pronounced horizontal aspect make it the first mature example of the in-line type. The linear deployment of the main body of the Husser House can be traced back to the McAfee House, but the cross-axial entry achieved by sliding along its side to a vertical circulation zone that bifurcates the house into living and dining zones is presumably the theme that Wright was to extract from the Heller House.

The Tomek House is of the raised living room type with entry below. It is located on an oblong corner site with driveway entry on the rear flank and a frontal pedestrian approach on the opposing side. The structure is an important transitional link between the Husser and Robie houses. Its elongated plan is modeled on the Husser type but with significant differences in its volumetric expression. On the exterior it plays to the street. Its entire length is unbroken along this side, acquiring a pavilion-like aspect that belies the complication to the rear of the attached service wing. Its extreme linear proportions are made more emphatic by continuous ribbon windows and deep, cantilevered eaves. The plastic unity is emphasized by similar treatment at both of the narrow ends in the form of alcoves and dramatic cantilevered roofs that enforce the notion of a pavilion.

Next to Fallingwater, the Robie House[12] is perhaps Wright's most famous residential design. It has an immediately appealing unity and drama with sufficient incident and detail to qualify and give scale to an otherwise overwhelming singularity. Its unrelenting horizontal composition is reiterated at every level of detail. The roof overhang, raked Roman brick, cantilevered terrace, continuous stone coping, and continuous ribbon windows conspire to give a dynamic sense of movement and even levitation. Wright is claimed to have invented the term *streamline*, and surely this work more than any other from this period embodies the kinesthetic that term evokes. The Robie House is, above all, the fruits of the disciplined development of an idea that seems to unfold with an irresistible scientific logic from the McAfee House onward. Even though its dynamic form, as portrayed in perspective and countless photographs, is its best-known aspect, its final resolution is generated at least as much from Wright's attention to the plan.

The house, which is located on an elongated corner site on the south side of Chicago, has its broad face open toward the south with a view of the park beyond from its raised living level. Significantly, Wright decided not to make the major entry frontal from its broad side but rather indirect from the less narrow frontage to the west. Service yard and garage occupy the extreme eastern edge of the site to the south.

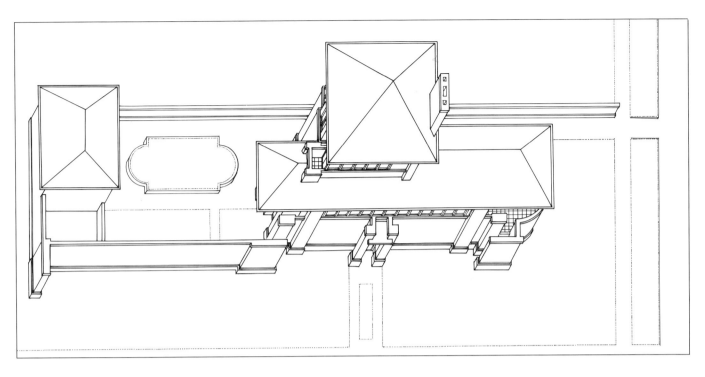

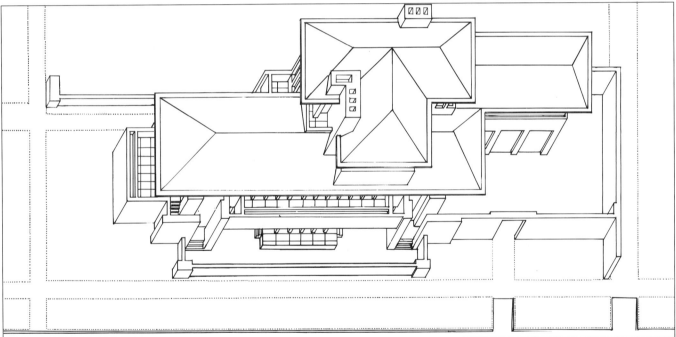

4-37 Plan projection of Tomek house

4-38 Plan projection of Robie house

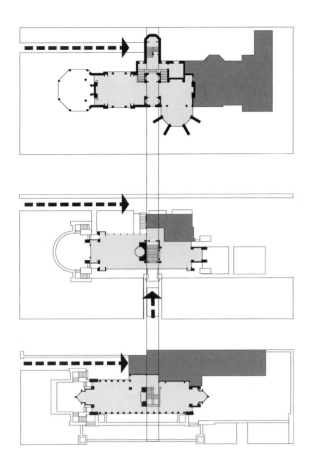

4-39 Comparative plan analysis of Husser, Tomek, and Robie houses showing thematic continuities of access, zoning, and cross circulation core (mirror view of Tomek house is shown to reveal a common plan composition)

The Husser House plan organization is established by the typical baseline axis. It becomes the first step in the design of the plan and acts as a datum for its development. The ensuing longitudinal volume built around it comprises the major elements of the house. The two different ends of the structure suggest a dynamic directionality. At one pole the living room terminates in an outward burst formed by an octagonal porch—a typical motif for Wright during this period. The other pole ends in a service zone comprised of kitchen, servants' rooms, and a stable, which tends to stop the building like a bookend. Projecting from and opposing the linear treatment are two secondary axes. One is formed by the stair and its attendant entry zone, the other by the dining room and its projecting octagonal bay. These secondary volumes are shifted off-axis so that they do not align in plan. Furthermore, their extensions occur on opposite sides of the house, the dining bay toward the lake and the stair toward the landward side. Both of these factors induce a dynamic pinwheel motion, a preferred compositional mode for nearly

all of Wright's mature domestic work. The opposing volumes are stabilized by the in-line volume itself, which is interpenetrated by yet another bounding volume defined by the alcove dining in the kitchen zone and the stair landing and its entry hall. From here the long extension toward the porch is punctuated with a living room bay. The system creates a complex weave of overlapping planes and interpenetrating volumes that could be elaborated ad infinitum.

This compositional approach allows for great continuity in the major living spaces but also acts to give a degree of definition to each minor space. The seemingly contradictory need for individuality of part and unity of the whole is here brilliantly resolved and is a premonition of what was to follow in Wright's other domestic work. The interior-exterior relationship is such that every internal volume finds its external expression. The equilibrium Wright has been able to establish in this manner was a step forward in his quest to unify interior space and achieve a plasticity in the whole.

The Tomek House plan is also organized along a baseline, but here the service zone is placed to one side to create a continuity of major interior spaces and exterior spaces projecting from both ends of the baseline. The living room and dining room on the main level seem to have been conceived as one large room, in contrast to the more incidental spatial treatment of the Husser House. The fireplace and stair have been moved to the center of the living space to punctuate it rather than separate it into two distinct rooms. The hearth at the center simultaneously anchors the house to the land and suggests vertical spatial continuity between levels. The rotational cross-arms and bookend garage of the Husser disappear to be replaced by a disengaged garage and cubic service wing that interlocks the main living level and is completed three-dimensionally by the action of the bedrooms on the level above. The stair volume of the Husser has been withdrawn into the body of the Tomek like a retracted tongue, leaving only a vestige in the form of an entry terrace. The extreme formal and spatial

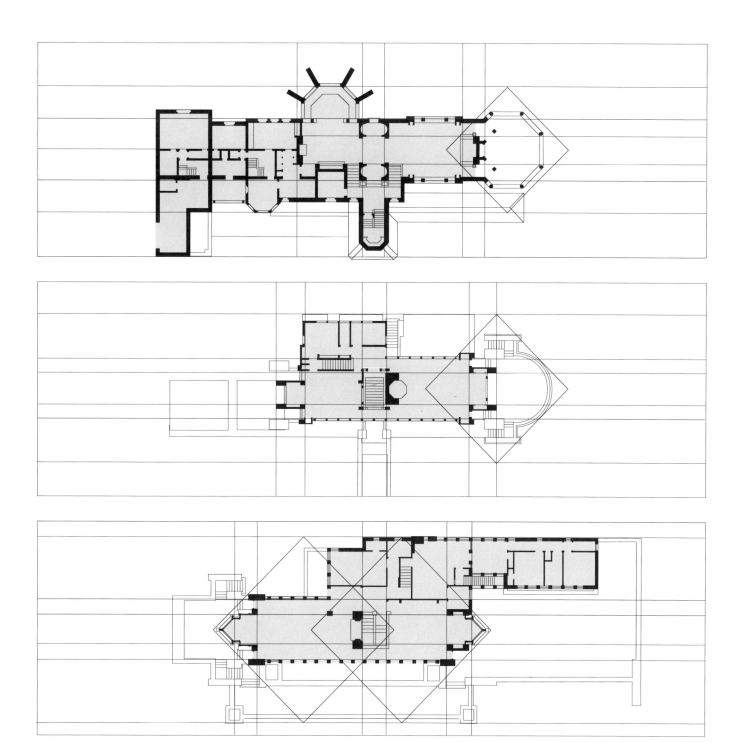

4-40 Plan of Husser house

4-41 Plan of Tomek house

4-42 Plan of Robie house

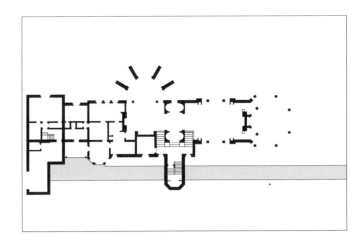

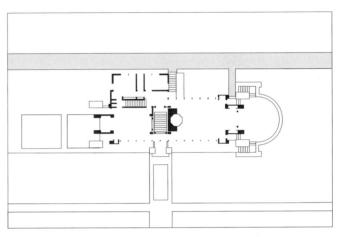

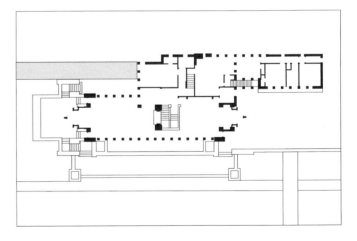

unity of the Tomek House becomes the measure by which Wright develops his ultimate, bold statement along this theme embodied in the Robie House.

The Robie House footprint reveals a longitudinal volume similar to that of the Husser and Tomek houses. This house, however, is even more articulated than either of them and gives the sense of an explicit pavilion that is about to disengage itself from its service wing. This effect is most apparent from the oblique vantage point of the southwest, which effectively obscures the service wing's presence. This vantage point is Wright's classic perspective and photographic view of the house, which underscores his concern about the "photogenic" aspect of his designs. The two prowlike end bays of the pavilion support this reading and suggest an overall shape and proportion akin to that of a sailing vessel. As at the Tomek House, the hearth pierces the center space like a ship's mast. Both the living and ground floor levels are conceived as continuous spaces punctuated and not separated by the hearth. The continuity of space achieved in the plan is elaborated through consistent secondary themes that are particularly apparent at the living room level. The pierced opening in the chimney above the mantel and the stepped ceiling, which gives the impression of an inverted ship's hull, act to unify and express the space.

4-43 Comparative plan analysis of Husser, Tomek, and Robie houses:
Access;
Circulation armature and spatial hierarchy;
Spatial weave and geometry

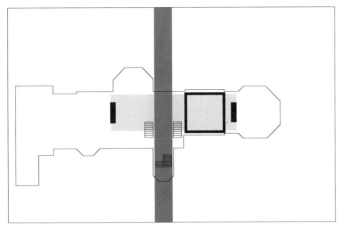

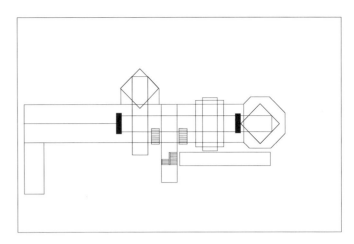

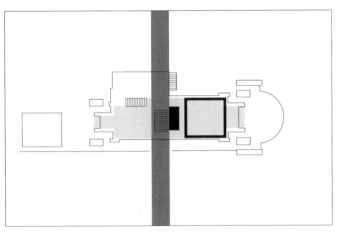

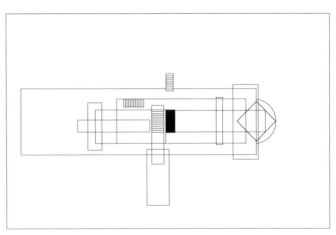

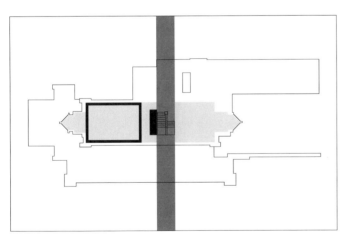

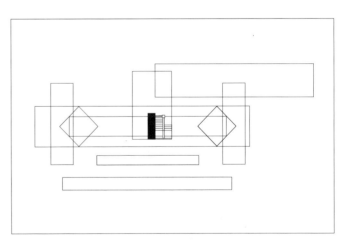

The proportion and unity of the space thus achieved on the living level of the Robie house are remarkably similar to those of the River Forest Tennis Club of 1906. Its prowlike ends display a similar formal treatment, and its broad terrace facing the tennis courts parallels a similar motif in the Robie so much so that it looks as if the two plans were made in collage fashion. The tennis club is only slightly lifted above grade and its plan opens to a central space for gatherings. The Robie, it might be imagined, takes this theme and simultaneously elevates the main level and collapses the central space by fusing the three peripheral fireplaces into a single central core.

The main pavilion seems to be docked alongside its service wing. The kitchen, servants' rooms, garage and other secondary spaces have been so condensed and positioned in parallel orientation that they emphasize rather than counter the movement implied by the primary volume. However, the two volumes do not simply slide by one another. A cross-axial movement appears in the form of the stair and circulation, which literally help to knit the two sides together. Stabilizing their relationship, the bedroom level above interlocks both the living pavilion and the service wing. It is based on a square in plan like that of the Tomek House and is almost symmetrical about the cross-axis, which is further developed formally and spatially to the south with a symmetrical raised terrace and a lower garden that are articulated with extended walls and capped off by broad urns. The fireplace is centered on the principal axis described by the living pavilion. This axis is further reinforced by the symmetrical composition of the cantilevered terrace, doors, garden walls, and urns.

The Robie House represents the climax of Wright's first career and comes at a time when his mastery of an architectonic language was at its peak. Although other projects of the in-line type followed, none captured the imagination of the twentieth-century like the Robie House. Wright subsequently designed versions of the in-line house, but none parallels the Robie House in the same direct way that the Johnson Wax Administration Building parallels the Larkin Building.

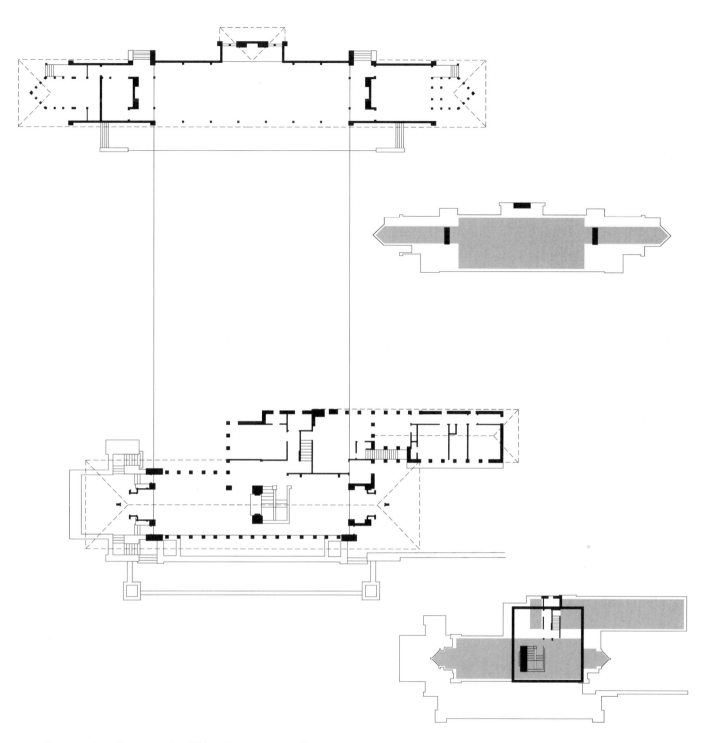

4-44 Comparative plan analysis of River Forest Tennis Club
and Robie house showing similar organizational themes

OTHER VARIATIONS

Characteristically, whenever Wright found a solution to a problem, he embodied it in a formal concept. These concepts frequently reemerged in other designs, strongly etched on the house plan, whereas the expressions in three-dimensional form might be considerably varied. The following pairings of houses help to illustrate some of these formal concepts that provide added dimensions to his work.

The Pinwheel Plan

Precursors of the pinwheel composition can be found in Wright's early house plans in which offset parallel axes induce a dynamic 'twist'. In breaking out of Palladian inspired symmetry the Blossom house plan extends offset axes in the form of semicircle enclosures of the entry porch and the conservatory to the rear. The Winslow house plan, especially the version showing the unexecuted octagonal tea pavilion, also shows divergent 'twists' of elements. The opposing driveway and dining axes are shifted along the 'x' axis, and the porte cochere and tea house extensions suggest a near equivalent shift along the 'y' axis. The beautifully proportioned and symmetrical street facade belies a much more dynamic garden facade. From the rear the rotational movement of the plan is revealed as the opposing volumes of tea house, dining room, porte cochere and even the vertical octagonal stair hall make clear.

There are two different strategies for resolving the confluence of these axes, both of which produce a vertical 'z' axis. The Heurtly house demonstrates the strategy of joining the horizontal axes at a space. Its central stair hall is the vortex of a pinwheeling movement which

joins living, dining, kitchen and bedrooms on the upper level. On the exterior, the prow-shaped bay windows and entry porch express this movement pattern ; while the symmetrical arrangement of the large veranda acts to stabilize the spinning.

The second strategy receives the pinwheel movement of the horizontal axes in a solid vertical core rather than open space. The first house designed in this manner is Wright's simple house in Oak Park of 1889. Although based on Bruce Price's shingle style work, the plan shows distinct tendencies away from the stability and containment implied in that prototype. The curved terraces, extended dining room, rear service stair and porch extend beyond the basic square of the structure in a clear rotational manner. The theme is picked up at the hearth and inglenook which seems to extend rotating arms to embrace a dynamic composition of space. Rotation is also implied by the shifted axes of the hearth and bay window at opposite corners of the living room.

This strategy is continued in Wright's 1903 project for a studio house. It exhibits a complex set of tendencies which might be said to fluctuate between the closed compositional mode with defined central axes and a more open peripheral composition with shifted axes. This plan is interesting because of the ambiguity of incorporating both compositional strategies. The hearth marks the center of a square that acts as the unifying, stabilizing force in the plan. Dynamic rotation is induced by extending arms on shifted axes. The prow-shaped porch is opposed by the bedroom and the studio opposed by the sitting porch.

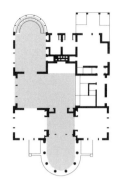

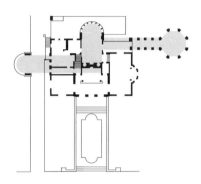

4-45 Comparative plan analysis of the Blossom and Winslow houses showing implied pin-wheel organization

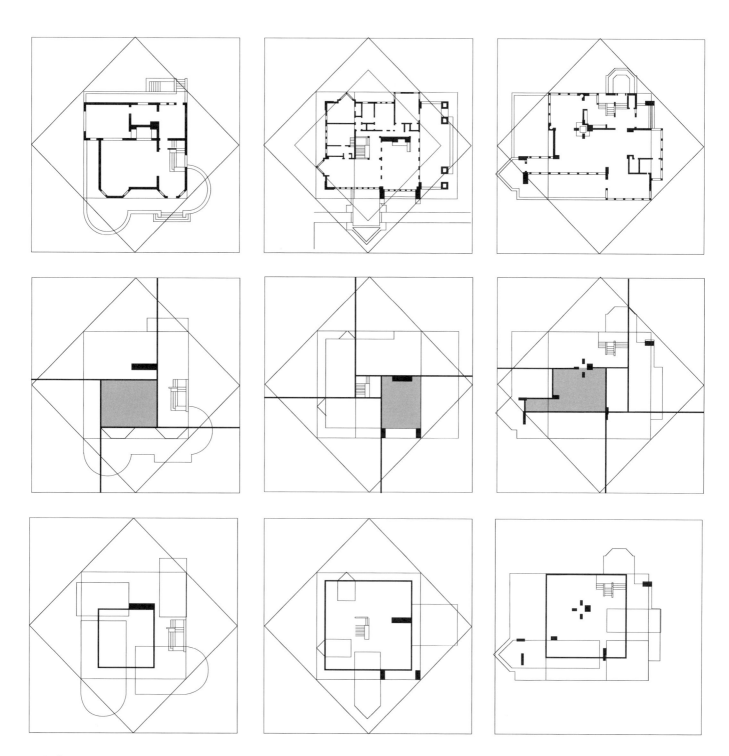

4-46 Comparative plan analysis of the Pin-Wheel Hearth type variations: F.L. Wright Oak Park house, Heurtly house, and F.L. Wright Studio house

The pinwheel appears first in its pure form as a site plan. The Quadruple Block houses of 1901 show a square land parcel divided into four equal parts. Each house is oriented and approached in a consistent but rotated manner. This organizational device results in a series of rotationally symmetrical groupings. Wright claims that this composition insures variety and privacy. Wright's belief in the possibility of infinite variety through mechanical means is here demonstrated in an example which was to inform all his late housing projects. St. Mark's Tower, Price Tower, and Suntop homes develop this theme of rotational symmetry in individual buildings for multiple housing.

A literal use of the symmetrical plan for the individual dwelling is rare. The Johnson house, 'Wingspread' is the exception that proves the rule. It is modeled on the earlier Booth house which sits on a ridge surround by ravines that are crossed by the entry bridge and bedroom wing. The spatial arms extend into the landscape but converge at the center living room space which is developed as a large volume with its own vertical axis. Although these arms are shifted they still develop along two primary axes. The Johnson house is more emphatic. It is organized around a central living room 'teepee' space similar in scale to that of the Booth; its bedroom and service wings rotate around this center like an enormous windmill.

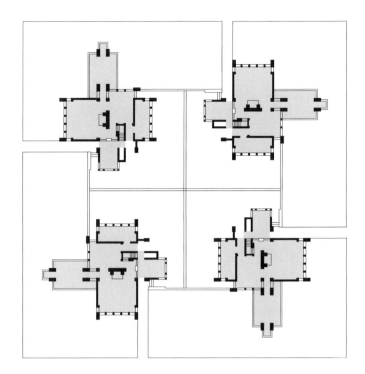

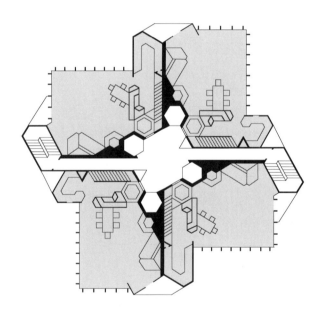

4-47 Plan of Quadruple Block houses exhibiting ideal pin-wheel site organization

4-48 Plan of St. Mark's residential tower project exhibiting ideal pin-wheel site organization

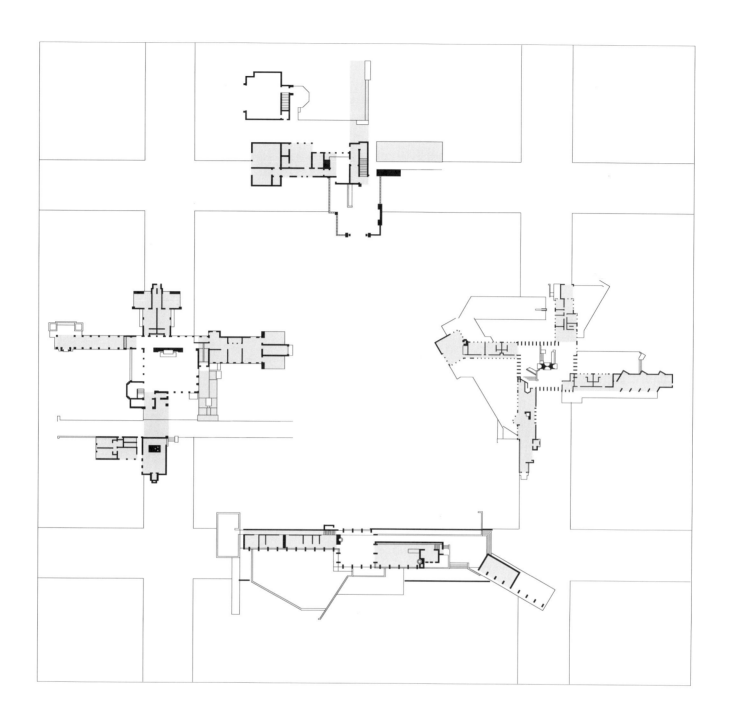

4-49 Plan array showing variations of
the Pin-Wheel type:

Walter Gerts house, Booth house,
Wingspread, H.C. Price house

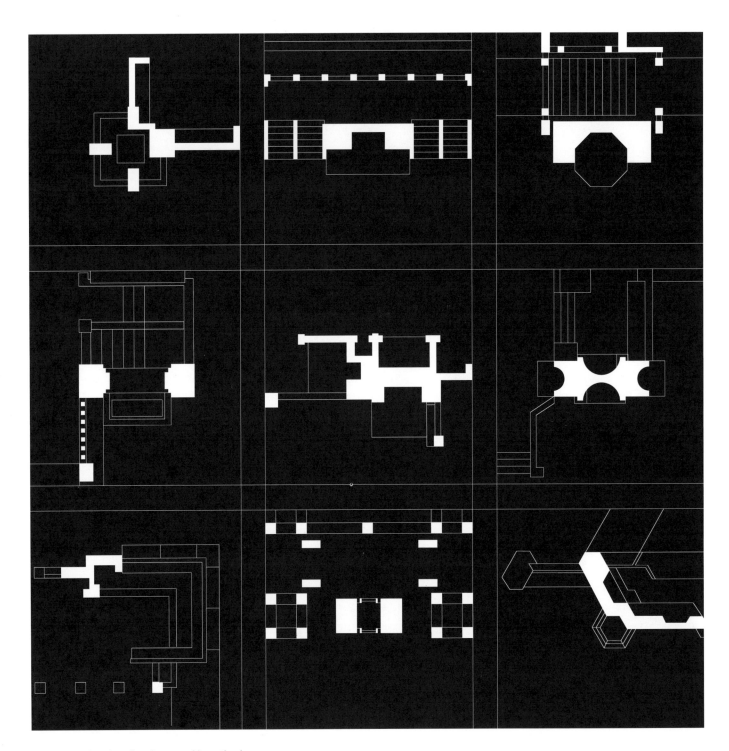

5-1 Array showing fireplace and hearth plans:

F.L. Wright Studio house, Hardy house, Tomek house,
Robie house, Willitts house, Wingspread,
Life house, Martin house, Hanna house

Hearth Themes and Variations

Because residential design accounts for the largest portion of Wright's work, that he would address his principal concerns and evolve most of his concepts within the realm of the hearth type is understandable. In the previous chapter we reviewed the basic variations of the hearth type: the cruciform, hillside, in-line, and pinwheel. These examples illustrate the persistence of organizational concepts throughout Wright's career and the flexibility and inventiveness with which he addressed changes in needs, context, and time. This compact overview represents the trunk and branches of the tree of his thinking as embodied in his designs for the hearth. In this chapter we look at the continuing themes that distinguish his residential architecture, the principles of growth for this tree. We also focus on specific variations or elaborations on Wright's domestic themes.

The relationship between variation and theme is an important part of the realization of the art of architecture just as the successful integration of personal expression and universal concepts lies at the heart of poetry or music. The themes connect Wright's designs with the known, shared world of architectural ideas including determinants of form such as order, unity, geometry, proportion, and hierarchy. The variations on themes connect his designs to the special features or qualities of the site, the client, and the architect. The theme relates to an intellectual, abstract realm; the variations relate to the emotional, experiential realm. However, in the juxtaposition of theme and variation we can fully appreciate the value of both.

In the first part of this chapter we examine a few of Wright's basic themes about the realization and experience of three-dimensional space that consistently place a unique stamp on his domestic work. The themes include space, spatial weave, zoning, siting, unit system, structure, construction, and materials. Wright's persistent point of view about these features of defined space are the source of the energy and sophistication we experience upon entering his houses and a critical part of the means by which he translated principles into forms. The second part of the chapter reviews variations on these themes by comparative analysis of the plans of several pairs of houses: Coonley and Lloyd Lewis, Studio House of 1903, and the second Malcolm Wiley, Glasner and Goetsch-Winkler, Francis Little and Rose Pauson, Robie and Hanna, and Jacobs and Jester houses. Each of the pairs illustrates that even in variations on themes design concepts might reemerge at distant points in Wright's career.

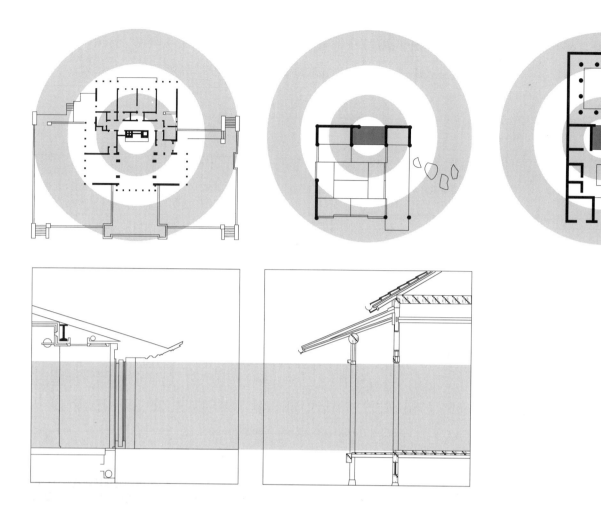

5-2 Cheney house hearth

5-3 Japanese house tokonoma

5-4 Roman house tablinum

5-5 Comparative partial sections of Robie house and a traditional Japanese house showing similar spatial extension

DOMESTIC THEMES

What are the themes Wright pursued in his house designs? Foremost was a notion of centering, with the earth symbolized by the hearth at the core of the dwelling. The hearth provides the focus for the interior space and anchors the house in the landscape. Although drawn to the hearth (and its architectural adjunct, the inglenook) for warmth, shelter, and fellowship, the inhabitant can never occupy its center. Horizontal spaces extend and expand outward from the hearth toward the light and views at the perimeter of the house to suggest continuities with the landscape. Wright's houses have this quality not simply because they have a fireplace. The hearth, at the center of gravity of the dwelling within its dark, intimate

recesses, acquires an intimacy and mystery akin to that of a shrine. In this way Wright's hearth echoes themes found in other architectural traditions, such as the tokonoma of the Japanese house and the tablinum of the Roman house.

SPACE

A unifying theme in all of Wright's houses is his distinctive idea of space.[1] Within the context of domestic design, this development had two interrelated expressions. The first was to conceive of interior and exterior space as a single phenomenon that could move with an unimpeded horizontal extension into the landscape. Glass screens and enclosing walls fracture like louvres pivoted

outward to direct the space to the landscape. The second was to minimize or eliminate altogether the interior divisions of the house. They act more like screens than solid walls. The traditional compartmentalization of interior rooms is replaced with a continuity of space that unifies living rather than segregating it into discrete parts. The realization that the essence of architecture was the space contained and not the container is akin to Lao-Tzu's dictum about the reality of space.[2] Wright's architecture is above all generated by an inner spatial sense seeking expression on the exterior. This quality is the sense of plasticity that Wright so often mentioned.

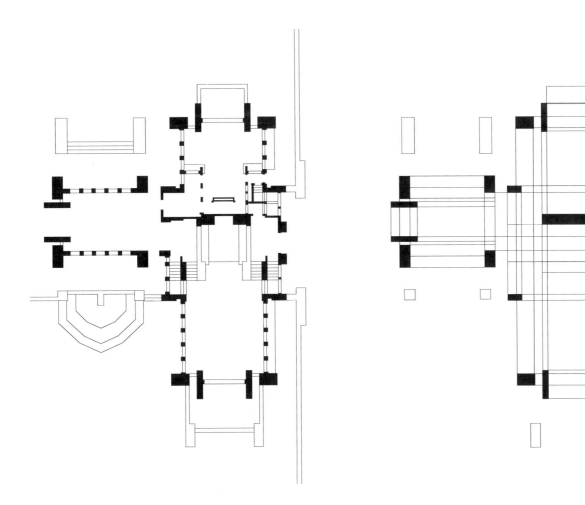

5-6 Plan analysis of the Ullman house
showing spatial weave

THE SPATIAL WEAVE

Space described in such terms can still be inert or yield indifferent results. Wright's fertile imagination, aided by his training in abstract design, seized upon the metaphor of weaving to describe and perhaps help to formulate his ideas about space. Even a casual look at one of his early Prairie houses such as the Ullman House of 1905 reveals a complexity of overlapping, interweaving spaces. The two-dimensional plan overlap becomes a three-dimensional volumetric interpenetration. These volumes are not described literally by four walls but are only implied, some-times to a greater or lesser extent, with piers, roof overhangs, ceiling recesses, terraces, garden walls, plantings, paving, and so forth. "True beauty could be discovered only by one who mentally completed the incomplete" is the essence of this attitude, an attitude foreign to the classical tradition but embraced in Eastern philosophy by Lao-Tzu and Okakura.[3] Within this world of multivalent space, we can experience a multiplicity of events simultaneously. All Wright's houses, including those from his Prairie, Wilderness, and Usonian periods, possess this dynamic weave that renders a shimmering spatial fabric rare in the history of architecture.

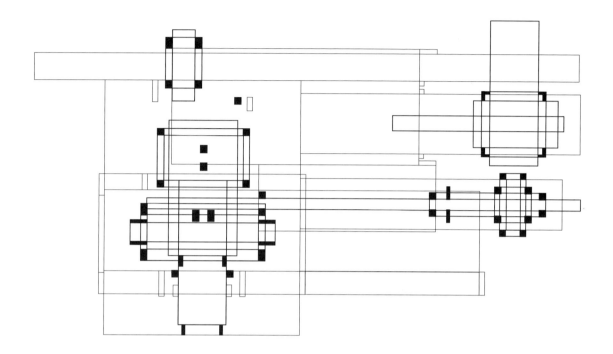

5-7 Plan analysis of the Martin house showing spatial weave

The great variety, which is an irrefutable aspect of Wright's work, when over-emphasized can mask the underlying order that is common to the work and an integral part of his approach to creativity. This order at its simplest level can be reduced to a systematic development of major and minor cross-axes. These become the armature or "seed-germ" for the spatial volumes or other architectural elements they describe. To describe this system of crossed axis upon axis, Wright used the verb *weave* and called himself "the weaver." This textile analogy is perhaps a more descriptive term, for it captures the essence of what Wright had in mind: the continuity of space passing over and under and through other space. *Axis* was perhaps too architectural a term for Wright and conjured up negative associations with

classicism and the Beaux Arts method of composition. Furthermore, it may have suggested a less continuous relationship, one with terminations and crosses rather than the fluidity suggested by the woven thread.

In applying axes to the design process, Wright seems to follow the advice of Louis Sullivan: "There is always supposed to be a main axis: however much it may be overgrown or over-whelmed by the vitality of its sub-axes. Herein lies the challenge to the imagina-tion."[4] The establishment of a horizontal axis, referred to as the *base line* by Wright, was the very first primal step in the design process. It may take the role of the centerline for a primary spatial volume, an edge, or another key organizing element, such as a terrace,

drive, or pathway. Its placement in context was important and usually influenced by the natural site features, including topography and view. Wright could then proceed to cross or weave other volumes with this primary one. In the design process the original primary axis might be eclipsed by one or more of its cross-axes, thus rotating the plane of reference by ninety degrees. This changed orientation seems to be a common trait in his work, and some plans of this type can be oriented about one of two plausible primary axes.

Wright's axes were not just "built axes"; they did not necessarily all occur in the same plane, and often they were layered or stacked vertically. His driveways and paths and even natural elements such as ravines or streambeds

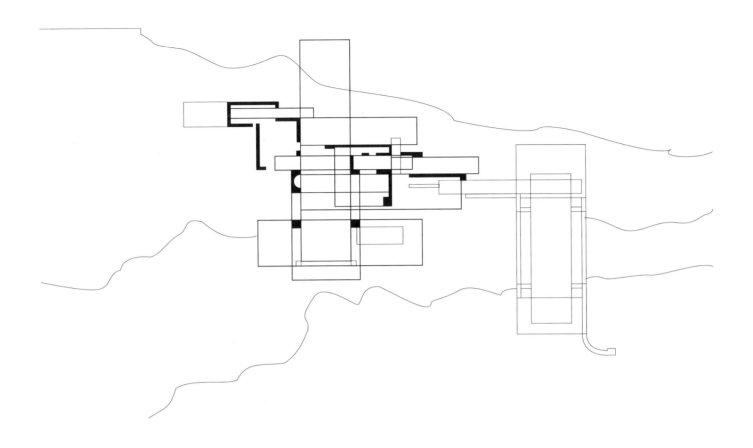

5-8 Analysis of spatial weave in the Fallingwater house and site

could assist in describing axes and corresponding shafts of space that became integral parts of the spatial weave, often occurring in layers below, above, or through the main house. In some house designs Wright's predominantly horizontal spatial weave was complemented by a vertical spatial weave where vertical spaces, chimneys, or other building elements expressed vertical axes.

The most splendid example of this kind is to be found in Fallingwater, where the landscape is beautifully woven into the structure. A visitor encounters this theme immediately upon approaching the house. The drive crosses the entry bridge spanning the mountain stream and connecting to the main house by low retaining walls. The drive continues up a gentle slope between the structure and the rock ledge. At this point visitors may enter underneath a porte cochere formed by concrete beams spanning the gap between house and natural hillside. Continuing ahead, the visitor drives through and around to the upper-level garage and guest house. From here the visitor continues across a second bridge, which reiterates the theme of the lower. It spans the drive and ties the house back to the rock ledge. The visitor has just experienced a rhythmic spatial weave of movement over, under, and through that was accomplished with a mixture of architectural, architectonic, and natural elements. The resultant composition effectively unites architecture and nature as one.

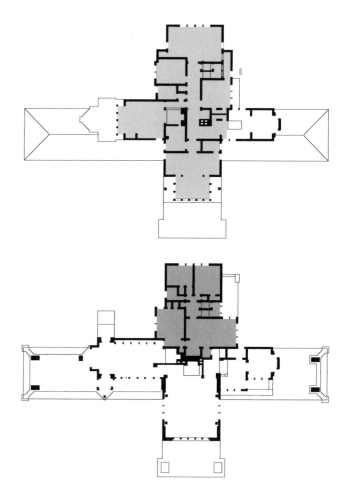

5-9 Zoning of upper and lower levels
of Willitts house

THE ZONED HOUSE

During the Prairie years Wright tended
to separate and articulate program
elements into distinct volumes that were
expressed as such on the exterior. The
houses usually have three distinct
zones: living and dining, private and
sleeping, and service, including garage
and outbuildings. Besides formal living
and dining rooms, the first zone often
contained a range of other minor
spaces. Typically a study, library, or
similar intimately scaled space would be
found in addition to a reception area or
entry hall. The inglenook was a prominent feature positioned next to the
massive fireplace it embraced. All
spaces in the living zone were usually
on the same level or separated by a few
steps. When the living level is raised,

the ground floor directly beneath usually
contains a playroom or other common
room. Rather than being assigned to
separate rooms, living functions were
interconnected as a single spatial
continuum. When a greater degree of
privacy was necessary, screens were
used. Wright had banished the door
from the living area forever.

The service zone consisted of the
kitchen, pantry storage, and so forth,
along with servants' rooms; sometimes
a garage or stable was included in this
zone as well. Often the services
occupied an entire wing and therefore
were expressed as separate and less
hierarchically important elements. The
disposition of these rooms was straightforward and efficient and lacked any
special architectural treatment. The

services could occupy one or more
levels, although they usually were
clustered on the living level but separated from the rest of the family activi-
ties; a separate service stair linked all
levels of the house. The garage or
stable might be attached to the house,
but even when detached these structures were integrated into the design.
Often they were connected to the house
by garden wall, pergolas, or another
landscape element that defined exterior
space. Sometimes the automobile is
recognized by a porte cochere, typically
integrated into the main house, as a
continuation of the broad cantilevered
eaves that provide protected entry to the
house for passengers.

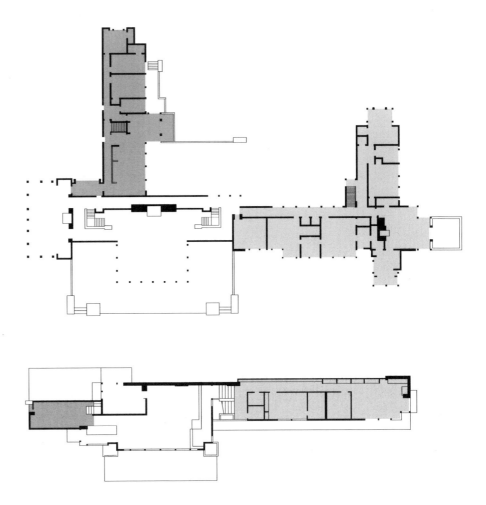

5-10 Raised living plan of Coonley house showing functional zoning

5-11 Raised living and split level bedroom plan of Lloyd Lewis house showing functional zoning

The bedroom and private zone was frequently lifted to an upper level and connected to the ground floor by the primary family stair. The bedrooms were usually given less attention than the living zone in terms of their accommodation and architectural design, and some display clumsy planning. Relatively few plans of the upper sleeping levels were published by Wright, perhaps an indication of his view of their importance. Typically he imposed a compact symmetrical arrangement on this level, modified by the stair and hearth core. The expression on the exterior was carefully controlled, however, and the symmetry of the upper plan was brought into harmony with the rest of the design.

The Willitts House is a good example of this programmatic arrangement, but the later Coonley House shows to what extent the theme could be extended and proliferated across the landscape.

During the middle years and especially during the Usonian period, Wright reduced the number of program elements in his house designs to reflect his interest in the changing living patterns in the American household. Consequently, the house is developed in simpler terms than the Prairie House. It typically consists of two rather than three zones. The living zone contains a living area focused on the hearth, a dining alcove integral with the larger

space, and a "work space," or kitchen, defined as a prominent volume attached to the hearth. The kitchen behind closed doors, serviced by the maid and butler, was replaced with a more democratic system; the Usonian House had no "menials." The garage was replaced by a carport to eliminate the gaping hole of the garage door. The private zone might include a study, guest room, or workshop in addition to the bedrooms. Usually these spaces are treated as cells and efficiently lined up along a single loaded gallery or corridor. The end of the wing is articulated as a special formal event and may contain the master bedroom or other specialized program element.

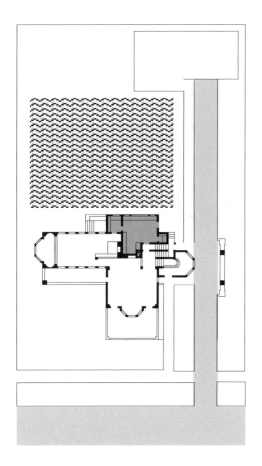

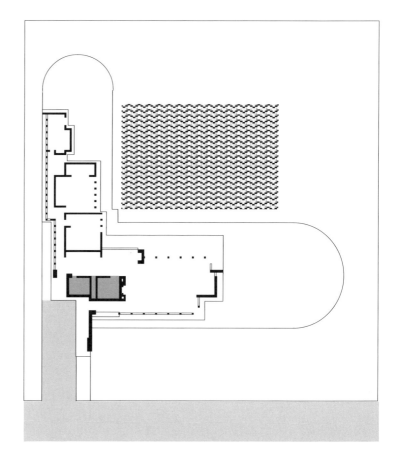

5-12 Plan of Second Ladies Home Journal house showing living area oriented toward the street

5-13 Plan of first Jacobs house showing living area oriented toward a private rear yard

SITING

Wright's ideas about siting the house in the landscape are among his most poignant architectural observations. Contained within this seemingly neutral preference for seeing building in the round is a deep antiurban bias. Buildings that lack frontality can be said to be incapable of defining the space associated with the traditional city, such as streets, squares, and open space. They are conceived more as objects to be placed within space or alternatively to generate space rather than define its edges. Wright's houses were conceived without the context of corridor street in mind; the closest he gets is the rather loose alignment along suburban sites such as Oak Park that do acknowledge front and back to a limited degree by the location of services toward the rear and major rooms toward the street. However, Wright's Usonian houses deliberately turn their backs to the street and open instead to a rear garden. The gaping carport, a remnant of the porte cochere, seems to inhale its visitors like a vacuum. The statement is emphatic: The relationship to the private world and the landscape is to be cultivated. The public world of the street (or what is left of it) is to be denied.

Although Wright's houses do not normally configure space at the scale of urban form, they are crafted supremely well to modulate exterior space associated with the individual dwelling. Courts, gardens, terraces, fountains, and the like form an integral part of the dwelling and become extensions of it. The entry court at Taliesin and the cantilevered terraces of Fallingwater are only two of the more conspicuous examples. Even the modest Usonian houses never lose their intimate connection with the exterior, as both the Goetsch-Winkler House and the first Jacobs House demonstrate so well.

The spatial connectedness to landscape is further enforced by its grounding on the earth itself. The building grows out of the earth; it does not levitate above like a Villa Savoye. Even though dramatic cantilevers are prominent from time to time, they are carried back to the ground on sturdy supports. The earth, whether flat or sloped, high or low, is embraced. Wright said of Taliesin West that he did not so much build it as "dig it up."

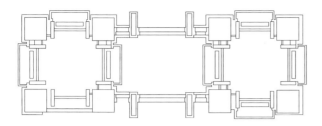

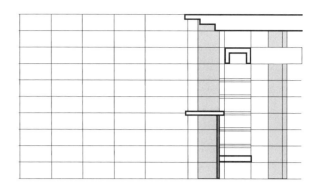

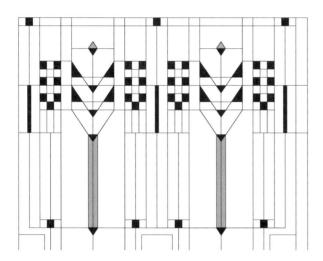
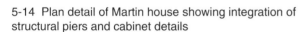

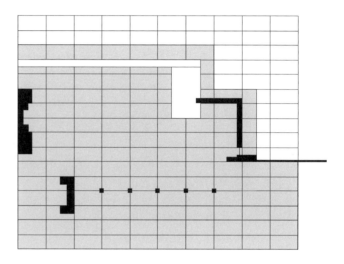

5-14 Plan detail of Martin house showing integration of structural piers and cabinet details

5-15 Detail of leaded glass design for Martin house

5-16 Partial elevation/section of first Jacobs house showing vertical unit system

5-17 Partial plan of first Jacobs house showing horizontal unit system

UNIT SYSTEM

All the buildings I have ever built, large and small, are fabricated upon a unit system as the pile of a rug is stitched into the warp. Thus each structure is an ordered fabric; rhythm, consistent scale of parts, and economy of construction are greatly facilitated by this simple expedient—a mechanical one absorbed in a final result to which it has given more consistent texture, a more tenuous quality as a whole.[5]

The importance of the grid, or "unit system," as Wright preferred to call it, provides an important underlying structure that has profound consequences for his architecture. His preoccupation with this method of design probably stems from his early Froebel training, as Richard MacCormac has convincingly demonstrated.[6] Once implanted in Wright's fertile imagination,

this idea flowered under the tutelage of Sullivan, as Wright's designs, especially for tile, prove. His interest was further supported by Owen Jones's *Grammar of Ornament*, a pivotal text that demonstrated that an infinite wealth of design riches could be created based on a simple system of grids and overlapping grids. These examples proved to Wright that "mechanical means to infinite variety" was not an impractical dream.

The term "unit system" is more descriptive than grid and more inclusive in its meaning. Not only is there a pejorative cast to the term grid that associates it with inflexible monotony but also it implies a purely two-dimensional understanding. The unit system can imply a three-dimensional spatial weave whereby elements appear and disappear and then reappear through spatial

manipulation of elements. This is the warp and woof of which Wright so often spoke.

The practical dividend of this system was to allow for standardized planning and building construction procedures and parts that were to result in economic advantages, at least in theory. The horizontal module was often four feet by four feet or four feet by two feet, thus capitalizing on the building industry's standardized dimensions in wood and masonry. The vertical module, also based on wood and masonry practices but less directly so, was more varied in treatment. The Usonian homes were based on a one-foot, one-inch stratification that cut through the entire house like an egg slicer, governing mullion placement, sill and door heights, and built-in furniture and bookshelves.

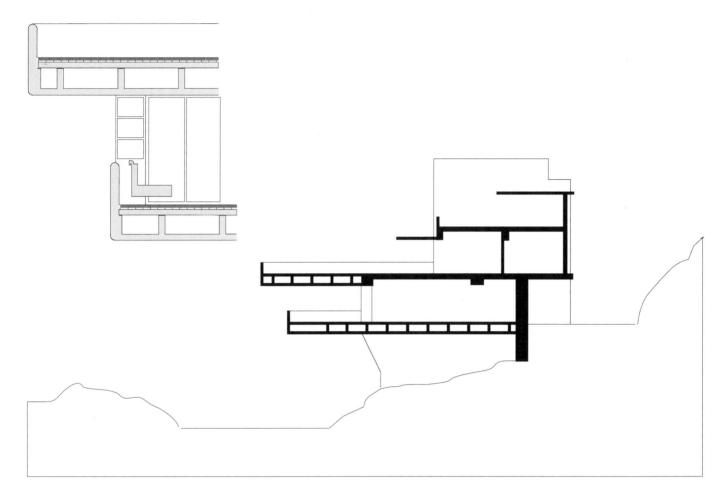

5-18 Detail section of Fallingwater showing integration of structure with mechanical system

5-19 Section of Fallingwater showing reinforced concrete slab construction

STRUCTURE AND CONSTRUCTION

When viewed in a technologically deterministic way, Wright's houses occasionally embody engineering or construction innovations; the mechanical systems at the Martin House and the structural design at Fallingwater stand out. However, technology was not the ultimate determinant of form. Occasional forays into innovative structure and construction such as his textile block houses result in serious technical shortcomings, no matter how intriguing the initial premise may have been in the abstract. The plastic results are always more satisfying than the pragmatic necessities. We look to the Robie House for reasons other than structural or constructional methods. Even though Fallingwater makes a conspicuous show of structure, it is always in the service of

a larger idea—which is why Fallingwater is more interesting than a simple collection of dramatically cantilevered trays.

MATERIALS

Wright's sense of materials lent a special flavor to his vocabulary of abstract forms and interpenetrating space. The "nature of materials" expressed an attitude that attempted to harmonize all aspects of the design with nature or, paradoxically, the machine. Its message was not to fight the material at hand by making it behave like another; therefore, wrought iron should not be made to look like stone and stone should not be asked to behave like iron. The inherent qualities of each material should be understood and allowed to govern an appropriate expression. His

houses give a good indication of where this approach leads and perhaps reveal some of its contradictions. Fallingwater is no doubt the supreme example of the synthesis of materials and architectural expression. Nevertheless, many of Wright's identical plan types are executed in a variety of materials. The Martin-Barton House in brick and wood served as the plan type for the Hollyhock House, which was built in stud and stucco but was really intended to be built of reinforced concrete. The Prairie House could switch from wood and stucco to masonry and hidden steel without markedly influencing the form and certainly without changing spatial qualities. Although undoubtedly stimulating Wright to new invention, the materials seem to aid rather than rigidly determine any given design.

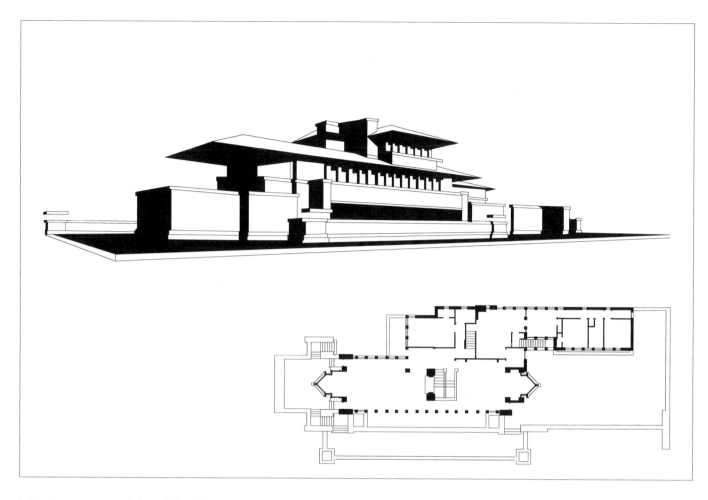

5-20 Perspective and plan of Robie House

ORGANIC VERSUS CLASSICAL

For Wright, organic form did not mean
the literal imitation of nature but an
abstraction based on an understanding
of natural principles. In his usage of the
word to describe organic design, he
seems to have relied on two very
different traditions. One is linked to a
nineteenth-century idea of growth
expressed by Herbert Spencer.[7] He
could liken animal or vegetable growth
to mathematics and specifically makes
an analogy to crystals and their forma-
tion. The other notion of organic design
has a classical base. When Wright
insists on a relation between the part
and the whole and the whole and the
part, he is simply paraphrasing Alberti
and other Renaissance theorists.[8]

Wright's domestic architecture is usually
characterized as informal. For the most
part this observation is correct. Wright
cherished this quality as a distinct virtue
in his houses and never tired of comparing his "organic" informal approach to
the rigid symmetries and axes of
classical design and Palladianism. In
contrast, his public buildings were often
rigidly symmetrical and organized about
one or more major and minor axes.
However, a strict, informal classification
of Wright's residential work fails to
acknowledge the more complex attitude
toward classicism that this work exhibits.

Wright was not an advocate of the
picturesque, even though many of his
admirers have tried to label him as such.

He made his position clear when he
discussed his perspective representation of his designs:

The schemes are conceived in three
dimensions as organic entities, let the
picturesque perspective fall how it will. While
a sense of the incidental perspectives the
design will develop is always present, I have
great faith that if the thing is rightly put
together in true organic sense with
proportions actually right the picturesque will
take care of itself.[9]

101

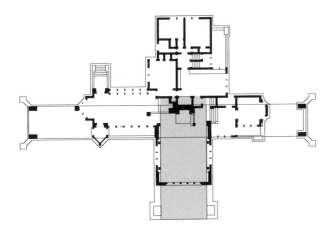

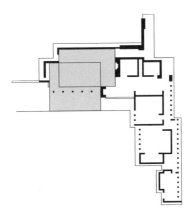

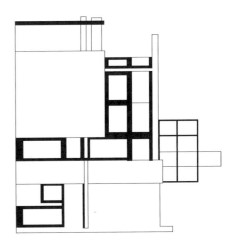

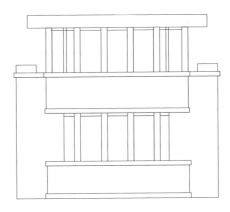

5-21 Willitts house plan showing the classical symmetry of the living room

5-22 Jacobs house plan showing informal asymmetry of living room

5-23 Rotated elevation of Schroeder house by Gerit Rietveld demonstrating anti-gravitational composition

5-24 Elevation of Gale house demonstrating gravitational composition

CLASSICISM

Almost all the Prairie houses exhibit a debt to classical precepts of design. The Willitts House, for example, is neatly organized about two major axes with minor cross-axes occurring at intervals. Each end of the resultant cruciform is carefully designed with a symmetrical terminus emphasizing the axiality of each. These precepts are evident not only in the hierarchically important spaces such as the living room, porte cochere, dining room, and porch, but also in the service wing, where twin maids' rooms are expressed as a symmetrical volume on the exterior. The building is further divided into a tripartite organization in both plan and elevation. In general, local symmetries can be discovered in Wright's work at any period, although Wright's domestic work tends to become more asymmetric over time, climaxing in his Usonian homes, which almost, but never quite, relinquish classical principles.

The classical base, shaft, and capital organization appears in Wright's work as well. Wright's "water table" or raised podium was rationalized in practical terms as a means to combat moisture, but it also provided a visual base on which to place his building, a kind of stylobate. The middle section of horizontally banded walls and ribbons of glass were then emphatically capped off by the deep, overhanging eaves. The proportions evident in the plan and elevations employ simple whole-number relationships and especially make use of the square. It reveals a mastery of proportion that went far beyond his more overtly classical contemporaries. Wright's buildings always acknowledge gravity, even though they may display a derring-do attitude with cantilevered members. Unlike De Stijl examples, his building elevations do not make sense turned on their 90 or 180 degrees. Gerit Rietveld's Schroeder house, for example, would be able to sustain such an interpretation, but even Wright's most abstract houses, such as the Gale, could not. Gravity is a law that Wright chose not to transgress.

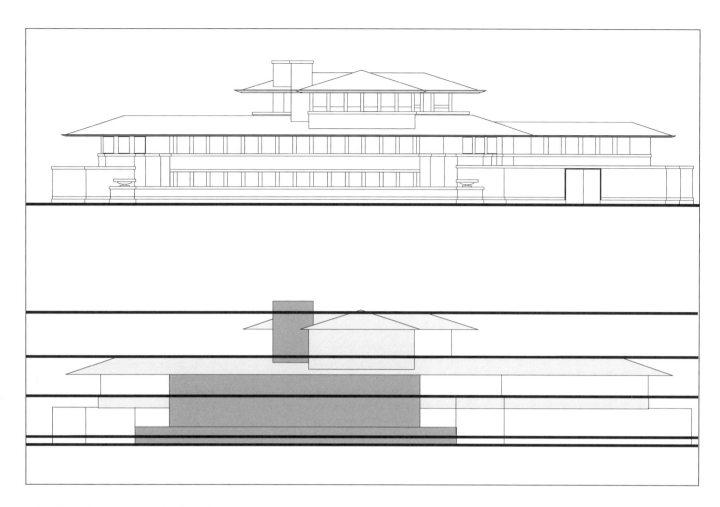

5-25 Elevation and analysis of Robie house showing dual symmetries

FRONTALITY AND ROTATION

Wright's houses do not have a facade in any ordinary sense of the word, and almost no elevations of his work were published during his lifetime. No elevations appear in the one hundred plates of drawings in his international debut.[10] Hitchcock's classic study, *In the Nature of Materials*, which was prepared with Wright's assistance, has more than four hundred illustrations. The preponderance consists of photographs, perspective drawings, plans, occasional sections, but only one elevation, the McCormick House project of 1907, is included.[11] Only since documents from Taliesin have been made available have we seen that elevations were not simply the literal translation of the plan but an important part of Wright's design process. His deliberate use of studied proportions and vertical axial relationships would have been impossible to achieve in perspective. Considering that other architects such as Le Corbusier make a conspicuous display of the facade in both drawings and photographs, why are they not illustrated in Wright's publications? Obviously Wright did not want his buildings to be understood as flattened planes but rather as plastic volumes, which is in keeping with his well-known disdain for the "paper-thin cardboard box" of modern European architecture. Virtually all his perspectives and photographs are taken from diagonal vantage points that emphasize the volumetric quality of the building. Wright's preference for the oblique view expressed his desire for dynamic formal and spatial relationships instead of the static relationship that he felt was implied by frontality. Seeing Wright's buildings in elevation is often a visual shock, and we might not immediately recognize even a familiar work such as the Robie House or Fallingwater.

THE VARIATIONS ON DOMESTIC THEMES

To further illustrate the potential of the domestic themes and Wright's creative approach to architectural design, we have selected a number of examples of residential designs to demonstrate variations on some of the themes previously discussed.

Spatial Weave: The Francis Little and Rose Pauson Houses

In their materials and construction, the Francis Little House of 1913 in Minnesota and the Rose Pauson House of 1940 in the Arizona desert demonstrate Wright's regional approach to design. However, their plans reveal strong similarities in interpretation to the in-line hearth type. Both exhibit a dynamic interpretation of Wright's concept of spatial weave. The Little House crowns the ridge of a gentle rise in the landscape. A large terrace acts as a focus and organizational datum for the house, which is conceived as a collection of more or less discrete elements that straddle the spine of the hill in a stepped diagonal line. A closer inspection reveals a clear progression from the contained bedroom wing at one end to the living volume at the other that becomes progressively more open and disengaged. The theme culminates in the screened pavilion, which completes the movement by turning its axis ninety degrees to the main terrace. An informal trail of garden terraces and stairs carries the system into the landscape. This movement is countered by a formal

entry stair and terrace perpendicular to the main terrace but parallel to the screened pavilion. These elements are set off axis from one another to suggest a rotational shift not unlike that of the Husser House entry stair and dining bay.

The entry axis thus established intersects the composition at the critical joint between living room volume and screened pavilion. This vantage point offers a view of the landscape beyond, and the visitor is made to prepare to spiral off axis into the great living room to the left or the screened pavilion to the right. The diagonal axis of the site is continued through the living room and dining hall by a movement system that connects diagonally opposite corners. A fireplace acts as a hinge between these spaces and stabilizes the main axis of the living room. The open terrace enjoys an oblique view to one side of the ridge, and the dining hall offers an equivalent diagonal prospect to the other side. The diagonal is continued to the elaborated bedroom wing that features a pavilion-like terminus at either end; kitchen services are below.

The tripartite division on the first level of the Rose Pauson House of 1940 and the cross-axial movement of the entry sequence recall similar themes in the Little House. The Pauson House responds to an entirely different regional context and employs radically different architectural vocabulary and materials. Desert stone fused by concrete into massive battered pylons and stepped terraces acts as an armature for the

wood-sheathed volumes that support and define interior space. The structure straddles a low ridge that affords spectacular views of the vast desert plain and the mountains beyond. The entry sequence begins at the base of its hill at the carport and gate and seems to harpoon the broad flank of the structure above and pierce through its skin to the other side. At this point the visitor becomes aware of the mountain range that was partially hidden by the wall-like structure. Almost immediately the visitor turns ninety degrees to finally encounter the entry. Underscaled and unexpected, the threshold passes through a dark, compressed gallery that finally climaxes in the two-story living room, which affords a magnificent framed view of the mountains beyond.

The living room is orthogonal in plan, but it is defined by a dynamic arrangement of solids and voids that conspire to give a strong diagonal axis. The visitor enters at the angle of the dining room and the fireplace mass, which turns as it meets its far corner. Diagonally opposite the entry is a glazed, two-story glass wall that also turns its corner. The resulting shift twists the space along an oblique axis. On the first level the entry passageway separates the house into a service core and a living, dining, and kitchen core. The upper-level bedroom and balcony bridge the gap like a giant beam to provide a visual and formal link of the two sides.

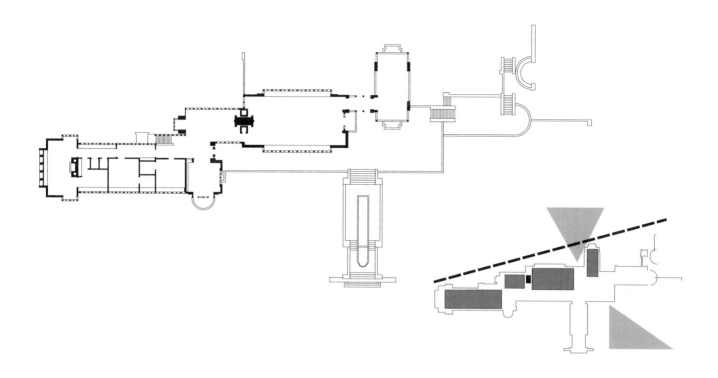

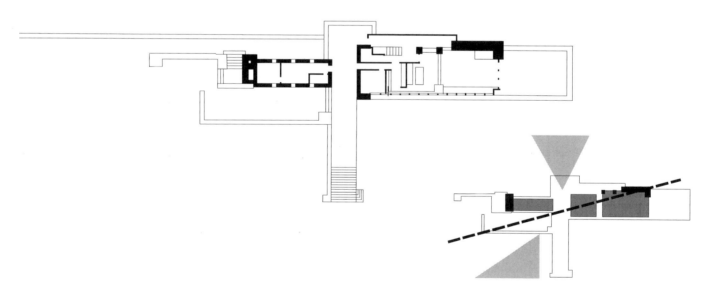

5-26 Comparative plan analysis of the Francis Little and Pauson houses
showing similar formal and experiential organizing strategies

Zoning

Early in his career Wright's project for a studio house (1903) demonstrates his desire to explore new interpretations of the zoning of domestic functions, particularly in the principal living areas. An unimpeded flow of space is created between the living, dining, and studio zones. Even the small bedroom can share in the dynamic configuration of space.

In 1934, Wright's design for the second Malcolm Willey House, on a gently sloping site in Minneapolis, combines living and dining in one large space with a separate, articulated bedroom wing. The entry through the living room wing makes through circulation necessary to the bedroom, a planning flaw that Wright later corrected in similar houses by placing the entry at the joint between the two wings. The organization could be seen as a "bent" in-line house because the bedroom wing makes a hook to enclose the yard like a garden wall. The innovation in the planning of the combined living-dining room arrangement with simplified kitchen and services, which was to lead to his Usonian House, stemmed from Wright's determination to build an economic and simplified program for the average American family.

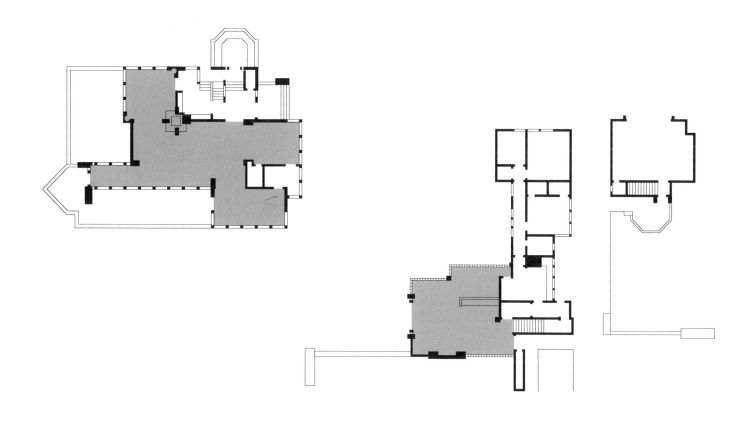

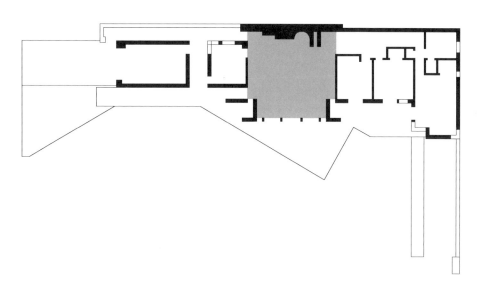

5-27 Comparative plan analysis of F.L. Wright Studio house, Gerts, and Second Willey houses showing spatial integration of living and dining areas

Siting: The Avery Coonley and Lloyd Lewis Houses

Important departures from the antiurban residential object floating in the landscape can be found in the plan compositions of the Coonley and Lloyd Lewis houses. Both designs capture and cultivate the landscape in the form of exterior spaces partially enclosed by building components. These exterior courts become principal organizers of the houses while preserving extensions of space into the natural landscape.

The wall-like Lloyd Lewis house faces toward the river and turns its back toward the land. This duality between its two long sides is qualified by the narrow ends, which terminate in pavilion-like cantilevers. The living, dining, and kitchen work space occupy an elevated position in the "head" with servant and guest quarters at the same grade as the entry below. The "tail," located a half level above the ground plane, contains bedrooms and is accessed by a long, single-loaded gallery corridor. The resulting split-level section is connected by a stair that connects the two parts and is accessed through the entrance loggia. The ensemble resembles a steam engine pulling a coal tender with the stair acting as the coupler. Although some similarities to the Robie House should be immediately apparent, a third example from Wright's Prairie years can make a connection to both the Robie and Lloyd Lewis houses.

Both the core portion of the Coonley complex and the Lloyd Lewis House display a similar disposition of functional elements. The living rooms act as the key to the plan. Although that of the Coonley is T-shaped and the Lloyd Lewis is oblong, both define a hierarchical locus of activity. Both act as a compositional lens that focuses energy outward toward the landscape. In both houses the axis originates in the hearth and expands into the living area, then to its terrace planting area, and then to the natural landscape beyond. The compression and closure at one pole transform into expansion and openness at the other. The analogous organization of the two buildings includes the water element; the formal pool in the Coonley has its equivalent in the flowing river of the Lloyd Lewis. Both water elements—one placid and the other dynamic—relate back to the hearth, which enshrines the household flame. The hearth is rooted to the earth but lifted into the air overlooking the water. The orchestration of the four primary elements in these two buildings defines a cosmological significance for Wright that is apparent in many of his houses, Fallingwater being perhaps the most striking example of a grounded hearth and airborne space over flowing water. The dining service and bedroom wings that attach to the living room help to define Wright's changing ideas about the programmatic nature of the house and his concomitant transformed notion of formal to informal composition.

A less symmetrical development of the Coonley unfolds as the visitor moves further away from the axis defined by the hearth and the reflecting pool. The paired symmetrical stairs at the edge of the living room act as hinges. One connects to the entry porte cochere below and the dining and service wing above. The other connects the playroom directly below and the bedroom wing above. All parts of the house are linked both vertically and horizontally to the living room by the stairs and by a narrow passageway behind the fireplace and its flanking screen walls. Although the overall organization is asymmetrical, individual and coupled instances of symmetrical rooms are imbedded within its length, a typical treatment for Wright in many of his linear plan elements. Similarly the bedroom wing is an asymmetrical, rambling, L-shaped wing. Here as well, however, symmetrical events punctuate its ends and midpoints.

The Lloyd Lewis House lacks paired symmetrical stairs, an elaborated service wing, and a separate dining room. Yet all these elements are present as vestiges and can be thought of as being partially absorbed elements in a new ensemble. This formulation allows a simple transformation process to explain the change. A simple attenuation of the Coonley bedroom wing would yield a similar plan.

The point of this analysis is not to insist that Wright used the Coonley as a specific model for the Lloyd Lewis. It is rather to serve as a vehicle that will allow us to speculate on Wright's design method and ultimately the buildings themselves. It suggests that even late in his career Wright valued the themes in his earlier work and was able to continue those themes in a transformed state. Novelty per se was less important to Wright than rendering appropriate form to the conditions at hand. In this sense, then, all his buildings were transitional buildings.

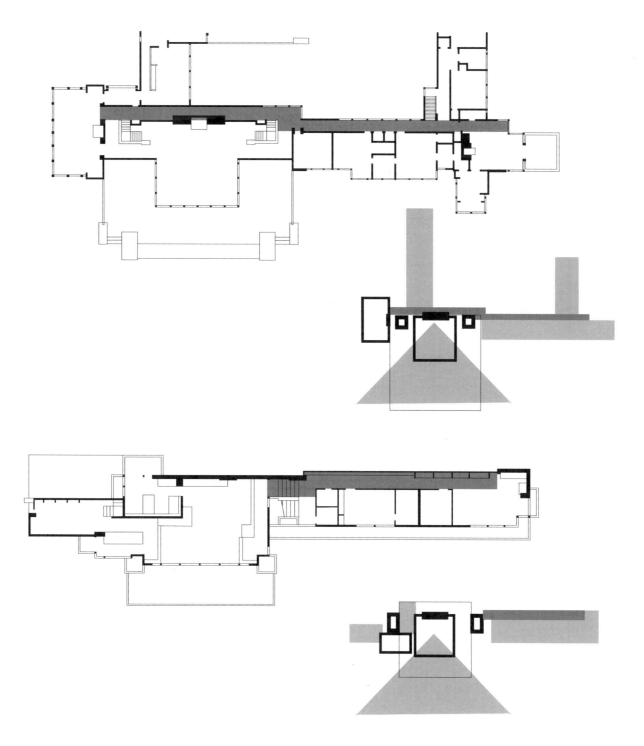

5-28 Comparative plan analysis of Coonley and Lloyd Lewis
houses showing similar organizational strategies

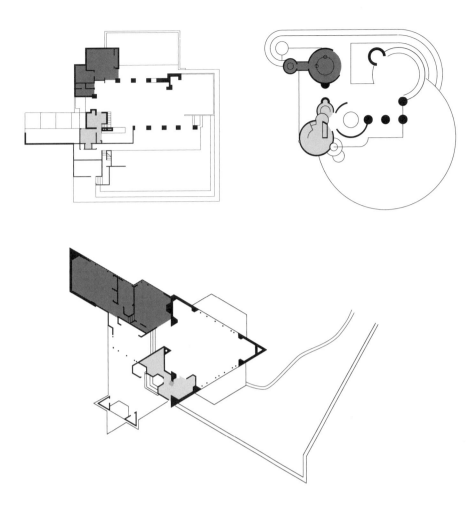

5-29 Comparative plan analysis of Life, Jester, and Sundt (mirror plan) houses exhibiting similar programmatic adjacencies expressed in three distinct geometric orders, from L. March and P. Steadman

UNIT SYSTEM: DIAGONAL AND CIRCULAR GEOMETRIES

Although the orthogonal grid or unit system dominated the bulk of Wright's residential designs, he explored a significant number of applications of diagonal and circular-based grids as well. These grids provided many new opportunities, but they also presented him with several problems, including the integration of major building components and the application of diagonal and circular geometries at different scales from site to interior furnishings. The following examples provide some insights to the challenges of these major variations on the orthogonal unit system.

Diagonal Grid: The Robie and Hanna Houses

Although Wright had used diagonal forms from the start, during the middle of his career he became enamored with the thirty-degree angle as a basis for planning grids. His desert projects of the twenties demonstrate several variations on the application of this diagonal, and it is integrated with orthogonal geometries in the St. Mark's Tower project of 1929. The Hanna House of 1937 is probably the best example of the application of the thirty-degree angle to a house plan. The dominance of this geometry leaves us with the impression of an isometric view of a basic in-line house plan; the rotation of some of the building components adds an effect like that of an Escher drawing. In the Hanna plan we can see the composition concepts Wright developed in his orthogonal, in-line houses. Spaces are organized about a longitudinal baseline in a way that recalls the Robie House plan; to one side of the baseline, major living areas are gathered in a continuous space punctuated by the hearth, and bedrooms and services form a group on the other side. Transformations from the Robie to the Hanna plan include wrapping the living room around the bent form of the hearth and the insertion of the kitchen into the living zone as part of the house. In an extension of the basic diagonal geometry, Wright overlaid the plan with a hexagonal grid to determine the shape and relationship of building elements at all scales to achieve a unifying aesthetic.

As we have seen in the massing of forms in the hillside houses and the shifting axes of the in-line houses, the diagonal was often implicit in the composition of plans for orthogonal buildings. Wright's later work reveals more explicit diagonal forms; that which had been an instrument of principle became expressed as form. We can speculate that this trend was a result of both a response to the more rural sites of his later houses and a determined effort to break away from orthogonal geometry in order to explore the possibilities of transcending geometric type.

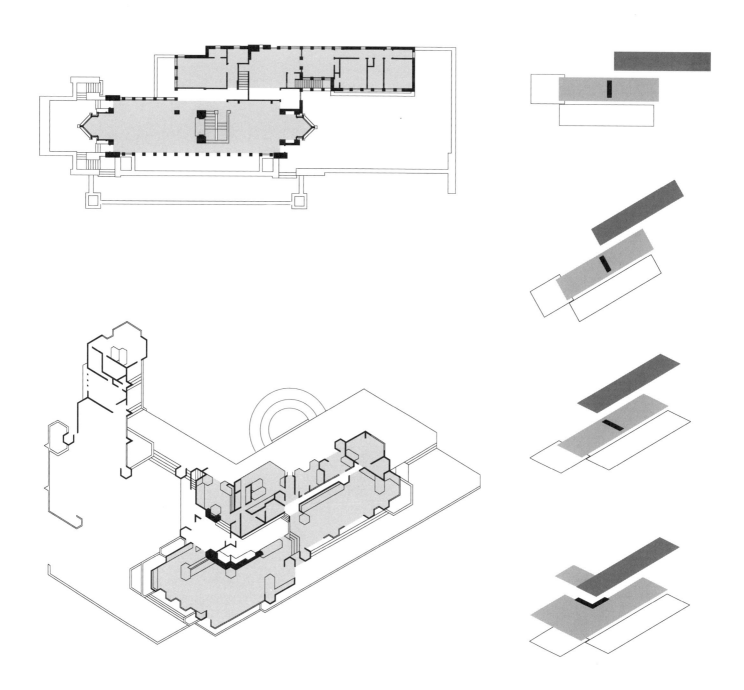

5-30 Comparative plan analysis of Robie
and Hanna houses showing hypothetical
transformation

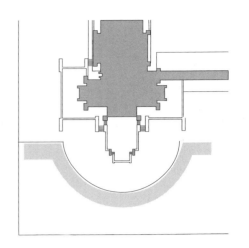

Circular Grid: The Jester and Jacobs Houses

From the beginning, Wright often used semicircular forms in his houses. At the Blossom, Winslow, and Tomek houses the semicircle defines alcoves, porches, and terraces. It is used to organize landscape at the Martin, Hollyhock, and Millard houses. However, his first attempts to develop house plans based on a vocabulary of circular forms emerge after the Johnson Wax Building of 1936, his first design that totally integrated linear and curvilinear forms. At first, curves are applied as a sort of streamlining of interior forms in the Johnson House in 1937 but are proposed as the dominant geometry for the Jester House project in 1938.

In the Jester design, several separate circular forms define areas for discrete functions including lounge and living, dining, sleeping, cooking, breakfast, hearth, and bathing. The loose collection of circles is held together by an orthogonal grid in the form of a flat roof that protects both the enclosed spaces and a central exterior patio. The total composition is anchored and the geometric theme reinforced through the dominant circular form of the swimming pool. In the strict sense, the Jester House plan does not employ a circular version of the unit system; rather, it derives its sense of order from the thematic unity of the circular forms.

When Wright pursued a curvilinear grid in designs such as those for the David Wright House and the second Jacobs House, his self-imposed constraints appear to be counterproductive. He seems to have had a fixation on the static aspects of the curve with its single central point of origin generating concentric rings or radial lines. This rigid system is univalent, seeing variations only in terms of itself. In his public buildings such as the Strong Planetarium project and the Guggenheim Museum, this approach was able to reinforce the idea of continuity by wrapping around a single unified space that could dominate all aspects of the design. Its unitary movement system seemed well suited for a single-goal processional experience. In the David Wright House, the circle simply provides a radial grid for transformation of the inline type plan. Here the processional curve could lead only to the entry door or to a master bedroom suite, where the continuity came to an abrupt halt. The unifying curve in the house might smooth over the cellular nature of its parts without spatially unifying interior space, as was possible in his public buildings. The scale of the move—the large, generous sweep of the Guggenheim climbing upward within and creating a large void—could not be matched in a small building where the gesture seems like overkill.

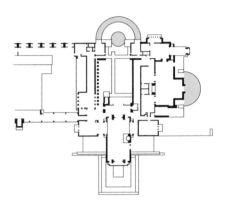

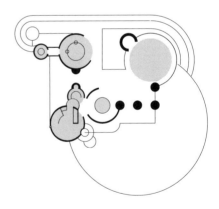

5-31 Comparative plan analysis of Martin, Hollyhock, and Jester houses showing use of circular geometry

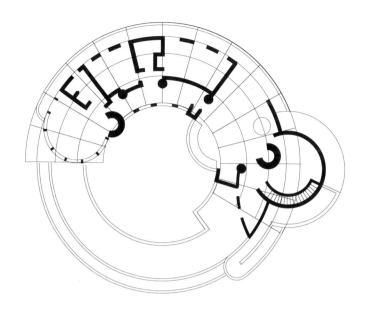

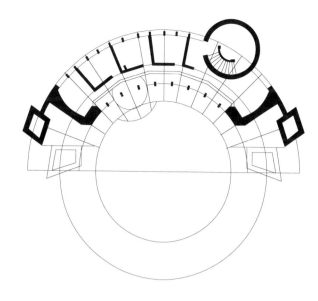

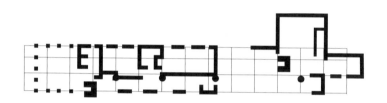

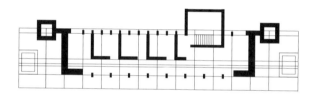

5-32 Comparative plan analysis of
David Wright house showing its affinity
with the Lloyd Lewis house plan

5-33 Plan analysis of the second Jacobs house showing its
possible derivation from a rectilinear grid

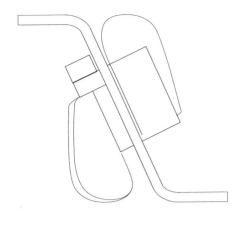

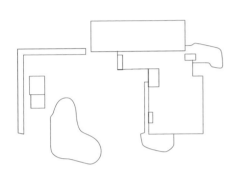

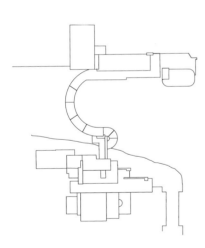

5-34 Plan of Carpenter Center by Le Corbusier

5-35 Plan of Villa Mairea by Alvar Aalto

5-36 Site plan of Fallingwater

Wright's vocabulary of curves also avoided the true or "natural" free forms used by other modern architects such as Aalto or Le Corbusier. Instead, his plans were based on complete circles or segments of circles. When Wright drew driveways and pathways that seem to demand continuity with natural land-scape contours, he combined circle segments and diagonals to approximate but never mimic the land form. These forms are particularly noticeable in the semicircular pathway between the Kaufman House and its guest house or in the awkward use of circles at the Hanna House. That Wright, the father of "organic" architecture, did not include biomorphic shapes in his work may seem strange, but Wright often stated that he sought to emulate nature's principles rather than imitate its external forms. No matter what the ultimate complexity of his buildings might be, the formal vocabulary was simple geometric shapes—the square, triangle, and circle—that are clearly discernible in the finished work.

Classicism: The Glasner and Goetsch-Winkler Houses

A comparison of the early Glasner House and the Usonian Goetsch-Winkler House provides important clues to the essence of Wright's integration of classical and natural forms to create organic plan composition, and it suggests how his approach might be extended and reinterpreted in a broad range of architectural styles.

The Glasner House of 1905 is an elongated structure sited on sloping land. It was originally designed to bridge an adjacent ravine with a connecting tea house that would have allowed the ravine itself to participate in the cross-weave of spaces. The extreme elonga-tion of the plan, terminated by identical octagonal ends and shifted cross-axes of livingroom and bedrooms, recalls compositional themes of the Husser House but with a new programmatic interpretation: it has a unified living and

dining room. In this plan we can find the basic compositional moves that would be developed in another modest but influential one-story house completed by Wright more than three decades later.

If there is an equivalent to the Barcelona Pavilion in Wright's work in terms of scale, siting, materials, structure, and spatial informality, it could be his gem in abstract planar composition, the Goetsch-Winkler. This diminutive structure is situated on a hillcrest overlooking a hollow. The approach to the house is via a broad, cantilevered carport and entry porch at one of its narrow ends. The entry is through one of several French doors on the long side of the house that faces up the hill. The plan consists of basically one open living space or "studio" with recesses for kitchen, dining, and alcove areas around the hearth. The bedroom wing is connected by a gallery. The compositions of both houses treat the baseline and the cross-axis as data for contrasting treatments of different sides of the plan. In both designs the symme-try of treatment of one side of the baseline contrasts with the dynamic informality of the spatial arrangement on the opposite side. The other contrast, about the shorter cross-axis, is that between the simplicity and larger scale of the living areas versus the relatively smaller and more complex bedroom suite. In both cases the siting of the houses on hills creates a dynamic relationship that seems to lift these modest structures into a realm of significance usually occupied by buildings of more imposing size.

These designs responded to functional programs embedded in two very different social contexts. The formal transitions between the two designs suggest how Wright's organic concepts might transcend future changes in time and place. With this expectation in our grasp we will now consider Wright's other major types, the atrium and the tower.

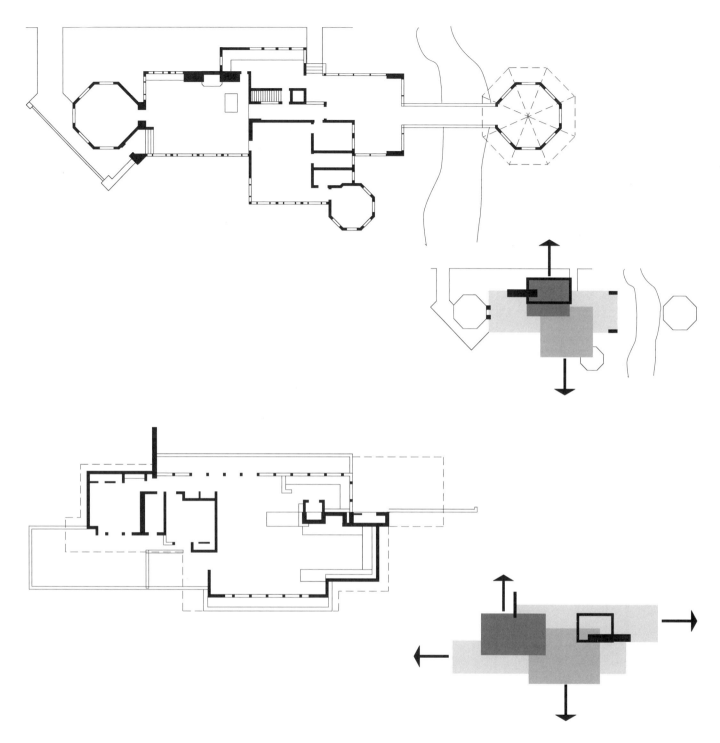

5-37 Comparative plan analysis of Glasner and Goetsch-Winkler houses showing similar organizational strategies

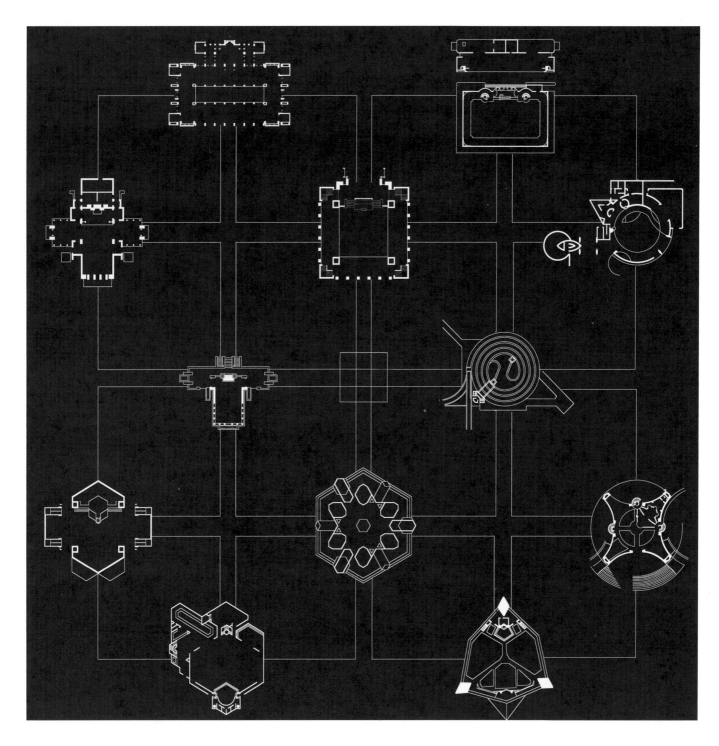

6-1 Array of four groups of Atrium type plans; top- bi-nuclear, left-
cruciform; right-circular; bottom-triangular

Larkin building, Johnson Administration Building,
Coonley playhouse, Unity temple, Guggenheim Museum,
Petit Chapel, Auto Objective,
Florida Southern Chapel, Steel Cathedral, Greek Orthodox Church,
Kansas Community Church, Beth Shalom Synagogue

The Atrium Type

6

Frank Lloyd Wright's non-domestic work displays a consistent approach to architectural issues involving the larger social world beyond the family. The atrium type describes his structures that serve a communal purpose. The concentrated development of the type throughout Wright's career suggests his deep commitment to communal values that he undoubtedly saw as a complement to the private aspect of his residential architecture. Although differing in formal and spatial precepts, the atrium type is no less important an embodiment of ideas; it equals the brilliance of his residential work.

The atrium category embraces any of Wright's structures that are intended to provide for gatherings that could engender a sense of community and shared purpose. In this definition, structures with diverse specific programs can be easily linked together. For example, the Unity Temple and Larkin Building present us with two differing "functions," namely, a place of worship and an office building. Yet each is clearly conceived as a spatial unit that encourages an extraordinary degree of community and shared purpose. Although the religious and secular distinctions between the two are obvious enough, the setting each suggests is that of an architecture that seems intent on confounding our conventional notions of worship and work. Unity Temple, displaying no overt reference to religious prototypes, seems rather secular, and just as assuredly the Larkin Building, with its towering cathedral-like central space, seems surprisingly sacred. A narrow form-follows-function argument, when applied to Wright's architecture, ignores these facts. Our thesis is that he formulated his architectural solutions according to program types rather than to specific literal programs. Formal and spatial ideas seemed to be as much cause as effect in this design process. Form could precede function. Form and program are linked, but only in a general way; once a program could be interpreted as "communal," then further design connected this function and the atrium form in a harmonious manner.

The distinguishing architectural impulse behind the atrium type is to provide an ample, light-filled space to preside at the core of the structure. Unlike the hearth type with its chimney core at the center illumined with the flickering glow of fire, the atrium building enshrines a central space ideally illuminated with light filtered from above. It shares the gathering and anchoring impulse of the hearth type but uses a contrasting composition of forms to express it. The space-centered rather than solid-centered organization is the central theme that motivates all of Wright's atrium work.

117

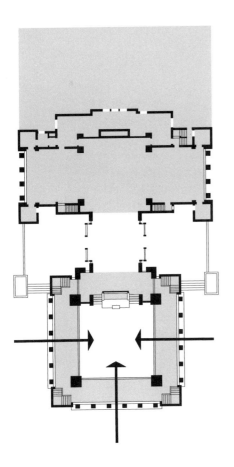
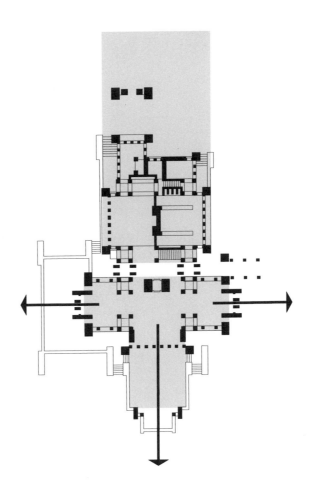

6-2 Comparative analysis of Unity Temple and the Martin
house contrasting introverted and extroverted spatial order

The formal and spatial characteristics of
the type are easy to define. Unlike the
suburban house, the atrium type is most
often set within an urban context (no
matter how sparse that may be), and its
natural tendency is to turn in on itself
and embrace a protected, inward-
looking space that essentially turns its
back on its surroundings. The spreading
peripheral energy of the Martin House
seems to have its perfect and opposite
counterpart in the compact, centralized
organization of Unity Temple. Three
decades later Fallingwater and the
Johnson Wax Administration Building
serve to illustrate the staying power of
the same dialogue. If we assume that
each of these two pairs exemplifies this
condition, then clearly the anchoring
core of both hearth configurations is
opposed by the centralizing space of
both atrium examples. The central
stabilizing core that excludes humans
has been exchanged for the central
vortex of space that willingly accepts
them.

118

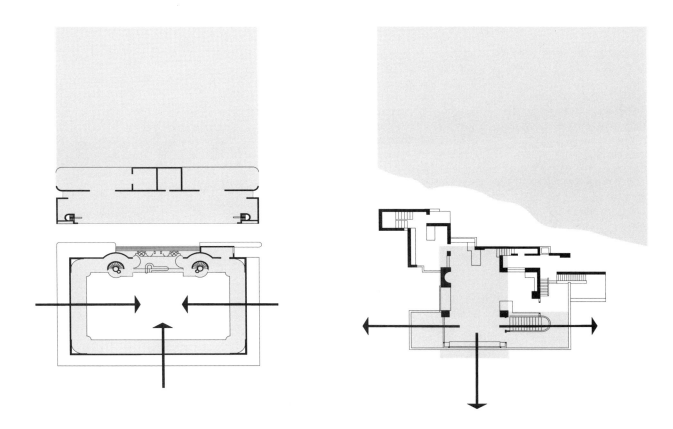

6-3 Comparative plan analysis of Johnson Administration Building and Fallingwater contrasting introverted and extroverted spatial order

The formal composition of the atrium type characteristically employs symmetry about major and minor axes. The more formal public building is thereby contrasted with the asymmetrical planning of the more informal private dwelling, thus keeping alive the ninteenth-century notion of decorum. Wright has been commonly regarded as the twentieth-century architect most facile with inflected asymmetrical planning schemes that rejected the "rigid" planning principles of the academic tradition. The atrium type demonstrates beyond any doubt that Wright relied on the academic planning tradition when he thought doing so was appropriate to the program type.

ORIGINS AND DEVELOPMENT OF THE ATRIUM TYPE

Wright's first serious study of the atrium type was probably his own studio in Oak Park. The structure, which was added to his house in 1895, occupies a prominent corner site. It consists of three parts, including a double-volume studio space on the east side of the structure, an octagonal library to the west, and a reception hall and private office "bridge" that connects the other two spaces. Significantly, the arrangement of this building exhibits virtually all the basic elements of the atrium type that would be used in future buildings. Although the elements of the studio do not show the marvelous integration of a Unity Temple, they nonetheless suggest that Wright was searching for answers to the problem of the communal structure and that he saw his studio as an architectural laboratory in this pursuit.

That Wright would interpret an architect's studio in such a spatially extravagant manner is worth comment. Unquestionably, this studio was to be an advertisement of his architectural wares. Beyond this consideration—and more germane to our present interests—Wright used the project to address both practical and symbolic concerns. The design of the major studio space seems to synthesize these concerns. Occupied as it was by Wright's staff, he has given them pride of place. Perhaps by sharing a large single volume, they would be better able to share a single higher purpose, namely, the realization of their master's ideas. Assuming that this arrangement symbolized a "democratic" workplace for Wright's charges might be an exxageration, but the design does suggest a benevolent, if paternalistic, common setting for work ennobled by space and light.

The tripartite disposition of the volumes with the special articulation of the two "nuclei" at either side of the entry obviously envisages this building type. Both the studio and the library are developed as large spatial volumes that contrast markedly with the spatially compressed reception hall. The experience of these end spaces is thereby dramatized by contrast in much the same way that the main congregation space in Unity Temple is experienced after passage through its extremely low entry hall. Light also plays an important part in the architectural organization. It streams into each of the end spaces from high clerestory windows, with particularly dramatic effect in the studio. The studio has an additional feature that was to play a major role in Wright's atrium buildings, namely, the balconied upper level, supported in this case by chains. The resulting layering of space serves to increase the impact of the atrium. The fluidity of space is supported at ground floor in the library nucleus and at the balcony level in the studio nucleus by an octagonal geometry. The off-axis entry into the studio exerts a kind of rotational spin that contributes to the overall dynamic effect.

Despite these precocious developments, the three parts of Wright's studio lack an overall unity, for they seem to be butted next to one another with little regard for the spatial and formal continuities that characterize his mature work. Yet, even with their obvious differences in architectural vocabulary and their separation by more than half a century, the Oak Park studio contains in embryo the constituent elements of the Guggenheim Museum. The Guggenheim Museum is also a bi-nuclear scheme with an entry bridge connecting articulated balconied volumes lit from above that "revolve" within a dynamic, fluid architectural whole.

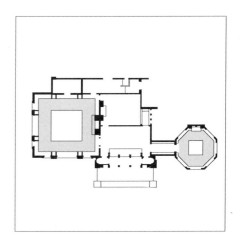

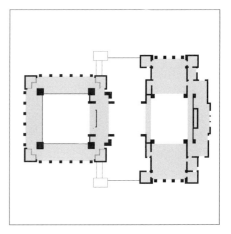

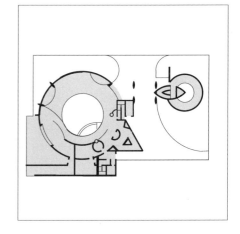

6-4 Comparative plans of F.L. Wright studio, Unity Temple, Guggenheim Museum showing similar organizations

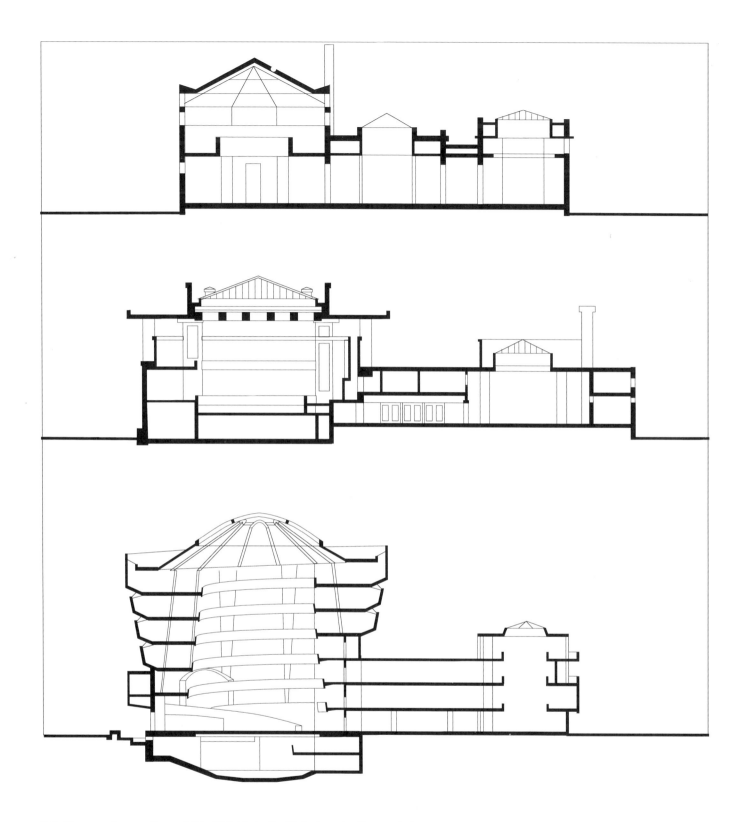

6-5 Comparative sections of F.L. Wright studio, Unity temple, Guggenheim Museum showing similar arrangements of major and minor volumes

Between the Oak Park studio and the first masterwork of the atrium type, the Larkin Building, were two important efforts that contributed to the development of the atrium type. The first was the Lincoln School, a disappointing episode in Wright's career that remains only partially realized because it was not constructed with the archtect's supervision. However, the four-square theme with articulated corner towers and the large central volume are a preview of both the Larkin building and Unity Temple. The second project, the small, gemlike Yahara Boat Club, is Wright's earliest essay in an abstract Froebelian vocabulary, a means of expression that in one form or another was to remain with him throughout his career. Its formal organization is that of a set of elongated, bilaterally symmetrical volumes with articulated corner elements surmounted by a unifying cantilevered roof and pseudo clerestory. Principles of this design can be seen at work in diverse examples, such as the Larkin Building, Unity Temple, and Midway Gardens. They also make an appearance in domestic work such as the Richard Bach House and again in high-rise structures such as the San Francisco Press Club, the latter seemingly grown from Yahara like an overwatered plant.

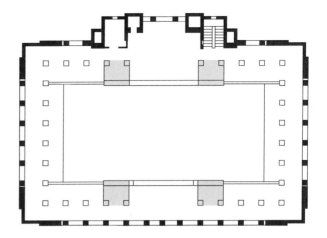

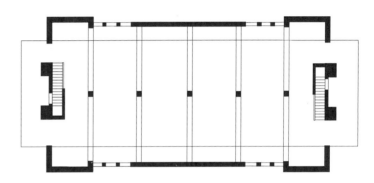

6-6 Plan of Lincoln School

6-7 Plan of Yahara Boat Club

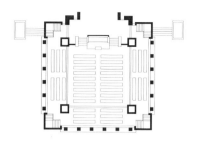

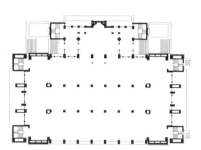

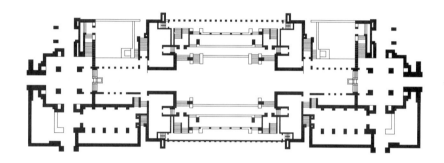

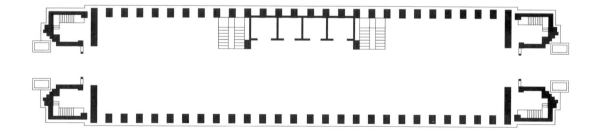

6-8 Comparative plans of Unity Temple, Larkin Building, Midway Gardens (partial), San Francisco Press Building, scale adjusted to show similar organizational strategies

THE BINUCLEAR TYPOLOGY

Because the binuclear composition is an important subtheme that embraces all of Wright's major atrium types and demonstrates his career-long preoccupation with the problem, the binuclear subtype serves as the chapter's extended analysis of the atrium type. Key buildings employing the binuclear organization include the Larkin Building, Unity Temple, the Johnson Wax Administration Building, and the Guggenheim Museum. The following discussion considers these four works as a distinct category and compares their characteristics. The single-nucleus variation of the type is discussed at the end of this chapter.

The Larkin Building and Unity Temple clearly establish the binuclear composition that was to dominate most of Wright's designs for public buildings. Whereas the two nuclei appear almost fused together in the Larkin building, they are clearly separated in the Unity Temple as active members of a dynamic balance. In both buildings the connecting element between the two nodes plays an important role in the reception of people into the building.

Compositionally the Johnson Wax Administration Building also conforms to the bi-nuclear arrangement of the type

and exhibits a completely symmetrical composition of the large office nucleus with major and minor axes. The exception to this symmetry is to be found in the other nucleus, where special offices and employee space are located. The entry sequence, although analogous to Larkin and Unity, provides for continuous through movement so that the connector bridge entry becomes a porte cochere for pedestrians and automobiles and occurs directly below the theater space. The entry proceeds from this drive through to an articulated lobby volume that is skylighted from above and encircled by balconies. This preamble to the larger space acts as an effective transition and provides a distribution zone to sort out movement into the building. The staged rhythmic sequence of compression and release, becoming greater through the axis of movement, provides a stunning climax to the sequence in the great office room.

With the Guggenheim Museum, the binuclear organization makes its appearance in what now must be seen as a canonical approach to such designs. The entry bridge or porte cochere recalls earlier examples, but the original plans for an automobile drop-off seems to make specific reference to Johnson Wax. The overall composition is not

symmetrical, although each nucleus has strong axes of symmetry. The smaller volume, the administration monitor, is a self-contained unit with its own central space and should be seen as a version of the larger. The main gallery space is, of course, defined by the spiral ramp, which both defines its edges and provides for the means of experiencing the space and the art work. A diamond-shaped "rudder" intersects the main volume and provides for services, elevators, and the like. It tends to stabilize the rotation of the spiral by providing a degree of orientation within the cylinder, just as the diamond pump element provides stability for the octagonal tower in the Romeo and Juliet Windmill. The entry sequence recalls that of the other buildings in the category. The visitor enters the connecting bridge in a low compressed space and then breaks out into the larger central volume. The intended sequence was to take the elevator to the top and then spiral down. The resulting orchestration of movement (horizontal, vertical, and spiral) suggests a fluidity in perfect harmony with Wright's ideas of continuity of form and space.

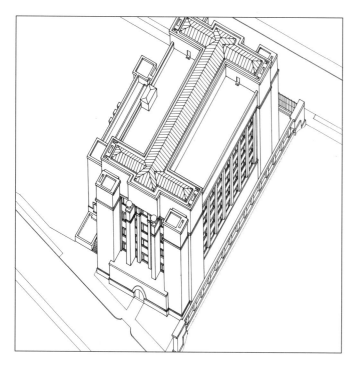

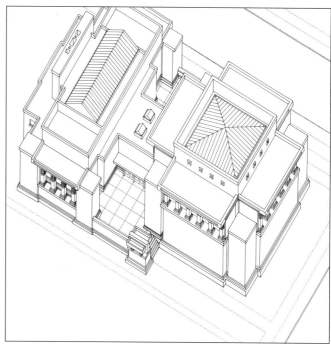

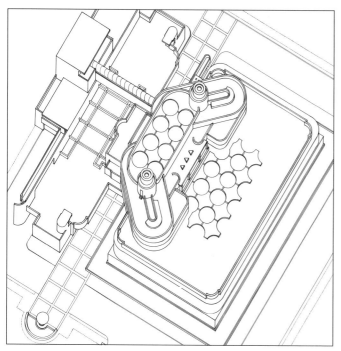

6-9 Plan projection of the Larkin Building

6-10 Plan projection of Unity Temple

6-11 Plan projection of the Johnson
Administration Building

6-12 Plan projection of the Guggenheim
Museum

Both the Larkin Building and Unity Temple share formal and spatial organizations that promote meaning at the highest level. They are both bilaterally symmetrical and composed about major and minor axes, underscoring Wright's unacknowledged debt to academic planning. The orchestration of carefully devised proportion systems for both buildings is nothing short of awe-inspiring and would please the most classically minded of Wright's contemporaries. Despite these characteristics, neither Larkin nor Unity Temple looks like a classical building. They lack any stylistic reference to the orders, and where ornament is used it is largely of Wright's own invention, without any suggestion of conventional systems of ornament.

The Johnson Wax Administration Building further demonstrates both the staying power of the atrium type and Wright's ability to take a fresh look at the formal expression of his architecture. In this building he explores the interaction of circular geometry and the rectilinear organization of the plan. The novelty of this space is that it is punctuated by a regular gridded forest of slender mushroom columns whose circular caps modulate the natural light from above. Nothing could be more different from the Corbusian, Cartesian grid or free plan, with its continuous floor and ceiling planes and cylindrical rather than tapered columns. The dominant horizontal spatial continuity of the Corbusian model is replaced by a very different system in which each column suggests a pool of space about itself generated by the central column shaft. Far from being a system of neutral elements subservient to larger continui-ties, the Johnson Wax columns retain their identity. They act more like an aggregate of independent elements like so many tree trunks, making the forest analogy particularly apt. The effect is that of a nonhierarchical but consistently modulated space reminiscent of the Great Mosque at Córdoba.

Surrounded by controversy, the Guggenheim Museum is often seen as Frank Lloyd Wright's most radical statement. Its most distinguishing features, namely, its cylindrical form and spiraling ramp, make it seem completely unlike anything that preceded it in Wright's work. When discussing this work, critics, with few exceptions,[1] concentrate on what is unique rather than what is similar to other Wright buildings.

The Guggenheim stands as a monument to Wright's tenacious hold on his architectural principles and a disciplined transformation of themes developed throughout his career. Wright had experimented with nonorthogonal geometries before, but in this building he brought this fluid geometry fully under the control of guiding principles and emulated his example of the seashells that was discussed in chapter 1. The museum looks new and in many ways it is, but the structure is also part of that exploration of form and space that began for Wright in Oak Park many years before. Our contention is that the Guggenheim Museum shares the basic principles of other atrium buildings. Therefore, we feel that confronting Wright's final masterpiece within the context of other atrium buildings whose themes and continuities it shares is especially appropriate.

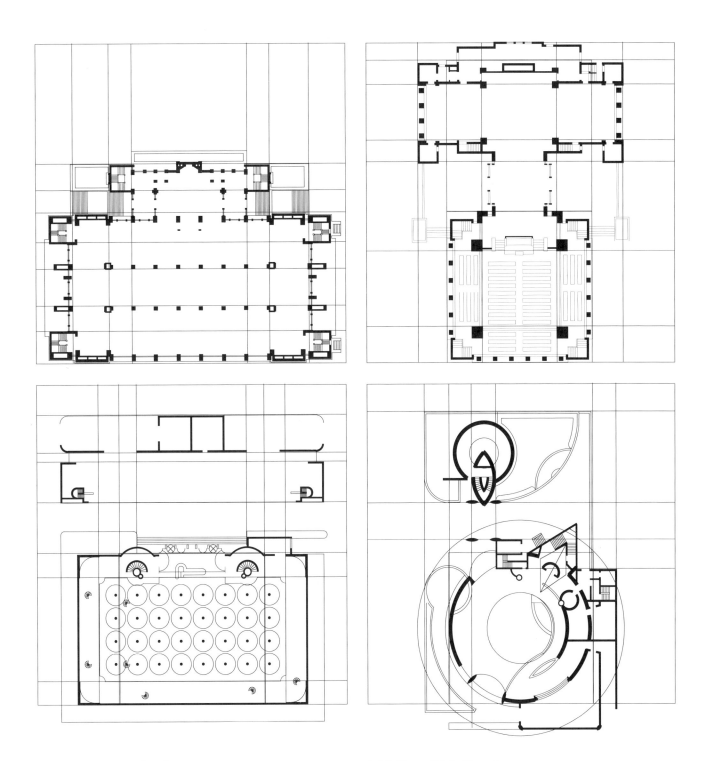

6-13 Plan of the Larkin Building

6-14 Plan of Unity Temple

6-15 Plan of the Johnson Administration Building

6-16 Plan of the Guggenheim Museum

SITING

The Larkin Building is set within an industrial zone. Little in the site per se could have appealed to Wright; consequently, the structure mainly turns inward for its sustenance. The severe exterior contrasts with the soaring light-filled atrium within, and this dichotomy imbues this scheme and others of the type with an extraordinary power. The Larkin Building was designed for a progressive Buffalo mail order house and was to contain their office headquarters. The selection of this parti for an office building is unusual. We may be justified in attributing part of the decision for a large central atrium to consideration for illumination and perhaps even efficiencies in office management. More likely Wright's wish for such a commanding interior was akin to that for his own small office. He wished to make a large unitary space to emphasize and express the shared purpose of those within. In Sullivanian terms this statement could possibly be about the broad economic forces at work within American society. The European visitor Henrik Berlage interpreted this space as an expression of American democratic values.[2]

Unity Temple's parti is identical to that of the Larkin Building. Although it is set within a suburban context, it is located on the corner of a busy street. Its inward orientation can be partly explained by the site; obviously, the requirements for a quiet, reflective atmosphere were uppermost in the minds of Wright's clients. The clerestory windows and skylights allow ample light to penetrate but maintain privacy. The sacred quality of the auditorium space depends on its ability to shut out the mundane distractions of the everyday. The common purpose of the congregation and the "unity" it so aptly symbolizes contribute to the appropriateness of this spatial organization. Similar to the Renaissance centrally planned church and unlike the Latin cross plan with its implied hierar-

chies of authority, the Unity Temple's central space is the focus and anchor of the building. Occupying this privileged space, the congregation rather than the preacher dominates the action.

The Johnson Wax Administration Building conforms in many particulars to the Larkin and Unity buildings. It occupies a full block site next to a series of factory buildings and small houses that impart no special contextual pressures. The introverted character of the office building could therefore be justified with the same site argument as the previous examples. Similarly, the interior contains a large central volume surrounded by a balconied space illuminated from above by linear strips of clerestory lighting and skylights. The programmatic reasons for this space must rely, as they have with our previous examples, on questions of symbolic intent rather than practical necessity.

The urban setting for the Guggenheim is unique in that it is located on New York City's Fifth Avenue facing the open space of Central Park to the west. No industrial zone or derelict neighborhood can explain its introverted nature. Rather, we must try to understand this solution in light of the program and Wright's ideas about appropriate exterior expression for the museum building type. The museum program was new for Wright; given that the Guggenheim was specifically to house contemporary art, Wright may have been inspired to seek a new solution to the problem of "museum" to measure up to the novelty of the works to be contained therein. The main gallery volume provides a clear hierarchical focus for the entire museum; it underscores the unity of the composition, always relating the part back to the greater whole. Its engulfing volume, balconied galleries, and skylighted space are all features that recall other examples of the atrium type going back to the Larkin Building.

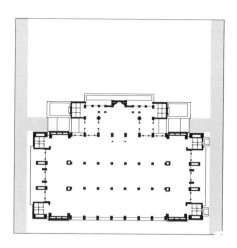

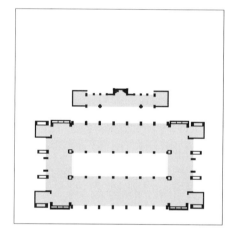

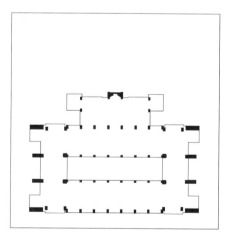

6-17 Comparative analysis of Larkin Building, Unity Temple, the Johnson Administration Building, and the Guggenheim Museum:

Site access; Bi-nuclear organization; Structure

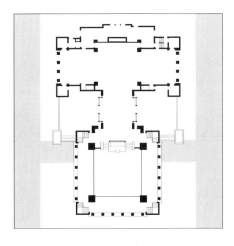

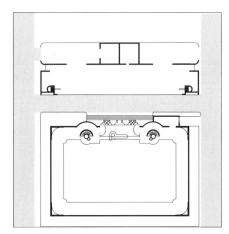

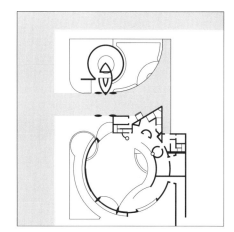

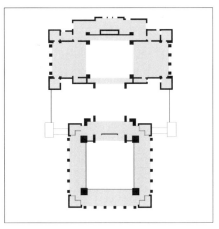

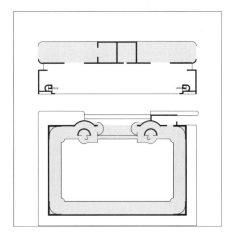

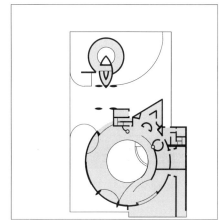

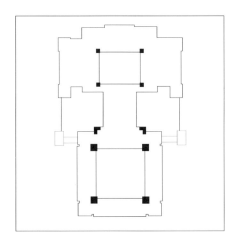

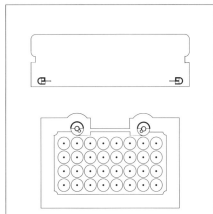

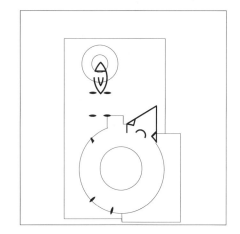

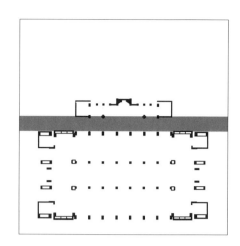

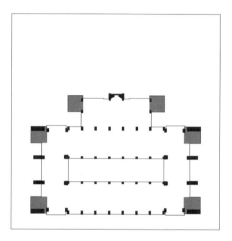

THE DYNAMICS OF MOVEMENT

Another important departure from the classical tradition is that a visitor never enters a Wright atrium building on axis but instead is directed off axis in a spiraling movement pattern. Asymmetrical movement is played against a symmetrical composition. This aspect of Wright's nondomestic architecture recalls his residential work, which similarly favors an elaborated spiral entry. Both the Larkin Building and Unity Temple structures have been designed with two identical entries that could be justified by through-block sites. However, both sides of the sites are not equal, having in each case major and minor streets that the rigid symmetry and identical entrances do not acknowledge. This discrepancy could have been solved by providing one entrance on a central axis rather than two entrances off axis, but to do so would have sacrificed the integrity of the central volume and the entry sequence to it. Furthermore, the side, spiraling entry encourages the visitor to take in the building from a diagonal viewpoint and better experience the plastic excitement of interpenetrating volumes. The net effect of such an approach is to increase the dynamic aspect of the building that, if approached frontally, would seem static. The spiraling motion generated by the approach could also result in two identical but opposing systems of circulation within the building, one left-handed and the other right-handed.

The curving theme is obviously a part of the Johnson Wax parti, echoed in the columns and in many details, including the furniture design. The implied fluidity may be taken as a more literal manifestation of the spiraling movement noticed in the earlier examples. The non-orthogonal geometry is a particularly effective promoter of this increased sense of mobility. The later additions, including the laboratory tower, reinforce these earlier ideas. Finally, the striking geometry of the Guggenheim Museum witnesses the literal transformation of the spiral movement into primary form.

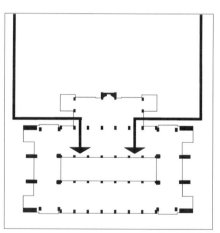

6-18 Comparative plan analysis of
Larkin Building, Unity Temple,
the Johnson Administration Building,
and the Guggenheim Museum:

Major circulation armature; Vertical
circulation; Entry sequence

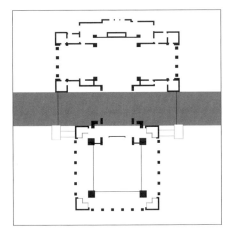
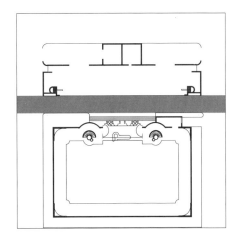
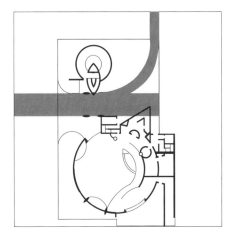

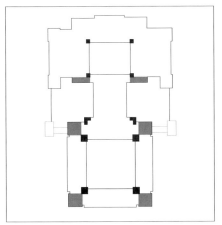
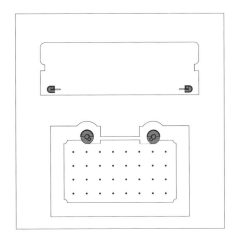
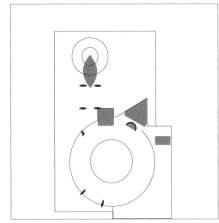

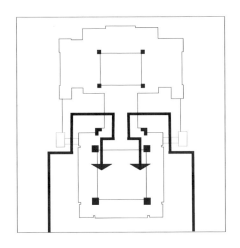
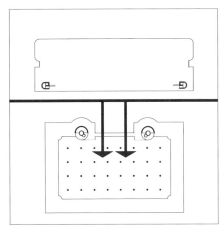
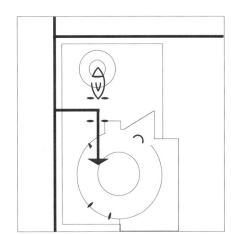

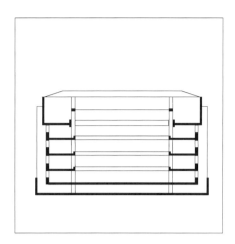

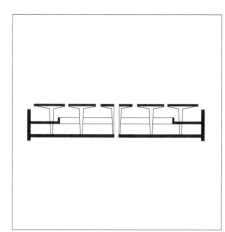
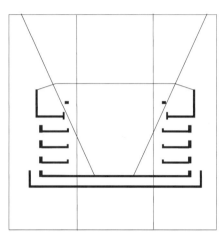
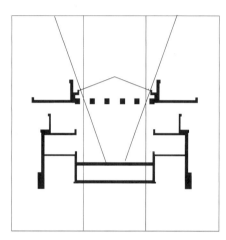
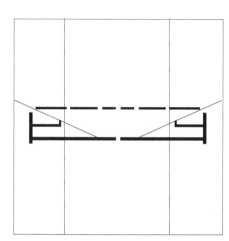

6-19 Comparative section analysis of Larkin Building, Unity Temple, the Johnson Administration Building, Guggenheim Museum, Spaulding Print Shop, and Beth Shalom Synaggue showing similar modulation of interior space

VOLUME

A section of the four buildings we have been discussing reveals Wright's special sensitivity to the connection between interior space and exterior form. It is particularly evident in the resolution of the stair volumes. In commenting about the Larkin Building, Wright was to remark that the major breakthrough in the planning process of the building came when he realized that the stairs should be pushed to the exterior and expressed as separate, articulated volumes. Not only could this deft move express the interior and therefore make the building more perfectly an integration of parts (organic) but also it could

serve to break down the overall mass of the structure into a series of articulated volumes. The scale of the structure was thus modulated from large block to intermediate and smaller volumes, all of which were ordered by the strict discipline imparted by the geometry and composition.

The Guggenheim section further reveals that its volume slants outward on the exterior and tilts forward on the interior. The resulting section is that formed by the intersection of two cones. The tilted surface with its dynamic aspect is not a new feature in Wright's work. It occurs in

his tower designs for St. Mark's and interestingly in a small, centrally planned gallery for the Spaulding Print Shop. The sloped display surfaces imply a funnel-shaped space and open it to the skylight above. The Guggenheim's intersecting section also recalls similar triangular intersections, including the Mile-high Skyscraper and Beth Shalom Synagogue. All seem to have at least partial structural rationale based on triangulation, but all enjoy an increased dynamism that avoids the static "butt and join" approach of a trabeated system—a system Wright was to reject in principle in his work in the forties and fifties.

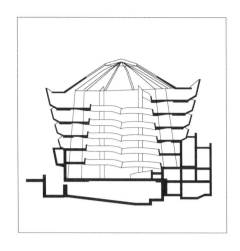 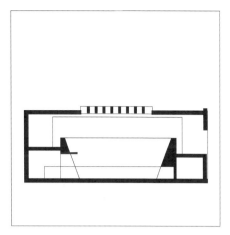 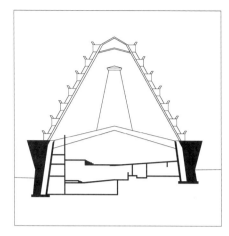

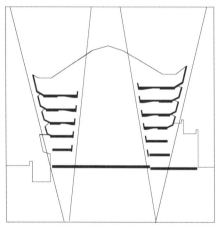 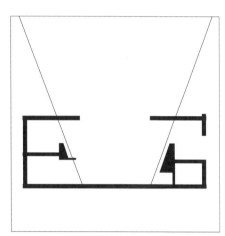 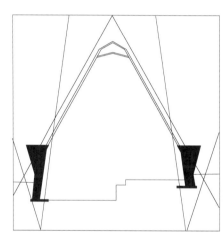

133

OTHER ATRIUM BUILDINGS

Wright employed the single-nucleus atrium type on numerous occasions in diverse settings and programs throughout his career. Although it is more varied in some respects than the binuclear version, definite patterns emerge and help to define subthemes within the grouping. For example, two basic strategies seem to characterize the type. The cruciform and modified cruciform constitute one evolutionary branch of the tree. Early projects such as the Belvedere Chapel of 1906 and the Coonley Playhouse of 1912 exemplify the type. Both were to be sited in park-like settings and were apparently conceived as a species of garden pavilion. This introverted, centralized version of the typical atrium type lacks clerestory lighting and instead is tensioned by a strong horizontal extension into a lush green landscape. Obviously the type is informed by Wright's Prairie houses of the period but shifts the solid hearth focus out of the center to allow the central space to dominate. The opposing centrifugal-centripetal pull results in a hybrid somewhere between the hearth and atrium types.

During the twenties Wright conducted a number of experiments that explored the dynamic potential of non-orthogonal plans. The Auto Object of 1925 and the Steel Cathedral of 1926 illustrate this tendency. Both suggest an important departure from Wright's earlier work but emphasizing the differences too much would be a mistake. Each of these works continues to develop planning themes articulated earlier, namely, centralized symmetrical planning with spiral movement systems implicit, all organized by a large central unitary space. The Auto Object scheme, turned on its "head," becomes a close approximation of the Guggenheim Museum. Likewise, the Steel Cathedral previews a number of religious projects, including the Florida Southern Chapel (with its cruciform plan) and the Beth Shalom Synagogue, based on a hexagonal geometric system. The circular theme explored in the Auto Object appeared two years earlier in the Little Dipper project for Aline Barnsdall and reappears with a kind of baroque flourish in Wright's Greek Orthodox Church of 1956.

In the design of his communal structures, Wright provided inspiring evidence of the power of the clear, unifying building concept when it is anchored in a fundamental understanding of the human condition. In characteristic fashion Wright pursued the complete realization of the concept through the highly disciplined orchestration of construction, detail, and ornament in each building. Whereas the "originality" of some of Wright's ideas might be questioned, his tenacious professional perseverance is not in doubt.

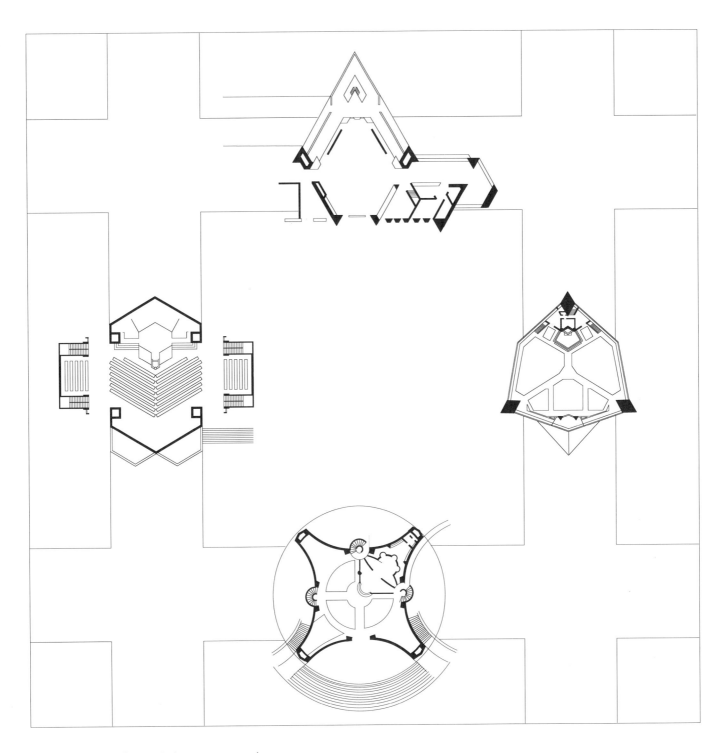

6-20 Plan array of other Atrium type examples:

Unitarian Church,
Florida Southern Chapel, Beth Shalom Synagogue,
Greek Orthodox Church

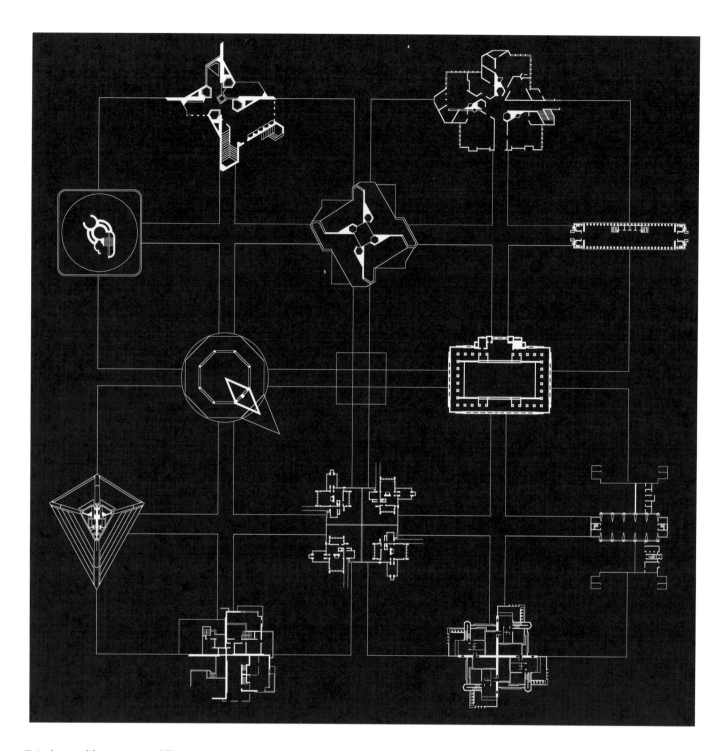

7-1 Array of four groups of Tower type plans and related housing:

Price Tower, Crystal Heights
Johnson Research Tower, St. Mark's Tower, San Francisco Press Building,
Romeo and Juliet Windmill, Lincoln School,
Mile-High Skyscraper, Quadruple Block Houses, National Life Insurance Building,
Suntop Homes, Pittsfield Housing

The Tower Type

7

Even though Frank Lloyd Wright realized only two tower buildings during his career (the Johnson Research Tower of 1947 and the Price Tower of 1956), his many unexecuted projects on the theme demonstrate his fascination with the problem of the tall building. If we include his early Romeo and Juliet Windmill of 1896 and the Mile-high Skyscraper project designed three years before his death, we see that Wright explored this theme in a variety of building contexts and programs.

Wright's changing approach to the design of the tall building became a vehicle to clarify his ideas about the landscape and the city as well as his notions of structural and spatial integration. His investigations into this problem indicate a determined search to discover the essence of the tall structure as form and meaning and to define a type that would once and for all settle the architectural problems involved. Its verticality should be viewed as a complement to the horizontality of his domestic work and the spatial centering of his congregational work. The St. Mark's Tower project of 1929 embodies meaning no less potent or distinctive than the Willitts House and Unity Temple. We shall see that the tower is linked to his other work and yet retains its identity as a unique expression in Wright's architecture.

FRANK LLOYD WRIGHT AND THE CHICAGO SCHOOL

That Wright, Chicago's most famous architect, should treat the high-rise building seems logical enough. What is quite extraordinary, however, is his ambivalence toward and final rejection of virtually all the lessons of the Chicago frame.[1] In formulating his personal vision of the high-rise building, he ultimately shunned the cues of urban context and insisted on a synthesis that unified structure and space instead of a dialectic that separated them into distinct elements. Although the product of his research may seem inevitable, these explorations did not unfold with the inexorable momentum that characterized the evolution of the Prairie House or the development of the binuclear plan. Wright's search for an appropriate form for the tall building found resolution rather late in his career and only after a series of detours and long periods when the problem remained dormant. When clarity of the type was finally established in the St. Mark's Tower, his interest in the tall building accelerated, and he never tired of using the type or its principles.[2]

137

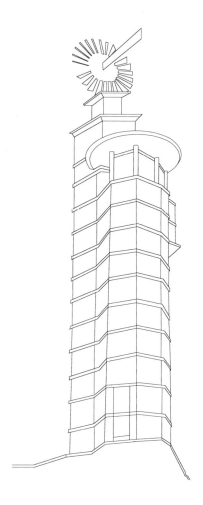

7-2 Perspective view of Romeo and Juliet Windmill

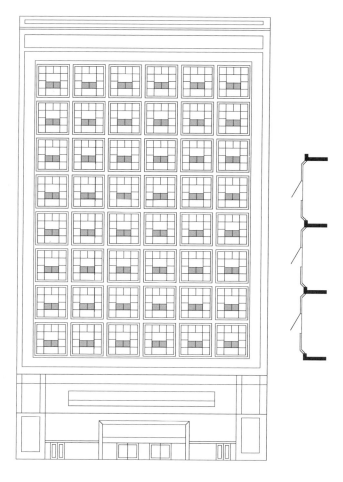

7-3 Elevation and wall section detail of Luxfer Prism Building

TWO TYPES OF TALL BUILDINGS: THE URBAN BLOCK AND THE TOWER

The Luxfer Prism Building of 1895 and the Romeo and Juliet Windmill, built a year later, illustrate Wright's contrasting approaches to the problem of the tall building. These two themes, the urban block and the free-standing tower, occupied distinct phases in Wright's development. The urban block theme was the focus of his studies during the Oak Park years and the teens and finally climaxed in the National Life Insurance Skyscraper project of 1924. At this critical juncture his interest in the urban block waned and was replaced by the tower theme. By the late twenties the tower became the exclusive means by which Wright explored the problem of the tall building. It reappeared in various transformations for the next thirty years and capped off his career.

The Evolution of the Urban Block

The tall building as urban block began as a classicized cubic volume, picking up cues, no doubt, from Sullivan. The initial compact statement transformed into an increasingly complex series of interpenetrating volumes within a Froebel vocabulary. Neither his approach to composition nor structural expression was challenged, however, until the design of the remarkable National Life Insurance skyscraper.

Wright's first skyscraper project was barely ten stories tall. The Luxfer Prism Building was to house offices for a glass manufacturer, which may explain the extensive use of glass on the exterior but cannot explain the specific resolution. Given that Luxfer followed the important achievements of the Chicago School and Sullivan's Wainwright and Guaranty buildings, it is curious that Wright seems to have rejected these

lessons in a setting that seems to demand them. The expression of the frame (if indeed there is one—no plans of the project apparently exist) is ambiguous; the three-bay structure implied at the base is surmounted by a six-bay division above. The doubling of vertical elements could be connected to Sullivan's treatment of the Wainwright, and yet Wright is both more ambiguous and more consistent than Sullivan. Whereas Sullivan implies a structural role for all piers even though in reality it is only true for every other pier, Wright makes no such commitment; both vertical and horizontal framing elements are treated identically. The result suggests a weightless screen and implies separation between structure and surface. The glass panels, which may have at first appeared to be a version of the Chicago window type set within the structural frame, now seem to be following other rules.

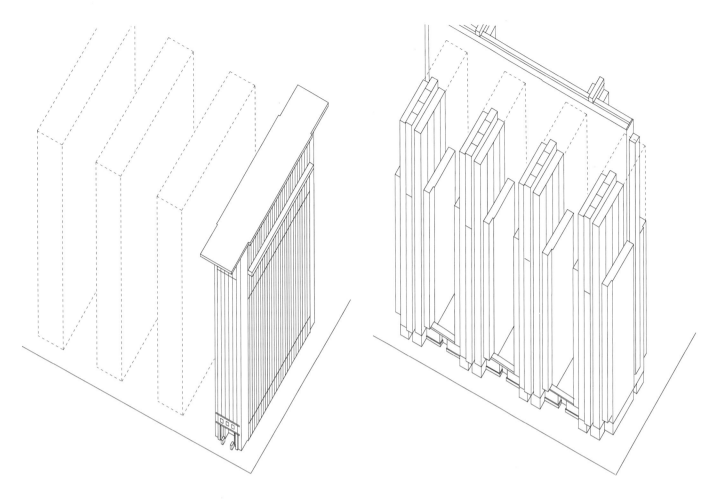

7-4   Plan projection diagram of San Francisco Press Building illustrating its potential as a prototype for the National Life Insurance Building

7-5 Plan projection of the National Life Insurance Building

A closer inspection of the wall section reveals that the glass sections actually project in front of the framing elements to create the impression of volume rather than infill. The picture-frame-like border enclosing the glazed portion of the facade is another important departure from Sullivan's pseudostructural expressionism and further contributes to our impression of a weightless, omni-directional glazed membrane, a kind of proto-curtain wall. The volumetric glazing of Luxfer is further enlivened with the operable tilted glass panes at the center of each bay; in the perspective drawing of the project, each unit is opened to the same angle, which, coincidentally, is the identical angle of the entry canopy. The resulting play of light suggests a special sensitivity to the material qualities of glass and its ability to dematerialize structure by reflection and refraction. The Luxfer Prism

Building should be considered as an early essay on the possibilities of glass as a building skin and not as a comment on the tectonics and expression of the structural frame.

The Lincoln School.   The urban block type as seen in the Lincoln School is characterized by a heavy masonry wall that folds into external volumes of closure. Glazing recedes both literally and metaphorically as mere background so that the major exterior element, the masonry wall, can find expression. The corners in particular are emphasized, suggesting a compositional if not structural stabilizing role.

San Francisco Press Building. The conclusion to the urban block approach is the San Francisco Press Building of 1912. This building was to occupy a

dense urban site in the center of the city and reach over twenty-five stories in height. Its soaring aspect, elongated plan, and dramatic play of form should not obscure the fact that these qualities are derived from earlier experiments in the Froebel manner. The masonry structure, heavy corner piers, and exaggerated cantilever at the top seem to emanate from much smaller build-ings, such as the Larkin Building and Unity Temple. Their structure, the overt symmetry of their plans, and the classical interpretation of their vertical extension into capital, shaft, and base are not challenged. In the end we are left with the feeling that Wright had the uncomfortable realization that he had created a stretch-limo version of the Yahara Boat Club.

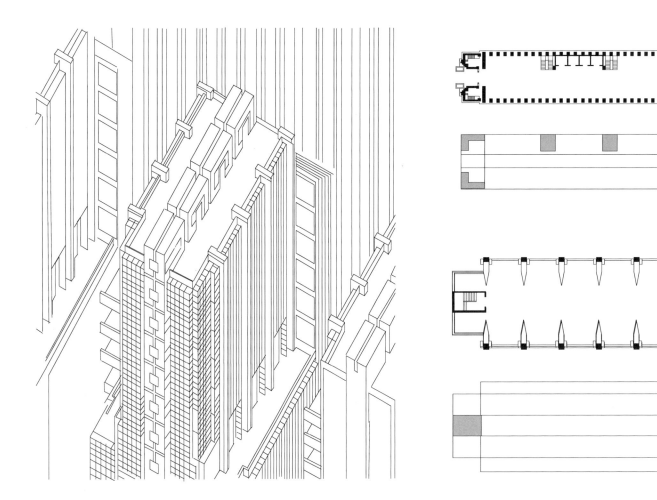

7-6 Detail plan projection of the National Life Insurance Building

7-7 Comparative plan diagram of the San Francisco Press Building and a typical wing of the National Life Insurance Building

The Transition to the Tower

The National Life Insurance Company Building of 1924 was an important turning point for Wright in his formulation of the tall building and a crucial step toward his eventual development of the tower. The project was to embody a radical reevaluation of the type in terms of urbanism, architectural form, and structure. Although this Chicago building represents an important transitional phase in Wright's development, it is a significant achievement in its own right, one that was to inform his explorations into other building types as well.

The insurance building emphatically dispenses with Sullivan's concept of a unitary classical volume in favor of an assemblage of interlocking volumes. As a result the building loses the frontality and wall-like continuity that normally helps to define the street. The bi-laterally symmetrical plan favored until now disappears, along with the classical tripartite vertical formula. Although the project retains a strict symmetry along its broad surface, the irregular massing as seen from an oblique vantage point dominates our overall impression. The building is conceived as a series of five transparent volumes. The highest volume acts as a continuous datum for four fingerlike projecting volumes that form entry "courts" on street level. These volumes are made increasingly sculptural as they rise skyward, finally shedding their skin of glass to reveal the structure beneath. The intricate texture of the overall facade and the ornamental enrichment toward the top remind us of Wright's decorative designs, especially his compositions for leaded glass windows.

The National Life project rejects the Press Building's approach of heavy masonry walls and piers with cantilevered roof in favor of a weightless skin of glass in which virtually every floor is cantilevered. The building skin, demate-rialized by glazing, is free of the outer masonry shell that is conspicuous in the San Francisco Press and Larkin buildings. The simple device that makes it possible is the structural cantilever. Wright attributes this innovation to lessons he learned while building the Imperial Hotel in Japan. He describes the system as "Floor slabs stiffened and extended as cantilevers over centered supports, as a waiter's tray rests upon his upturned fingers."[3] The glazing no longer acts as a passive infill but as the principal player in an architectural drama. The curtain wall is delicately suspended as a thin membrane in front of the structure. In the process the glass develops qualities of volume and prismatic luminescence reminiscent of the Luxfer Prism Project. The liberation of the skin from structural necessity—"the free facade"— did not have the same meaning for Wright as for Le Corbusier; Wright's facade never became completely disconnected from the building surface or the internal

7-8 Perspective view of St. Mark's Tower

7-9 Perspective view of Johnson Research Tower

7-10 Perspective view of Mile-High Skyscraper

spatial subdivisions within. Wright always insisted that the interior and exterior "organically" relate, unlike the dialectical contrast of Le Corbusier.

The National Life Insurance Company design shows Wright critically reappraising the urban block type. He was able to embody new ideas of structure and resuscitate earlier ideas about glazing that allowed him to achieve a startling new architectural expression. His dynamic mastery of form and increasing tendency toward highly articulated volumes in space hint at his growing impatience with the constraints implied by the city. That this building was never realized is unfortunate. Wright did not have further opportunities to explore this potential form prototype and its response to specific urban contexts. Such exploration might have led to an explosion of creativity equal to or exceeding his Prairie School houses. Instead, we find Wright extending his

experimentation with the issues of structure, enclosure, and composition within his approach to the St. Mark's Tower commission.

The Urban Implications of the Block and the Tower

Wright abandoned the block type and embraced the tower at the moment in his career when his vision of the city changed into the "disappearing city" of Broadacres. The urban block building suggests an urban setting; it acknowledges the possibility of front, side, and rear. These hierarchical properties condition the space around it and imply continuities that could reinforce the spatial volume of the street corridor. The tower, especially in Wright's hands, lacks preferential treatment on any side. Furthermore, Wright's tendency toward rotational or diagonal composition promotes a spinning spatial vortex that requires a degree of breathing room

around the building that a dense urban setting could not provide. The exurban setting demanded finds its first tentative application at St. Mark's Tower in a miniature park in New York City and later in the more spacious and rural setting of Broadacre City, where the irregularly spaced towers seem to spin like tops on a table. This condition of isolation is apparently necessary for the single tower; whether at the scale of Johnson Wax or the Mile-high Skyscraper, each tower operates as a centering instrument rather than a defining edge. Wright's tacit acknowledgment of the problem of adapting the tower to the city is demonstrated later in his grouped apartment towers for Chicago and his Crystal Heights project for Washington, D.C. In each of these instances, the towers form a glass palisade wall, thus implying an urban spatial role.

The Development of the Tower

Given Wright's well-known aversion to the city, we may ask why he was interested in pursuing a building form that grew out of a cultural and economic milieu to which he so frequently objected. The answer lies less in his endorsement of density and the open space rationalizations of Le Corbusier and the Bauhaus and more in his romantic notion of the tall building as a symbolic marker in the landscape. The Romeo and Juliet Windmill provides an initial clue to this notion.

The Romeo and Juliet structure stands on a hilltop overlooking Wright's ancestral landscape of rolling hills, cultivated fields, and winding streams. Later the Hillside Home School and then Taliesin were to unfold beneath its raking shadow. It thus came increasingly to fulfill its role as a marker in the landscape, suggesting, like the medieval tower, dynastic dominion over all it surveyed. For Wright the tower was a potent symbol of place and meaning that transcended the specifics of site and program.

Although Wright's first mature essay on the type is the St. Mark's Tower project of 1929, the Romeo and Juliet Windmill executed three decades earlier seems to have conditioned his response to the problem. The windmill is octagonal in plan, intersected by a rhomboid core. The octagon and the intersecting rhomboid are extruded upward and capped with a sheltered lookout and rotating blades. The plasticity of the interpenetrating forms and exuberant top presents a set of formal preoccupations that continued to be developed throughout Wright's studies of the tower. The triangulation and the resultant structural dependence of the two forms provide lateral stability that resists wind loads and any tendency for twisting or distortion. The one form, lofty, strong, and erect, embraces the other, which is lower, passive, and open. The decisive expression of supporting structure as solid vertical wedge and supported space as open surrounding volume is a theme that reappears in virtually all of Wright's tower schemes, including St. Mark's Tower.

The St. Mark's Tower embodies many of the ideas that were to characterize Wright's mature designs of the tower type during the following three decades. Wright has often likened his tower designs to that of a tree. It is rooted in the ground and springs upward with cantilevered arms emanating from its trunklike branches. The density of the core dematerializes toward the edges of the tower into crystalline surfaces of glazing. The bottom and top are likewise differentiated from the repetitive ribs in the midportion of the structure. The void of the lobby below emphasizes the cantilever, and the exuberant top emphatically crowns the structure as it pierces the sky. A further subtlety is the outward taper of the sides, which makes the upper floors cantilever slightly in front of the floors below. Wright has rationalized this feature as a natural means for self-cleaning the glass with rain. However, the recurrence of the outward tilt in other structures where no such rationalization exists (the Guggenheim, for example) suggests that Wright was more interested in creating a hovering, dynamic effect. The St. Mark's project consisted of nine levels of two-story maisonettes. The three towers (more towers were projected in another scheme) were to stand rather close to one another in the small green surrounding St. Mark's in the Bowery Church.

The Johnson Wax Laboratory Tower is similarly scaled to St. Mark's. It has seven stories and a system of mezzanine spaces comparable to the duplex arrangement of St. Mark's. The Johnson Wax Tower has a relatively subdued formal and spatial complexity compared to the explosive themes of the New York project. The structural system is directly analogous, with a single mastlike core and projecting cantilevered trays; however, the fragmentation into four separate quadrants and corresponding structural pylons vanishes. Obviously, the need for continuous, more flexible laboratory space dictated this more open approach. The integrity of the structure is ingeniously expressed, and the effect of streamlined corners and circular stacks deserves our admiration for the continuity of formal themes related back to the main building. However, we are left with the impression that once again Wright selected the tower as an a priori form type for reasons that went beyond functional necessity. The tower serves as a marker or beacon, especially at night. The Johnson Wax Laboratory Tower is surely less a statement of fact about the modern, efficient laboratory than it is a highly visible symbol for the enlightened and progressive values of the client.

The Mile-high Skyscraper is above all a public relations achievement proving that Wright could be as modern and daring as any member of the younger generation of architects nurtured by modernist schools such as the Bauhaus. In approaching such a monumental work, we are inclined to treat it as such. Its "function" is beside the point and no more important as an issue than it would be for the Eiffel Tower. Wright's list of facts does little to help us take the project seriously: 5,280 feet high with a 400-foot aerial, 528 stories, elevators "propelled with atomic power," parking for 15,000 cars and landing pads for 150 helicopters. If the Mile-high is a parody of a peculiar modernist folly, it nonetheless presents an interesting comment on Wright's development of the tower type, of which it is most defiantly a conspicuous member.

This building's cantilevered structure has a symmetrical, kite-shaped plan with a centralized tripod system of structural walls. The body of the building is further subdivided by an elevator core that pierces its center and breaks through the sloping sides of the building as it moves upward. The tapering needle-like structure is reminiscent of an upside-down icicle, the kind that scalloped the roof eaves at Taliesin in the winter. The triangular structure overwhelms us with a dynamic, faceted aspect of shimmering glass disappearing into infinity but recalling, nonetheless, the smaller-scaled faceted surfaces of St. Mark's.

The dematerialization of structure into space and the conquest of the sky with lightweight luminescent surfaces springing from the ground present a romantic vision of the high-rise building that elicits a feeling of awe and mystery. The tiny Romeo and Juliet Windmill and the polished Luxfer Prism Building are here reconstituted at a heroic scale. Wright proposed a complex interlock of prisms that overcame technical difficulties with a bold but simple structural concept that could serve as a marker in the sweeping landscape; it suggests dominion over all that it surveys.

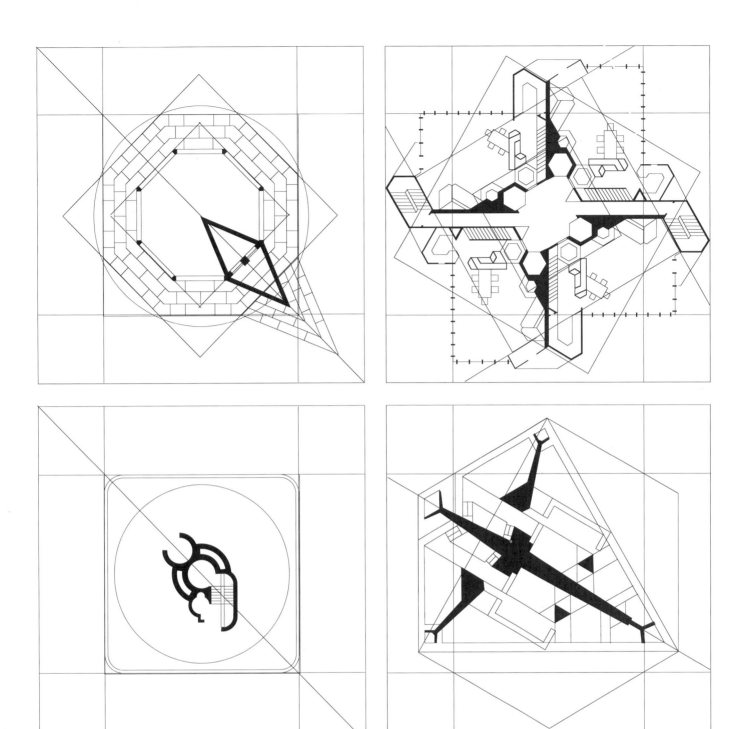

7-11 Plan of the Romeo and Juliet Windmill

7-13 Plan of the Johnson Research Tower

7-12 Plan of the St. Mark's Tower

7-14 Plan of the Mile-High Skyscraper

Comparative Analysis

Seen as a group, Wright's towers share a number of formal characteristics. All embrace the diagonal as a compositional motif. The plan of the Romeo and Juliet Tower, with its octagon and interpenetrating rhomboid, introduce the theme at a forty-five degree angle. The St. Mark's Tower scheme and others of its type, including the Price Tower and Crystal Heights, use a complex overlapping and shifting system of orthogonal and thirty- and sixty-degree diagonal grids. This complex pattern is based on simple overlapping grid systems and no doubt was influenced by Islamic tile design that was well known to Wright through Owen Jones and other sources. The St. Mark's rotated triangular pylons penetrate the basic building cube in a manner similar to the Romeo and Juliet Windmill. Although more subtly expressed, the plan geometry of the Johnson Wax Tower shares some of the consistencies of the tower prototype. The vertical support elements are aligned with the central core to create a forty-five-degree diagonal across the square plan. The plan geometry of the Mile-high Skyscraper also relates to the earlier experiments. The basic organization is that of a rhomboid or alternatively an equilateral triangle with one inflected side. This form, with its strong sense of the diagonal, is also found in the Boomer House in Phoenix, the Unitarian Church in Madison, and the stabilizing pier of the Romeo and Juliet Windmill.

The St. Mark's Tower best exhibits the possibilities for intricate manipulation of plan geometries. The tower has the spatial complexity of a Chinese puzzle, initiated by a shifted and overlapping thirty- and sixty-degree grid. The angle may have been prompted as a response to the site but, given Wright's predisposition toward experiments in diagonal geometries, it was more likely a felicitous opportunity upon which he was prepared to capitalize. A typical living level plan of the tower can be described as a square that has been divided into four equal quadrants by cross-walls that

almost meet at the center. The square is then sheared in both directions to accommodate fire stairs, access corridors, and services. The stair volumes project beyond the perimeter of the square in opposing directions to accentuate the pinwheel effect.

A second square is laid over the first at a thirty- and sixty-degree angle and serves as a foil to the first, increasing the velocity of the pinwheel spin. The space between the grid shift is not only a plan manipulation but also an important three-dimensional volume that serves spatially to link both floors of the unit. Both space and cross-walls are inflected in a rotational fashion to contain elevators and services. Secondary partitions respond to either grid as required while maintaining the integrity of the two overlapping systems. The formal and spatial virtuosity of the scheme comes through at every level of detail so that even paving, furniture, and open balconies and planters on the perimeter serve to articulate and clarify the complex interpenetration of the two systems, systems that in the last analysis are built up of very simple geometries.

The cross-wall—pier arrangement serves as the only vertical structure and provides the necessary stability for the dramatic cantilevers. The glazing is a curtain wall that projects in front of the floor slabs in the manner of the National Life Insurance Building and allows it to maintain its crystalline quality. The intersection of triangulated core with central volume recalls the same motif in Romeo and Juliet, where the roles of structural stabilizer and spatial volume are similar. Wright's expressed wish to integrate structure, space, and form are perhaps synthesized more successfully in St. Mark's Tower than in any other of his works.

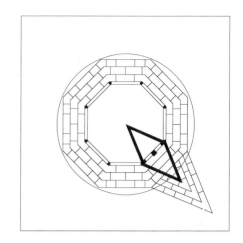

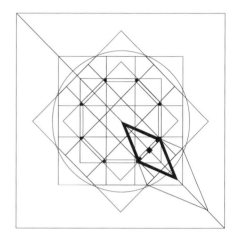

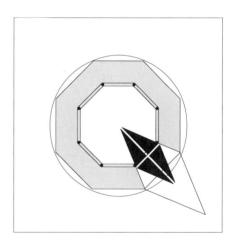

7-15 Comparative plan analysis of Romeo and Juliet Windmill, St. Mark's Tower, Johnson Research Tower, and Mile-High Skyscraper:

Plans
Geometric Order
Spatial and structural order

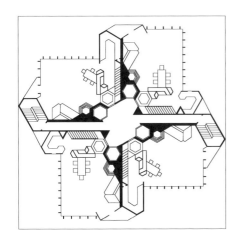

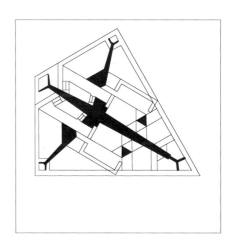
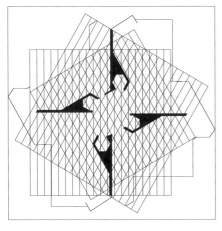
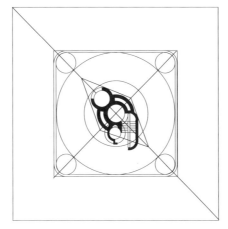
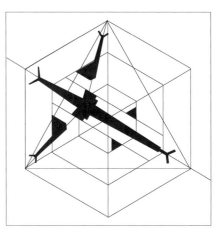
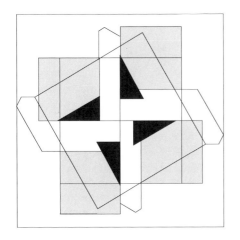
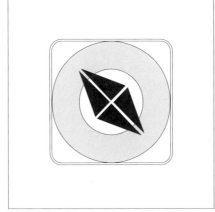
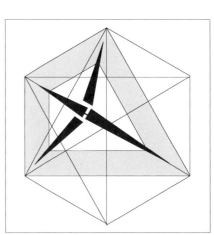

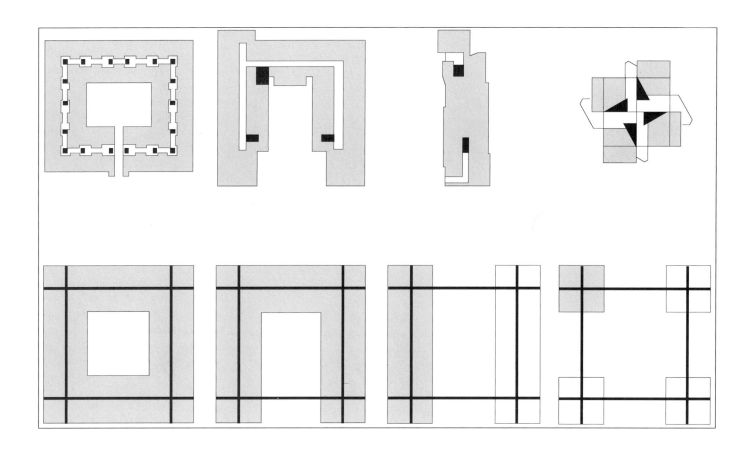

7-16 Plan diagram and analysis of Lexington Terrace Apartments,
Mason City Hotel, Noble Apartments, and St. Mark's Tower
showing transformation from courtyard type to point block type

Housing and the Tower

Unlike all of Wright's previous experiments with the tall building, the St. Mark's Tower is a residential complex with four duplex units on each major level. Until that point, Wright had conceived and executed a number of important low-rise housing schemes, especially if we consider the hotel as a member of this grouping. From the Francisco Terrace to the Imperial Hotel, these plans tended toward a distinctive spatial type, namely, the courtyard. In either square, doughnut, U-, or H-shaped plans, a strong sense of spatial enclosure always created a central community space. His housing in this vein should be seen as a larger-scale version of the atrium building type, with masonry walls replaced by "room walls." Wright's eventual rejection of courtyard

housing in favor of the tower might suggest a changed attitude toward individual housing residents and their relationship to the community. The quadrant plan of the tower appears to shift the orientation of the housing units from the man-made communal setting to the surrounding landscape.

The direct transition from Wright's courtyard type to the tower type seems unlikely. We are rather inclined to see this development as a complete break with Wright's earlier housing projects and indeed all his work up to that point. Housing in the form of a tower was new to Wright. We might find causes for his adoption of this form in such precedents as the American and European cross-shaped apartment towers. Did Wright conceive a diminutive version of the Plan Voisin, a kind of miniature tower in

the park scheme, or do we have a constantly evolving synthesis of Wright's attitudes about architecture and the city suddenly crystallizing? Wright may have been influenced by a contemporary sketch made by Buckminster Fuller of a high-rise building organized around a mastlike core with projecting trays. Realizing Wright's tenacious hold on ideas once articulated, however, we are inclined to place more weight on sources from within Wright's own world of form.

The tower shares a formal and spatial kinship with the hearth type. The tower possesses a solid core that acts to root the building to the earth much as the fireplace and chimney serve to anchor the house to the land. Its solid center and dematerialized edges provide for an open horizontal extension of space that

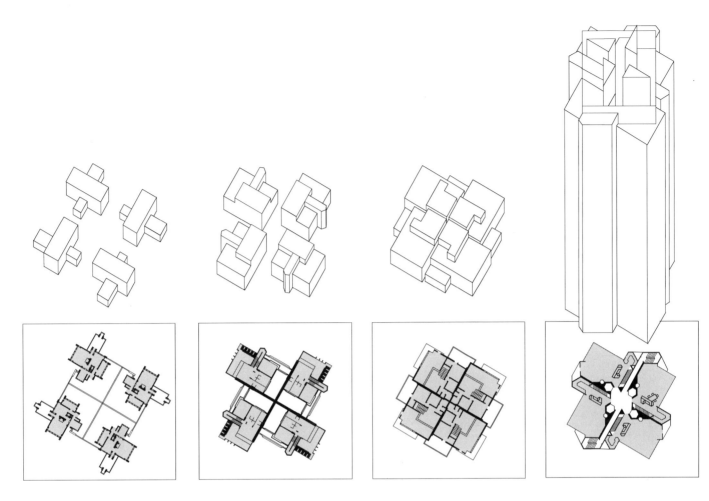

7-17 Plan projection and plan diagram of Quadruple Block Housing, Pittsfield Housing, Suntop Homes, and St. Mark's Tower showing volumetric transformation of the pin-wheel housing type

connects interior space with the exterior and stretches its sphere of influence, by implication, to the horizon beyond. Nevertheless, the tower is more centralized as a composition than the hearth type; it displays little, if any, preferential treatment of front, side, and rear.

Quadruple Block Housing

Another source of the tower form is the unexecuted Quadruple Block Housing project that occupied Wright for more than a decade beginning in 1900. It was published the next year in the *Ladies Home Journal*,[4] along with two prototypic Prairie House designs. This experiment provides a link between Wright's designs for the individual house and his concern for multiple housing and the prototypic form it could take. In the

Ladies Home Journal version, which was to be repeated in almost identical detail numerous times, his Prairie houses were interpreted as clusters of four identical units occupying a square parcel of land divided into four equal quadrants. The clusters were of two types. One type oriented front yard and house to the street, while the side yard enfronted a linear park. The second type arranged the four houses as a pinwheel. The linear street orientation of the former type contrasts with the centered, rotated symmetry of the latter. The theme was developed by Wright in a more compact version in 1939 with his Suntop Homes. In that instance the central service space is compacted into two cross-walls that provide separation between the four equal but pinwheeling units.

St. Mark's, the recognized tower prototype, appears to be a direct, vertical extension of the Suntop Homes concept. The rotational geometry evident in both projects recalls Wright's decorative designs, which, no doubt, served to inform these experiments. Rotational symmetry provided a dynamic aspect to the composition of identical units, and overcame the monotony of simple repetition. In St. Mark's, Wright demonstrates again that his variety-in-unity theme was more than a polemic; it was a design objective that could be realized through form manipulation informed by the principles of ornamental design.

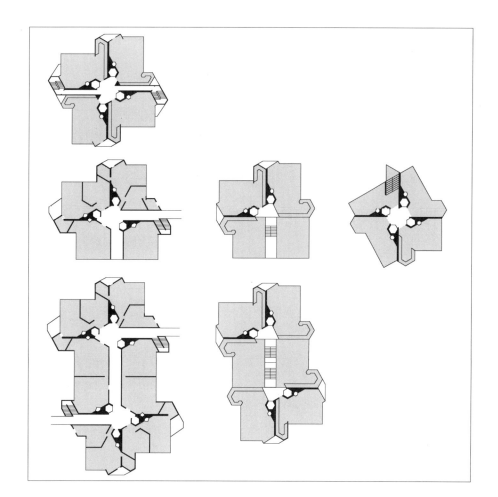

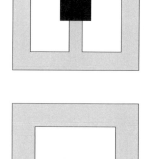
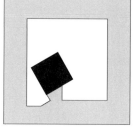
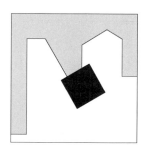

7-18 Comparative plan diagram of St. Mark's Tower (top) as the precedent respectively (left to right) for Crystal Heights Hotel, the Chicago Apartment Group, and Price Tower showing the single tower variations and additive arrangements

7-19 Comparative site plan diagram of Johnson Research Tower, Rogers-Lacy Hotel, and Price Tower

Seeking a Context for the Tower Prototype

After St. Mark's, Wright rejected his earlier experiments with the urban block building in favor of the tall building as tower or sometimes linked towers. His fixation on the tower image is so complete that he often imposes the tower form on projects in defiance of the logic of either the building program or the context. The following year, Wright designed a project for grouped apartment towers in Chicago and repeated the theme ten years later in the Crystal Heights project in Washington, D.C. Both schemes are virtually identical to St. Mark's, although the projecting stairs have been used to join the towers on

either side and thus provide for certain economies. The resultant wall made of individual towers has minimal horizontal continuity either in fact or in plastic expression. True to Wright's analogy, each is rooted like a tree to the earth independent of its neighbor in spite of the social or economic advantages that horizontally integrated floors might have provided. Another strategy for modifying the tower is shown in the Rogers Lacy Hotel, where one of the four pylons is enlarged to contain services. The hotel's base is implanted in a lower range and takes on a courtyard configuration. Later projects such as Broadacre City and the Golden Beacon in Chicago also follow closely the tenets of St. Mark's, with some minor variations.

The Price Tower

None of the apartment or hotel tower designs were realized, but in 1956, with the construction of the Price Tower, Wright was finally able to test his ideas in reality. His task was to design an office building, and he seems to have talked his client into increasing the scope of the project to include housing and to adopt the unexpected form of a tower. It was unexpected in that inexpensive land for horizontal development was not scarce. The Price Tower had a mixed program of offices and duplex apartments with a lower zone of shops and a pair of courtyards, one for the office portion of the tower and the other for residents. The typical upper-level plan displays a subdivision similar to that of St. Mark's, but with only one of

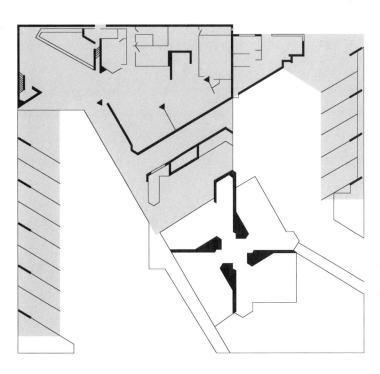

7-20 Site plan of the Price Tower complex

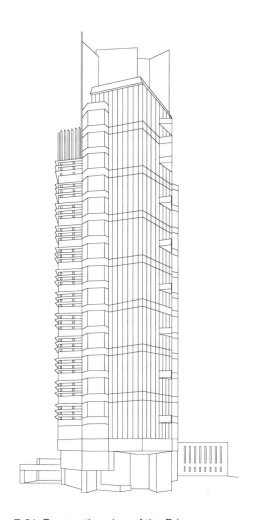

7-21 Perspective view of the Price Tower

the four quadrants reserved for a duplex apartment. The contrasting form and orientation of the apartment section lock the tower into the site and street grid at ground level while developing a special corner "rudder" that tends to stabilize the tower's pinwheeling movement and provide clearer orientation in the landscape.

At the Johnson Wax headquarters, Wright again imposes the tower scheme on the design of research laboratories and dismisses conflicts between function and form in favor of landscape and image objectives. The conflict between laboratory functions and their vertical disposition is perhaps more evident since Louis Kahn's attempt to house laboratories in similarly configured towers. The Richards Medical Center proved that a series of small floor spaces stacked vertically leaves fewer options for the flexible arrangements of labs. The Salk Institute's open horizontal loft space is an implicit critique of the earlier tower approach and provides for much more flexible laboratory space. If Kahn's lesson is valid for the Johnson Wax Research Tower, Wright's motivation for the use of the tower type is again called into question.

Wright's tower designs seem to illustrate the difficulties, shared with many architects of the twentieth century, of dealing with the urban condition. Like Le Corbusier, Wright seems to oversimplify or sidestep the issues of high-density habitation and the accompanying difficulties of resolving conflicts between individual and community identities. The insular quality of radially generated forms such as Wright's towers and Buckminster Fuller's geodesic domes is the source of their attraction and dynamics and is also the cause of the difficulty of integrating these structures with a larger built environment. Although his Mile-high Skyscraper seems to shun any pretensions of integration with an urban setting, Wright's incorporation of traditional linear geometries within his typical tower plan holds out the possibility of successfully integrating it with a clear community context. In the following chapter we examine variations on Wright's approach to site design that might provide clues to the possible integration of individual, internally generated units and the formal representation of their interdependence as a group.

8-1 Array of four groups of site plan patterns: top-unitary theme, left-spine theme, right-compound field theme, bottom-constellation theme

Wolf Lake Park, Monona Terrace,
Marin County Civic Center, Pittsburgh Civic Center, Florida Southern Campus,
Nakoma Country Club, Lloyd Jones house,
San Marcos in the Desert, Hillside Home School, Ocotillo Desert Camp,
Taliesin West, Taliesin East

Site Patterns

Frank Lloyd Wright's intention was that his buildings grow out of the land rather than impose themselves upon it. His ability to design within a natural context makes his architectural contribution among the most important of the twentieth century and provides an important bridge to landscape architecture. Of all the modern masters, only he and Aalto embraced nature as the great form generator. In their designs, both managed to join oriental and occidental concepts relating the worlds of humans and nature. The Western tradition sees the person in contrast with nature, whereas Eastern tradition sees people and nature as integral. Aalto took the abstract, man-made forms of the International Style and the geomorphic, curvilinear forms in nature and synthesized them within the natural environment; Wright adopted the abstract geometries that he believed to be at the heart of all natural phenomena, no matter how complex their physical manifestations might be. His search for first principles focused on this Platonic understanding of reality, although it was embedded within a vitalistic philosophy. The poetry of his work is derived from his emulation of nature based on his understanding of hidden truth rather than on a literal imitation of its external forms.

During his career Wright designed many large-scale projects: residential estates, housing groups and hotels, civic buildings, and urban design projects including the controversial Broadacre City. The compositions for these collective efforts exhibit many variations, but all occur within defined limits. These site plan strategies recognized critical issues such as the interface between man-made and natural form, the nature of growth and change, and scale and proportion relationships linking the part to the whole. An urban setting could dictate a different response than suburban or exurban sites; programs were organized differently for civic complex and group housing designs. All of these considerations evolved differently during the course of Wright's career. Generally the move was away from urban settings with collective exterior space to suburban groupings that only loosely defined place and usually did so in the private rather than the public realm.

OVERVIEW

The introductory chart shows an array of twelve building plans that represent a range of solution types Wright used at different times in his career and for different purposes. They suggest two major strategies for organization and growth at the site level: the closed system and the open system. In a closed system the formal organization of elements is fixed at the outset. It attempts to predict future needs in terms of itself and accepts growth only to the extent that it can be subsumed under

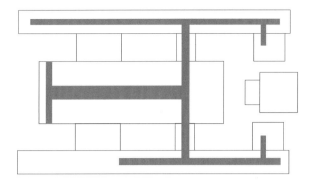

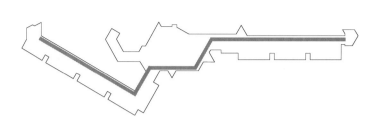

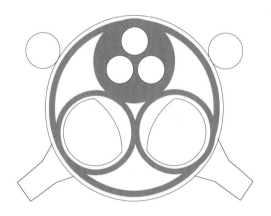

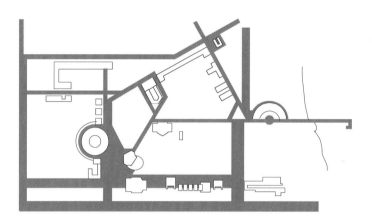

8-2 Plan diagram of Imperial Hotel and Pittsburgh Civic Center showing closed site plan strategy

8-3 Plan diagram of San Marcos in the Desert and Florida Southern Campus showing open site plan strategy

the original pattern. Most automobiles are designed as closed systems; any options or accessories must be carefully integrated with the original form. In an open system, form is organized to accommodate growth and change. Future needs are assumed to be unpredictable; they will continue to influence the overall organization of the form. An open system is basically a kit of parts with a set of rules for their relationships. Barn construction is a good demonstration of an open system. The kit of parts contains all the materials and fasteners needed to build a barn, and the rules are the known methods of construction that assure structural stability and protection from the elements. Unlike the automobile, the barn allows a great deal of flexibility in how to build the original structure and how to

make future additions or alterations. The overall organization of a barn complex can be adjusted to fit a specific site and may grow in unpredicted ways.

CLOSED-SYSTEM SITE STRATEGY

In Wright's hands the closed system approach to design characteristically produces formal, abstract compositions, predominantly in urban sites. The atrium type, as incorporated in the Francisco Terrace apartment block, is a clear early example of this approach. The disposition of all elements is set, and future growth is not a concern. The Francisco example is interesting for its two floors with upper-level galleried access flats surrounding a large garden. The units are paired with back-to-back services; corner towers, a projecting entrance

canopy at the upper level, and the monumental entrance are the only embellishments. The McArthur concrete apartment house of 1906 represents an attempt at moderate-cost housing. The U-shaped footprint of the plan resembles the earlier Francis Apartments and continues the closed-system approach. Although the geometry was to vary, the basic tendencies of the closed system appeared in several large-scale site designs.

The academically conceived Imperial Hotel was one of Wright's most treasured works, a building that he referred to throughout his career. Although the structural integrity of the construction and its miraculous survival of the Tokyo

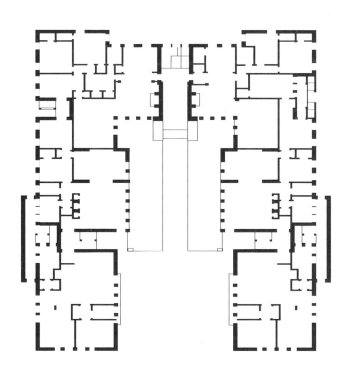

8-4 Plan of McArthur apartments

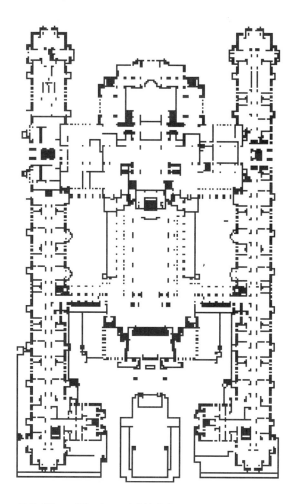

8-5 Plan of the imperial Hotel

earthquake seem to have been the objective reason for Wright's pride, its organization is an intriguing resolution to a difficult space-packing problem. The organization of the hotel could be seen as a modification of the McArthur Apartments. Besides growing very large, the U-shaped configuration has been modified in two important ways. First the building court has been split by the insertion of a pavilion-like communal block that includes the main entrance hall, dining, cabaret, meeting rooms, and support spaces. The central building is embraced by the unit wings on either side, which are woven together with two interconnecting bridges and stairs that link the entire complex. The spaces between the outer wings and the inner pavilion become a series of intimate courtyards. The central pavilion opens out to the gardens with terraces in a continuous movement of space. Although symmetrically planned about the longitudinal axis, a slight weight is given to one long side that accommodates a second entry point. Units open to both sides, inside and out. The increased fenestration and balconies enhance the relationship to the garden, and their more circumspect use mutes the relationship to the street side. The introverted, completed aspect of the plan supports our view of the hotel plan as a closed system. Nevertheless, the lateral circulation passages and their visual extension through the outer wings suggest possibilities for growth, even though limited.

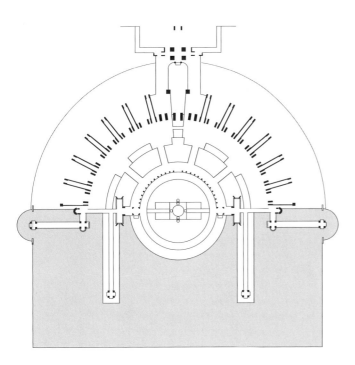

8-6 Plan of Wolf Lake Project

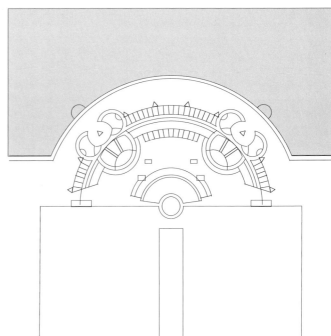

8-7 Plan of the Monoma Terrace Civic Center

The large building fragment conceived as a closed system is a characteristic urban strategy we associate with Wright's post–World War II work, although prominent earlier examples exist. Typically a large, inclusive organization is symmetrically organized about a major axis with one or more minor axes. It is usually a simple geometric form such as the square, triangle, or circle, precisely defined at its perimeter and tending toward a centripetal rather than centrifugal organization. His delightfully buoyant Wolf Lake project of 1895 proves Wright's mastery of academic planning. The play of major and minor axes, use of circular elements, mastery of circulation on both land and water, and the suggestion of spatial containment in the two extended pier arms with terminating towers create a richness of effect and spatial weave unparalleled in his early work. It is grounded in the urban academic tradition. What may Wright's work have been like had he taken this course at a truly urban scale during this period? The Midway Gardens picks up many of these themes, its large outdoor space being analogous to the water plaza of Wolf Lake. The terraced balconies,

towers, tiled wall surfaces, decorative sculpture, furniture, and the like made the Midway a magical place that summed up the very best in Wright's academic mode.

The later Monona Terrace is a more literal successor to Wolf Lake, and yet its net result is disappointing. The major difference between Monona and the two earlier projects is its object-centered rather than space-centered orientation. The generous relationship to the water suggested by the Wolf Lake structure is compromised by the broad parking terraces facing the lake in the Monoma project. The automobile cuts off the relationship between the internal building functions and the lake and results in a strangely introverted scheme for the given site.

The Point Park Community Center project for Pittsburgh of 1947 again shows a single organism, an overlapping triangle and circle, now grown very large and engulfing an entire portion of the city. The dichotomy between inside and outside is a crucial issue for the community center as well. The geometric center, the "shopping space" en-

circled by a car garage, has only two radial links to the community in the form of bridges crossing the two rivers. The role of the automobile becomes more obtrusive and enshrouds the inner space not unlike Wright's Automobile Objective and Planetarium project of 1925. The closing off of major functions that seem to deserve an outward breath of fresh air is strange. Could Wright be deliberately turning his back on the city, especially a city that at that time was infamous for its coal smoke and industrial pollution? This approach tends to make the large, urban ensemble look as if it were really a small building grown very large, resulting in a crisis of scale.

This problematic aspect of scale is most evident in his project for the Opera House and Gardens for Baghdad project in 1957, an example of his late rococo decorative tendencies. Throughout the project are problems of transition between different programmatic expressions in the closed-circle form and several awkward intersections. The initial circular opera house appears to have no graceful way to expand beyond its immediate boundary.

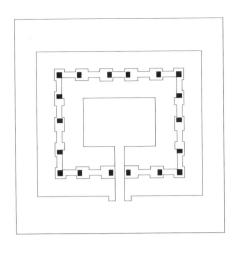
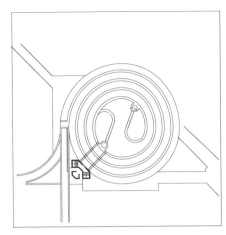
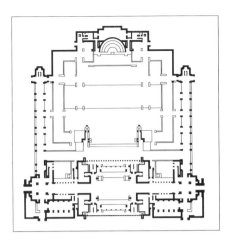
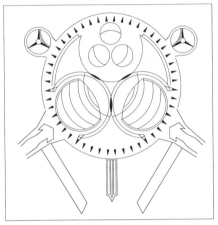

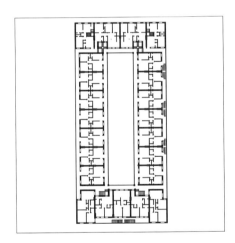
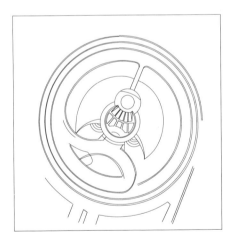
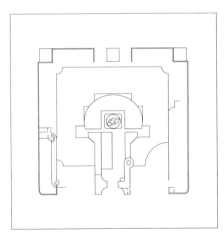

8-8 Comparative plans of the closed site plan type:

Lexington Terrace, Automobile Objective, Midway Gardens,
Pittsburgh Civic Center, Hartford Play Resort,
Francisco Terrace, Baghdad Opera, Johnson Research Tower and Base

OPEN-SYSTEM SITE STRATEGY

This other strategy, which dominated most of his site designs, adopts a set of parts consisting of epicenters connected by corridors, pergolas, or building wings stretching out from center to center like tentacles. This approach has an accretive, episodic quality that pervades the whole and often results in a constellation of building fragments. The parts are organized by adherence to a consistent, pervasive unit system or grid that is inevitably based on forty-five or thirty-sixty-degree angles.

From Hillside Home School to Taliesin West

When compared with Unity Temple, Wright's building for his aunts, the Hillside Home School of 1902, demonstrates the basic distinction between the open-system and closed-system strategies. Although the assembly hall, gymnasium, and studio wing are each centers based on the same compositional order as the worship space and community hall at Unity, here the centers are separated by long galleries. They are conceived as a series of pavilions that could be extended through the addition of other connecting links. The orthogonal geometry holds the pieces together as a constellation.

The Hillside Home School shows initial signs of integration with the natural site in the form of a horizontal shaft of space between the two major building masses.

In a series of house designs, Wright exploited this orthogonal constellation strategy and gradually shifted the focus of the plan from the building to exterior space, with its definition becoming increasingly clear. The Martin House is perhaps the earliest accomplished essay in which the Prairie House could grow and "embrace" the landscape. The site is conceived as a series of pavilions, each of which is either explicitly or implicitly based on a cruciform. These pavilions are then linked through landscape elements such as the pergola, garden walls, and planting beds. The buildings and subsidiary elements define exterior space. Yet the definition of space is, to a certain extent, ambivalent, and in the end the building commands our primary attention. This attitude changes with the designs of both the Coonley House and the McCormick House project, which followed shortly afterwards. Both of these later examples still insist on a epicentric grouping of important program elements such as the living room (singular but weighted with an asymmetric dining room above in the Coonley House; doubled up in dumbbell fashion in the McCormick House, where its large terrace and not the building itself describes the center of the composition).

The Coonley House has a preferred direction, which is outward; its back forms a large garden court that is loosely defined by its service and bedroom wings, as well as by a series of outbuildings. The McCormick project similarly displays an attitude toward defined open space, but in this case the weave of space is more complex. It includes a large entry court that simultaneously relates to the lakeside terrace and a secondary space at right angles to it that leaps across a ravine. The bedroom wing and services form a third, more private court that is bounded on three sides. The orchestration of public and private space woven through both the interior and exterior space allows the McCormick House to achieve a richness of site design unsurpassed by any of Wright's work up to that point.

The Hollyhock House has been described in stylistic terms and as an example of Wright's fascination with Mesoamerican themes.[1] Its planning has not been discussed or has been summarily dismissed as a new tendency toward classical precepts.[2] However, a closer inspection of the plan reveals a startling similarity to the Martin House complex. The key is the symmetrical triad of the formal living room suite, which duplicates those in the Martin complex. However, the fourth arm of the Martin House is compacted about the fireplace with flanking kitchen and reception rooms, whereas the Hollyhock is split open to form an oasis-like garden court.

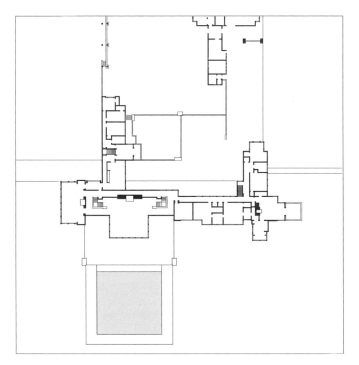

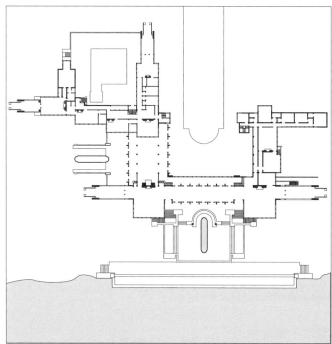

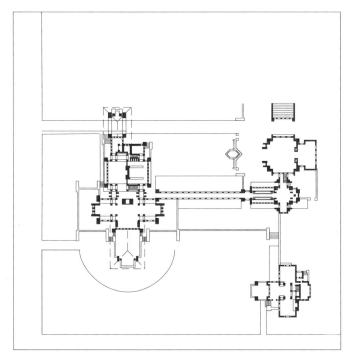

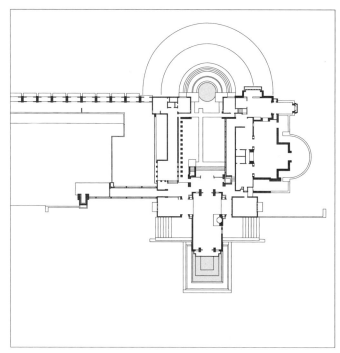

8-9 Site plan of Coonley house

8-10 Site plan of Martin and Barton
houses

8-11 Site plan of the McCormick house

8-12 Site plan for the Hollyhock house

The Hillside Home School was his first in a series of special building categories which could be loosely termed *educational*. Taliesin East, the Ocotillo desert camp, and finally Taliesin West all served to house Wright and his architectural establishment. Taliesin East was the first in this group to challenge this object orientation seriously and transform it with a focus on the space itself. *Taliesin*, Welsh for "shining brow," was conceived as a compound surrounded on three sides by buildings, with the focus of the space and the symbolic center the hilltop rather than the building. The fourth side is closed off in the distance by the highest hill in the valley, on which is perched the Romeo and Juliet Windmill. The sitings of Taliesin East and Jefferson's Monticello show striking similarities.[3] Each encloses a rear garden with embracing arms, and the open side of each is closed with the distant landscape, Carter Mountain in the case of Monticello.

The Ocotillo desert camp was designed as a temporary winter headquarters for Wright and his staff in 1927. The compound (formed to keep the rattlesnakes out) surrounded a small rise in the desert floor. It enclosed an irregular space with buildings made of wood and canvas canopies and diagonal wood walls. The plan, which at first looks haphazard, is actually formed with two primary grids, one shifted at a thirty- to sixty-degree angle to the other. Wright was to comment on the informality demanded by the setting:

> Out here in the great spaces obvious symmetry claims too much, I find, wearies the eye too soon and stultifies the imagination. Obvious symmetry usually closes the episode before it begins: so for me I felt there could be no obvious symmetry in any building in this great desert, one especially in this new camp.[4]

Taliesin West, similarly sited in the desert landscape, rests on a gently sloping incline facing a vast shallow valley and the city of Phoenix. To the rear the hill slopes gradually upward to the foothills and Camelback Mountain. Thus both building groups demonstrate a similar site strategy, Taliesin West's rear garden enclosure being provided by the distant mountain range. Both Taliesins display a similar program breakdown. Both separate Wright's private quarters at one end in a kind of T-shaped end pavilion. In Taliesin East it provides a splendid view over the valley and the artificial lake formed by Wright; in Taliesin West it terminates in an oasis-like desert garden compound that internalizes view rather than extending it into the distant landscape. The other major wing contains a variety of elements, but the major one in both cases is the studio and drafting room. The entrance for both Taliesins is circuitous and requires that the visitor take an indirect path. The visitor is provided with distant views of the complex that do not reveal entry. Only by moving from one entry cue to another—like hopping from one lily pad to the next—does the visitor finally arrive at the entry. Entry occurs precisely at the gap between Wright's living quarters and the work space thus providing a single entry point and functional link to both parts. The vertically compressed open loggia, a kind of porte cochere, presents a dramatic view of the landscape that one has just traversed. This spiraling theme—distant view, closer but mysterious entry, and final revelation back to from whence one came—is repeated countless times and is a theme present in his domestic work, as the Willitts house demonstrates.

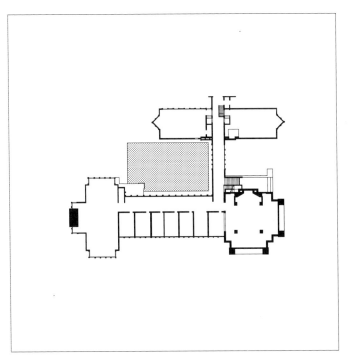

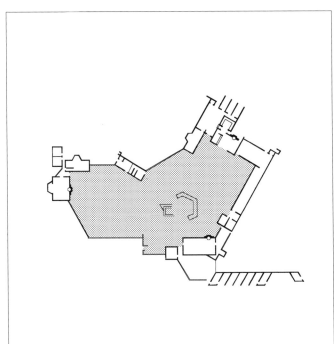

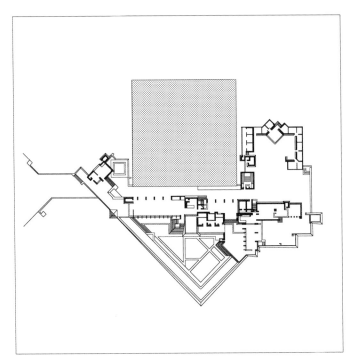

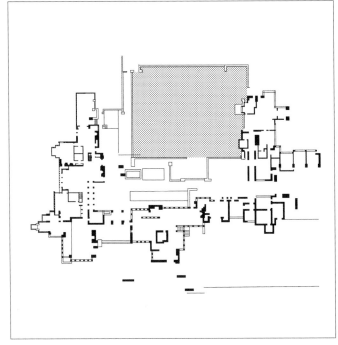

8-13 Site plan of the Hillside Home School

8-14 Site plan of Ocotillo Desert Camp

8-15 Site plan of Taliesin West

8-16 Site plan of Taliesin East

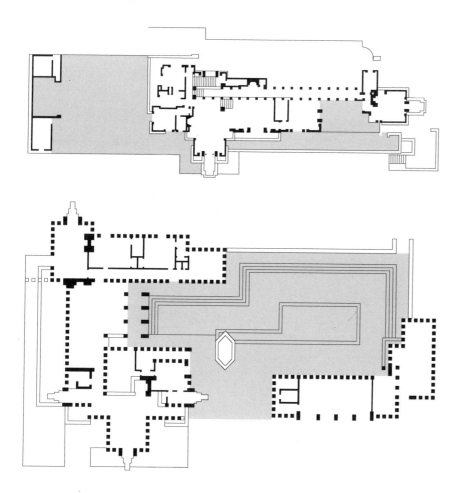

8-17 Site plan of the Ennis house showing defined exterior space at building perimeter

8-18 Site plan of the Lloyd Jones house showing defined exterior space at building center

The Ennis house of 1924 and the Lloyd Jones houses of 1929 show a variation of the open system strategy based on 'field' organizations which reinforce the notion of a compound in a more explicit way. In both houses the 'field' consists of a simple square grid. The Jones house in particular suggests a deviation from the constellation approach. Its outer perimeter is bounded within a regular orthogonal field described by major livingroom, bedrooms, and garage. A swimming pool and hexagonal fountain mark the central space, the latter acting like the campfire of the Ocotillo desert camp, and suggest a similar "sacred" place making.

The campus design for Florida Southern College is perhaps Wright's most poetic urban effort. The geometry of its plan is reminiscent of Wright's numerous decorative compositions employing circles, triangles, and squares, such as the mantel design of the Hollyhock House. The site plan suggests a large-scale approach that is neither so fragmentary as to fall apart nor so unitary as to be overbearing. The composition is structured by a "field" of orange groves whose grid extends like a carpet across the site. It can be compared to earlier decorative designs such as the thirty- and sixty-degree tile pattern designed for the Coonley House but not used. Smaller building groupings and the axis of a major east-west path

align with the pier on the water's edge which establish a connection between the heart of the complex and the campus chapel. The shifted thirty- and sixty-degree grid introduces a dynamic element within the grid and breaks the perimeter of the compound with its force, establishing a connection to the existing campus to the north. The multiple organizational readings suggest a layering transparent effect.[5]

160

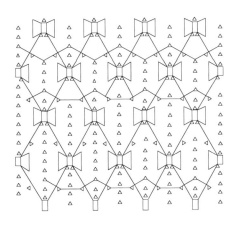

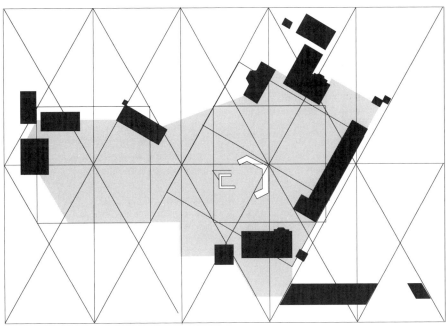

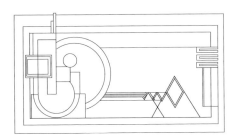

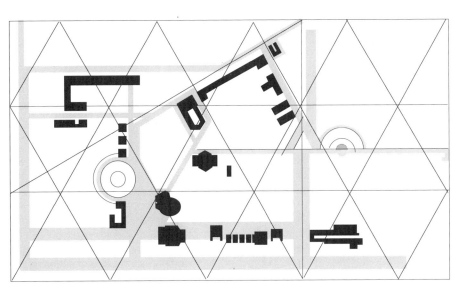

8-19 Comparison of early version of Coonley house tile pattern and site plan diagram of Ocotillo Desert Camp

8-20 Comparison of Hollyhock house concrete mantel relief and site plan diagram of Florida Southern Campus

THE SPINE

This last variation of the open system, also accretive but more openly sensitive to the natural site, appears mostly in the latter part of Wright's career. The spine organizes elements into a linear building with a series of epicenters that designate important program space and usually signal a change in axis. The Nakoma Country Club of 1926, the San Marcos Hotel in the desert a year later, and the Marin County Civic Center of 1959 all exhibit these traits. Enclosed space is only implied and less important than the wall itself, which may take on the form a bridge, dam, or aqueduct in the landscape.

The Nakoma Country Club on the historic Winnebago Indian camping ground is organized on the brow of a hill; it stretches its one long arm along the brow to make a wall punctuated at one end by the large lodge or wigwam. The octagonal motif with nearly symmetrical flanking arms is apparent in the earlier River Forest Golf Club, which was executed by Wright around the turn of the century and is the obvious precedent. Organizationally the octagon provides a hinge for a secondary arm of services that pivots at forty-five degrees. This formula is repeated in the Unitarian Church in Madison, where a similar ridge conditions the architectural response.

The San Marcos Hotel desert project of 1929 is a faceted linear arrangement that approximates the contours of the mountain slope on which it is sited, as well as miming the angle of repose of the distant mountain slopes.[6] The center of the hotel complex is the diningroom and other shared areas; they act as the pivot that links the arms radiating from its hub. The visitor passes through and under the major wing to arrive at an oasis-like court that is formed by the building and the hillside and is an intimate, luxuriant environment. The long wings extend out at a thirty- to sixty-degree angle and consist of units that step at a thirty-degree angle in section to pick up the theme of the plan. The units are connected by a single loaded corridor buried in the back toward the hill with storage. Pairs of units share plumbing services and steps, and each has a small pool. The overall effect is a careful marriage of site and building; the rather abrupt-looking angles effectively resolve themselves into the mountain landscape in perspective.

Marin County Civic Center does not occur as an edge condition on the brow of a hill; neither does it follow the contours of a hillside against which it is placed. Instead, it acts like an aqueduct, leaping from one hill to the next, an image that may have inspired its pseudostructural arches. The main center occurs at the the top of the larger hill and is reached from the major linear element. Similar to Nakoma it provides a hundred and thirty-five-degree angle relationship between the two wings.

Wright is well known for his masterful integration of interior and exterior space. His residential designs are overwhelming evidence of his commitment to the continuity of space. They also show that he recognized a boundary between man-made form and nature, even if it is subtly expressed. Private houses such as Fallingwater, swimming in a sea of nature, terminate their ordering geometries at the edges of balconies, terraces, or parapets. The clean, abstract shapes quickly give way to materials derived from the surrounding environment, such as the rough-laid sandstone of the piers. In these houses we are positioned between the security and comfort of the hearth and the powerful sweep of nature.

The resolution of human being and nature that was successful for the private building on a suburban or rural site was not easily transferred to larger-scale public works in urban settings. Like many architects of his time, Wright struggled with the relationship of the realities of urban life and his appreciation of the nurturing qualities of the natural landscape. As public functions and the need to unify large complexes of buildings increased human domination of sites, Wright had to address the relationship between man-made and natural exterior environments. Early approaches to this problem, such as at the Hollyhock House, provide a man-made container for controlled landscape, with the building and its extensions employed as a boundary between this exterior court and the surrounding landscape. The next concession to nature was the modeling of the plan shape of this exterior court to reflect major features of the natural site. The Ocotillo compound exemplifies this approach. In the Nakoma and San Marcos projects, we see the ultimate recognition of nature in the acceptance of its features as the central organizing force of the site plan.

Of Wright's two site-planning strategies, the open system is his most original and successful contribution. It recognizes both the interaction of human and natural environment and the realities of growth and change. The open system is reflective of oriental concepts of space and in sharp contrast with his closed-system strategy, which is rooted in classical Western composition.

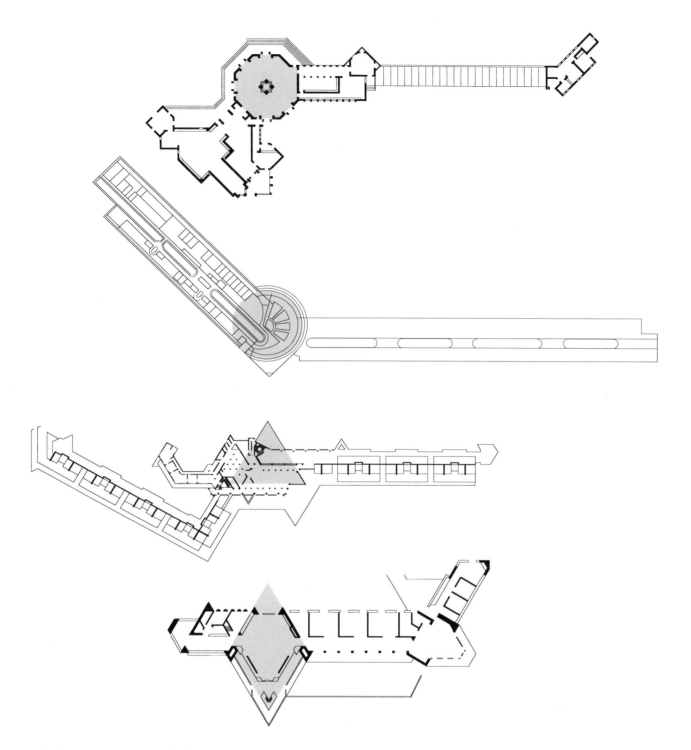

8-21 Comparative plans of Spine type site patterns:

Nakoma Country Club, Marin County Civic Center,
San Marcos in the Desert, the Unitarian Church

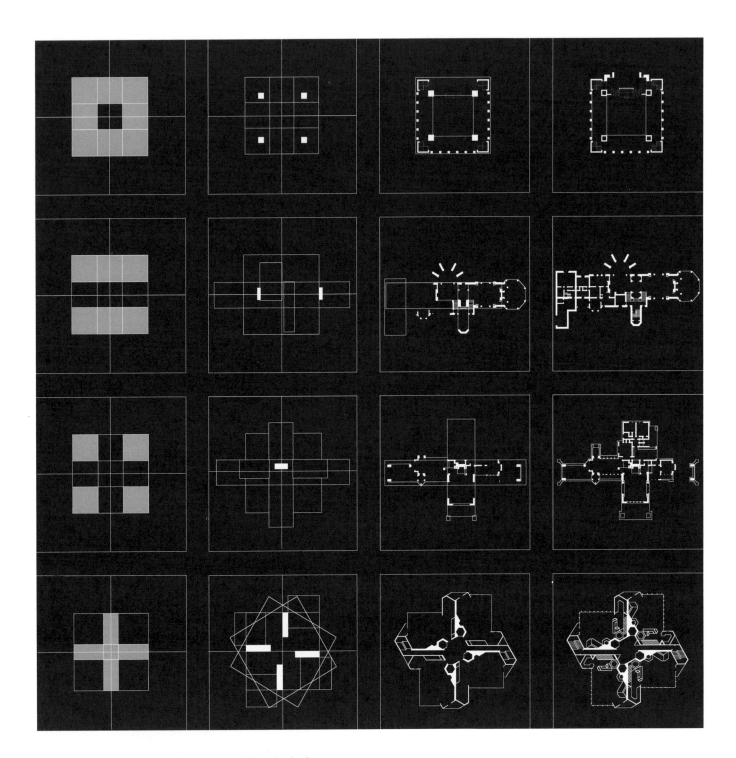

9-1 Comparative plan diagrams showing hypothetical
design process based on a square:
Unity Temple, Husser house, Willitts house, St. Mark's Tower

Between Principle and Form

In the preceding chapters, we have observed, described, and analyzed the formal structure of Wright's architecture and attempted to add layers of meaning to a typological view of his work. We have focused on the specific manner in which form incorporates principle and is an expression of it. In this chapter we speculate more broadly about Wright's ability to bridge the gap between principle and form. We are looking for consistencies in the way Wright designed. We are interested in the practical concepts or devices he applied throughout his career to achieve a unity of principle and form. Our purpose is to explore these issues of form and principle in order to make his process of design more tangible and accessible to other architects.

We have identified the following interrelated ideas that we believe played a major role in Wright's design process: type, order, space, and experience. Wright's conception of each seems to have originated in a deeply felt conviction that he then embodied in form. The means and devices that he used to explore these ideas in specific building designs reflect this larger frame of reference. Much emphasis has been placed upon Wright as a creative visionary, but another equally important side of Wright is the practical problem solver and strategic designer. Given his origins in crafts-oriented nineteenth-century culture and his prolific output, we can more easily see Wright as an architect committed to realizing his designs in built form, a creator who could invent practical, efficient ways to convert his principles into concrete forms of astonishing quality.

TYPE

Our contention is not only that formal groups or types exist in Wright's architecture but also that they constitute the essence of his approach to design. As we have seen in the previous chapters, the basic types of hearth, atrium, and tower are the starting points and guiding concepts for almost all of his designs. Wright spoke about function and form as a unity. Through the use of types, he is able to embody the idea of dwelling, community, and place that can transform to adopt a wide variety of expressions while retaining their basic integrity.

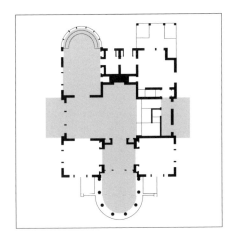

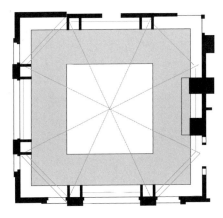

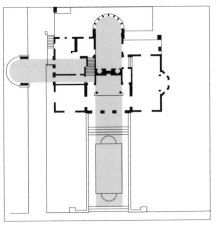

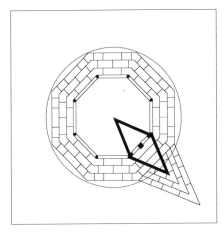

9-2 Plan of the Blossom House

9-3 Plan of the Winslow House

9-4 Plan of F. L. Wright Oak Park drafting room

9-5 Plan of Romeo and Juliet Windmill

Even in his earliest work we can see the emergence of the hearth type as a compelling idea. In both the Blossom and Winslow houses (1892-93), layered, interpenetrating space emanate from the hearth which is central to the resulting spatial dynamics. These innovations are trapped within a traditional housing volume for the most part with hints of the interior spatial dynamics beginning to poke through the shell. Over Wright's entire career, through the Prairie house

years and on through the Usonian houses, the spatial energy of the hearth type is released to the exterior and into the surrounding landscape without abandoning its primary identity. The other two types are also revealed early: the atrium in Wright's studio at his Oak Park home (1895) and the Romeo and Juliet Tower at Taliesin East (1896). It is extraordinary that these types, invented by an architect in his twenties, would provide the foundation for a full lifetime of invention.

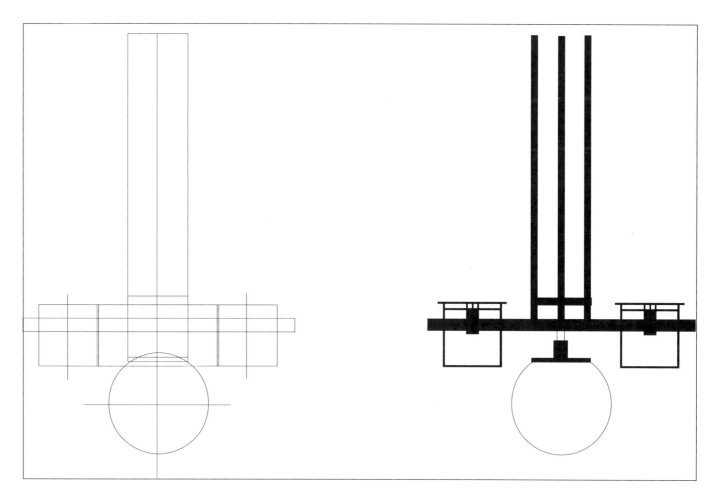

9-6 Detail of Unity Temple lighting fixture

ORDER

I confess to a love for a clean arris; the cube I find comforting, the sphere inspiring. In the opposition of the circle and the square I find motives for architectural themes with all the sentiment of Shakespeare's "Romeo and Juliet": combining these with the octagon I find sufficient materials for symphonic development. I can marry these forms in various ways without adulterating them, but I love them pure, strong, and undefiled. The ellipse I despise; and so do I despise all perverted, equivocal versions of these pure forms. There is quite room enough within these limitations for one artist to work I am sure, and to accord well with the instinct for first principles.[1]

Even a cursory review of Wright's buildings reveals a consistent identity that avoids monotony. Using a set of primary forms and "first principles," Wright could create an overwhelming variety of building designs that shared the Wright "signature". Pursuing the expression of "organic" architecture, he achieved unity and diversity at the same time. A major source of this achievement was his mastery of two basic types of order: compositional and thematic. Compositional order supports both architectural unity and diversity by employing traditional elements of design such as balance, alignment, hierarchy, repetition, and rhythm. The binuclear composition of Unity Temple, for example, incorporates symmetry about a major longitudinal axis with additional cross axes defining local symmetries at multiple and diminishing scales. The large vertical volume of the main worship space is balanced by a set of lower horizontal elements including the Unity Temple house and entrance steps, terraces, and loggia. The compositional balance is further supported by the equilibrium of the vertical and horizontal elements, solid volumes and voids, and large- and small-scale building components.

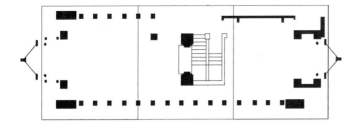
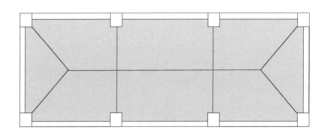

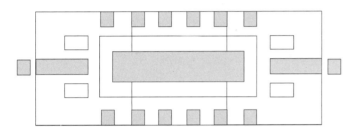
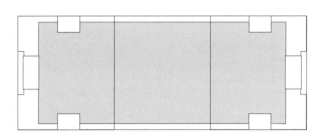

9-7 Analytical diagrams of designs for Robie house:
plan of living area, reflected ceiling plan with lighting
scheme, carpet pattern, dining table

Thematic order consists of a continuity of formal themes at multiple scales, from site plan, to building plan, to ornamental details, often including furniture and furnishings, to create an order based on aesthetics. This order is such as can be found in nature in trees or rocks or in the visual profile of traditional Mediterranean hill towns. The dining room table in the Robie House can be seen as a miniature version of the larger house acting like a nested toy doll that recalls the larger. In Unity Temple, thematic order is established through the consistent use of orthogonal geometry and the controlled application of a specific set of ornamental manipulations from the building footprint to the chandeliers.[2] The theme is further supported by the use of characteristic proportions and rhythms in form, especially simple geometries such as the square nested many times within itself, like the example of the Robie House.

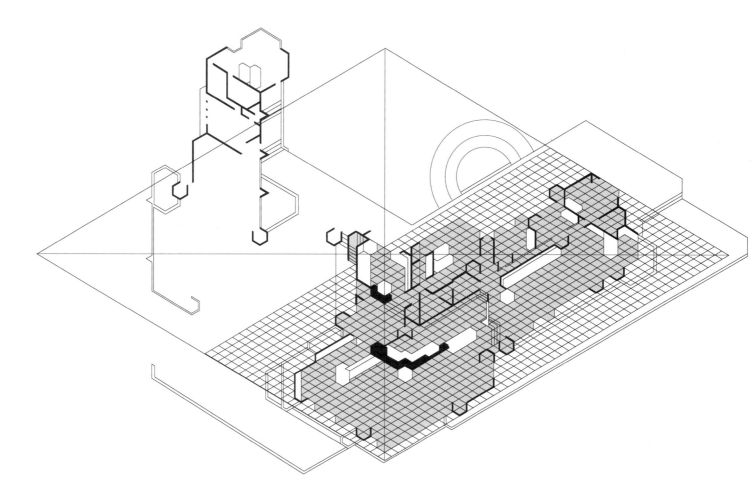

9-8 Plan diagram of Hanna house showing superimposition of 30-60 degree diamond grid

Part of the thematic order in Wright's work can be traced to his acceptance of the geometric limits inherent in his drafting equipment: the T square, the forty-five degree and thirty- and sixty-degree triangles, and the compass. Unlike Le Corbusier or Alvar Aalto, who derived curvilinear forms from other designed objects or nature, Wright used his basic set of drafting tools to generate his forms, which are inevitably abstract despite the use of natural materials.

Through the constant reliance on grids or a "unit system" as a structuring device, Wright incorporates both compositional and thematic order within the heart of his design process. The grid

becomes an armature or framework for experimentation with both the relationships between building elements and the expression of their common aesthetic. Wright's attitude toward the unit system was similar to Le Corbusier's attitude to his "modular" grid, that is, not as a formula for design but as a context within which to pose questions. For Wright the grid was the start and not the end; its application always assumed the presence of an experienced designer with sophisticated sensitivities and judgment who was already in possession of an architectural idea. Employing the grid to generate the forms of Unity Temple did not automatically generate its final design. Wright had to struggle

with many unknowns: the proportions and orientation of the site, the sequence of entry, the relationship between interior and exterior space, not to mention reconciling his clients' idea of a place of worship with his own.

Within the geometric range of his drafting tools, Wright experimented with many variations of the grid based on the rectangle, triangle, and circle. Demonstrating his distinctive ability to "design" his method of designing, perhaps inherited from Sullivan and Owen Jones, he freely explored a variety of interpretations of these grids and further extended the range of possibilities.[3]

SPACE

One of Frank Lloyd Wright's most significant contributions to modern architecture is his understanding of the role of space in design. As he readily acknowledged, his ideas of space were closely related to the fundamental concepts of Taoist beliefs expressed by the Chinese philosopher Lao-Tzu, namely, that the essence of that which is seen is that which is not seen. Translated to architectural design, the essence of a building is not the visible construction but the invisible, "negative" space that is embodied within. In oriental architecture we see numerous expressions of this deference to the continuity of negative space: the overhanging roof's eaves that tip up at their edges, to the structural beams that extend beyond their supporting posts, the elevated platform at the base of the building, the transom space above the doorways, and moveable screens that extend throughout the house. These elements are most clearly seen in traditional Japanese temples and houses, where everything exudes the sense of temporariness. Moveable floor mats and furnishings emphasize architecture as settings rather than structures. Negative space is treated as a river that flows through the building, only temporarily defined for habitation. The impact of Taoist philosophy on oriental architecture and Wright's interpretation of this tradition seems especially disposed to engage the imaginations of people who experience them.

Wright identified his concept of space as fundamental to the Prairie House and his break with the contemporary house design, which he expressed as "breaking out of the box."[4] His architecture would not be limited to space enclosure but would emphasize the continuity of space from indoors to outdoors; it would replace a static notion with a dynamic one. Wright gave form to his sense of space through strategies that support consistent themes in his architecture: interpenetrating spaces, both vertical and horizontal, and the dissolution of fixed corners. The three-part vertical composition of the typical Prairie house seems to have evolved slowly in Wright's work, starting with the Winslow House. In this house we clearly see three divisions: a base, a middle section under the eaves, and the large overhanging roof. As discussed earlier, the definition of the middle section seems not as clear as in later houses where the horizontal strip is recessed and dominated by ribbon windows. As Wright explores the elaborations of the three-part scheme, continuity of horizontal planes and the sense of deep recess in the middle horizontal section become more clear. Characteristically this sense of penetration of space through surfaces is expressed in various parts of the house, including the interior coves and moldings. Ultimately it led to the disintegration of the corner, the strongest spatial defining element.

The interpenetration of spaces emerges quite early in Wright's work, particularly in experiments in his own house and studio, which show a clear expression of spatial zones rather than rigid containers. A prime example of extended, overlapping space can be found in Wright's Unity Temple. The main worship structure is organized around a central cubic volume that extends upward through the skylighted roof that dominates the visitor's experience of the temple interior. Crossing horizontal shafts of space are defined by the four major vertical piers and the suspended balconies. The exterior extensions of the roof and large voids at the windows reinforce horizontal space, whereas the open gridded ceiling and skylight recognize the central cubic volume vertically. This centered, three-dimensional intersection of spaces provides the anchor and the theme for the rest of the building complex.

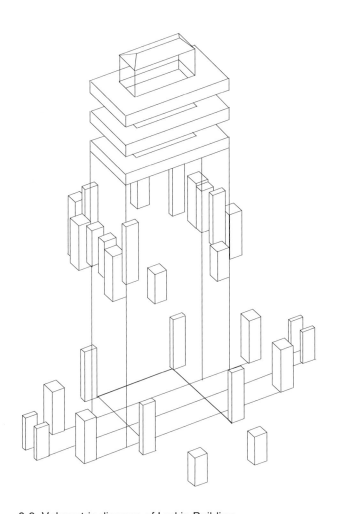

9-9 Volumetric diagram of Larkin Building

9-10 Volumetric diagram of Unity Temple

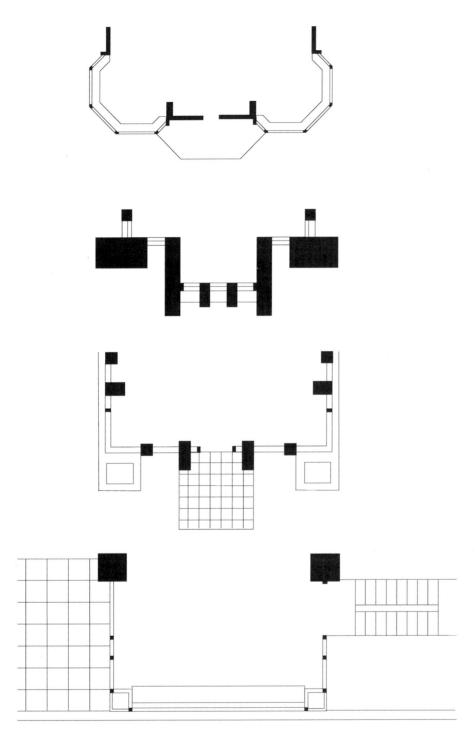

Wright's desire to break the corners of the traditional box plan is expressed early on in his 1892 design of the octagonal corner rooms for the Emmond House. The corners are further opened until they become dissolved in clusters of vertical piers in the Martin House of 1904. In the Freeman House and later in the Johnson Wax Tower, the corners are wrapped in glass with no vertical mullion or support. In Fallingwater we see a highly developed integration of extended space in a house that features horizontal layering, interlocking spaces, and the dissolution of corners with mitered glass corners. The protruding balconies appear to float over the cascading stream to provide "steps" that link the waterfall's rock ledges to the building and ultimately move skyward.

EXPERIENCE

In this book we have explored the underlying formal order in the work of Frank Lloyd Wright. Thus far we have dealt with the formal composition and expression of space whose permanent, visible imprint on Wright's architecture can be described and analyzed. Now we look at the less tangible but equally powerful orchestrations of experience with which Wright energized his work. Without attributing specific motives to Wright, we can observe consistencies in his designs that suggest the ways he intended people to experience the architecture.

9-11 Comparative plan details of Emmond, Martin, Freeman, and Fallingwater living rooms showing progressive dissolution of the building corners

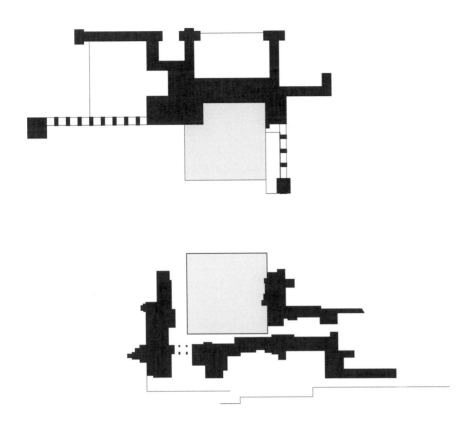

9-12 Comparative plan diagrams of the Willitts house hearth and the Taliesin East site plan showing the definition of sacred space at different scales

Many sympathetic to Wright's architecture have commented that only through the direct experience of his buildings can his mastery as an architect be fully appreciated. We believe that his ability to orchestrate experience is the result of consistently applied principles. They were developed as a response to important psychological and symbolic human needs that promote spiritual transcendency and energize the imagination.

The earliest artifacts of civilization record an awareness of an order or an entity larger and more powerful than the individual person. The desire to transcend the limits of a chaotic, finite existence and form a relationship to a more powerful, seemingly infinite, world is a strong force in all cultures but is often associated with more "primitive" civilizations in which celestial events involving the sun, moon, or a constellation of stars were particularly important. In Greek culture the link between the heavens and the human being was embodied in a pantheon of gods. The Greek myths consist largely of transactions and associations between these gods and mortal humans. Woven through these invented histories, we continually find tales of sacrifices made as a way of creating a bond between human beings and the supernatural.

In architecture this spirit of sacrifice has often been expressed as space set aside exclusively for the gods, holy spaces from which humans are excluded. An example surviving to modern times is the large, solid block that occupies the center of the principal shrine of Islam at Mecca. This gigantic block sits in the middle of an open-air forum. Muslim worshippers walk in a circle around this space but they may not enter it. By being prohibited from reaching the center of the space, the devout surrender or sacrifice dominance of the space to the symbol of their god. Sacrificial space can also be found in churches, monuments, and even some public buildings.

Similar transcendent spaces can be found in Wright's work, especially in his Prairie houses, where the great chimney and hearth fulfill this function. Although Wright extols the use of this device as a metaphor for kinship with natural organic form, we might also interpret it as a generator of the compelling intangible experience of sacrificial space. In his house designs Wright consistently forms a large solid area at the center, normally including the fireplace and hearth. This mass forms a dominant intrusion within the major space of the house so that the tension of being next to but never occupying the core of the house cannot be escaped. We are made to feel subservient to the architecture and to give the architecture a transcending sense of importance and permanence. In buildings such as Fallingwater and the Johnson Wax Tower, the psychological or symbolic subservience is reinforced by a literal structural dependence.

In this same tradition, the central atrium space at Unity Temple, for example, provides a clear expression of a sacrificial space. In deference to this unobstructed cube of space, much of the seating is tucked away in balconies couched between the four massive piers that mark the corners of the space. The vertical proportion of these piers and the skylighted ceiling reinforce the vertical, transcendental axis of the space. These spaces can also be found in other public buildings by Wright, including the Larkin Building and the Guggenheim Museum.

Another experiential theme explored by Wright is that of mystery. Human imagination appears to crave the experience of mysteries as much as or more than their resolution. Wright takes advantage of our curiosity by creating environments that deliberately lack the predictable clarity important to the classical tradition. From many viewpoints his buildings seem incomplete to the viewer. The combination of large, overhanging roofs, deep parapets, and segmented stained glass windows provides us with an intriguing, almost impenetrable sense of space that heightens our anticipation. Light seems to penetrate deep into the recesses of the walls without revealing the inner sanctum of the building. In urban settings the use of an elevated first floor and outrigger parapet walls provides an added phenomenal distance between the exterior and interior that guards privacy as it provides the inhabitants with clear visual access to the exterior.

Having created a "sacred" core and attendant central space for the building, Wright develops our sense of mystery to create a protective psychological distance between the building exterior and its interior. If we trace the typical route of entry to the core or central space of any of his mature buildings, we find a consistent pattern of sequential redirection, anticipation, and suspense, until the climax occurs upon arrival at the hearth or central space. To reinforce the sense of anticipation and heighten the impact upon reaching the main destination, Wright manipulates the height, scale, and intensity of light and carefully orchestrates experience through contrasts. This theme is related to the oriental conception that the essence of experience is not what is immediately evident but rather what is imagined or anticipated. In many of his houses and particularly in Unity Temple, Wright creates an experience much like a Japanese garden, where the complete scene is never evident. We cannot comprehend the total space at once; a part is always left around the corner to provoke the movement and the imagination.

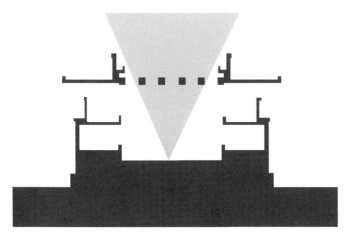

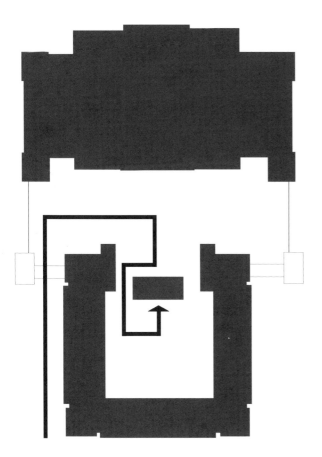

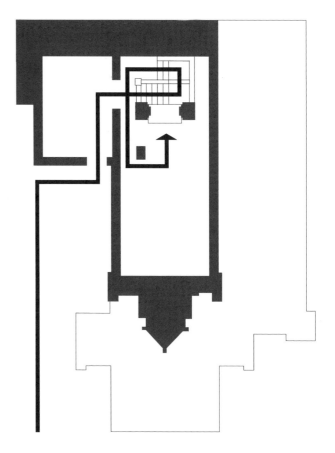

9-13 Section diagram of the Unity Temple showing the vertical disposition of interior space

9-14 Section diagram of the Robie house showing the horizontal disposition of the interior space

9-15 Plan diagram of the Unity Temple showing indirect entry sequence

9-16 Partial plan diagram of Robie house showing indirect entry sequence

Most of Wright's work is distinctive for its intensity and vitality. Much of the energy in the architecture is derived from the dynamic tension he creates between opposing forces: the universal and the particular, the community and the individual, the prototypic and the contextual.

The tension between the universal and the particular is represented by the juxtaposition of strong abstract geometries and the special, often natural characteristics of the site. The geometry, often in the form of a pervasive grid, acts as an anchoring or stabilizing element in tension with the fluid forms of nature. Fallingwater house most clearly demonstrates the manner in which Wright orchestrates the dynamic interplay of these two forces.

The central tension of civilization, between the individual and the community, is another dynamic force played out in Wright's houses. Whereas the powerful expression of the hearth, central space, and dominating roof reinforce the social, communal nature of the family, the dynamic extensions of space, terraces, and roofs express the expansion of each individual's potential. The way these forces are resolved within the building creates unity and harmony without diminishing the importance of either the individuals or the community.

Further examination of Wright's architecture will, no doubt, uncover additional bridges between principle and form. Our aim here is to demonstrate plausible connections and to suggest that their recognition may provide avenues for understanding Wright and avoiding "mere imitation." We hope to convey a richer understanding of Wright's means of joining of principle and form that might serve to inspire architects.

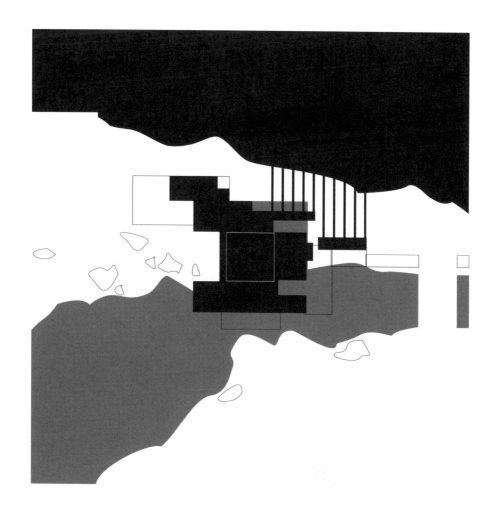

9-17 Site plan diagram of Fallingwater showing the dynamic
tensions between natural and man-made orders

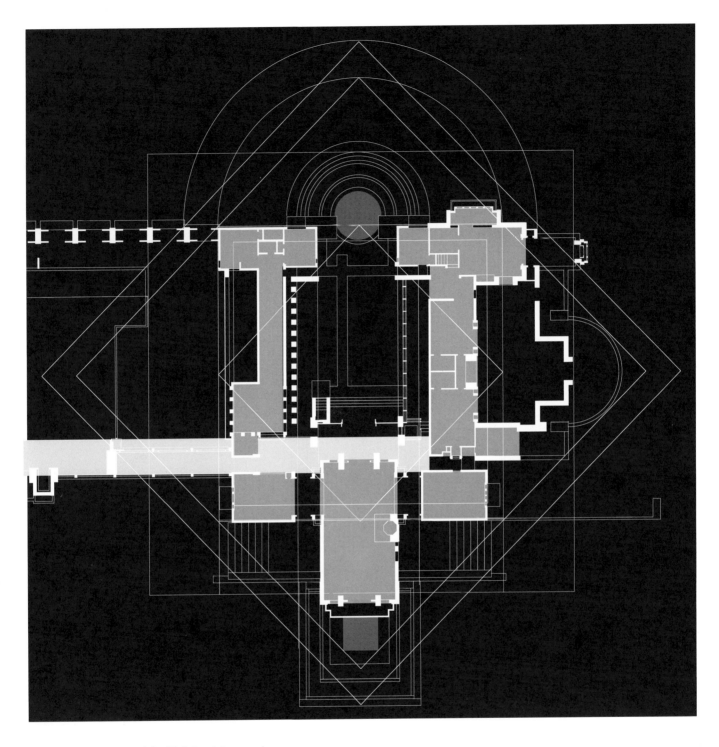

10-1 Formal analysis of the Hollyhock house plan

Architectural Implications 10

A book like this could have been written about any one of a number of architects. We chose Wright because of his recognized preeminence among American architects and his unmatched output of projects and completed buildings. We hope our typological approach will encourage researchers to study the designs of other architects in a similar way. As our investigation has provided a number of insights into the architecture of Frank Lloyd Wright, our understanding and appreciation of his accomplishments and the potentials of typological research has grown. In this chapter we share some of these insights in the belief that a lot more can be learned about both Wright's work and typological research.

THE IMPLICATIONS OF WRIGHT'S WORK

An overview of the architecture of the twentieth century, particularly in America, provides plausible evidence of Wright's broad influence. At first consideration, the dominant influence of his work appears to be the concept of thematic unity. We do not refer to the imitation of his specific aesthetic, but rather to the continuity of form at all scales of a building, irrespective of style. Much of the strength and integrity of designs by architects such as Louis

Kahn, Carlo Scarpa, Paul Rudolph, Mario Botta, and Faye Jones hinges upon the refinement of forms in constant reference to a unifying theme. In this light, Wright contributed to the liberation of modern architecture (as distinguished from International Style) from dependence on one style or aesthetic. He promoted a method of form generation that could accept a range of formal or experiential preferences.

Our comparative studies of Wright's building plans show that he also demonstrated the possibilities of integrating formal, academic composition and the informal fluidity of natural rhythms. The full potential of these plans was exploited through his adoption of oriental concepts of space. This "hidden dimension"[1] of his architecture accounts for the undiminished experiential power of his best buildings. This approach introduced a dynamic mode of expression that has been pursued by many architects.

However, Wright's architecture seems to have escaped the formal analysis accorded the works of several prominent contemporary architects. Several reasons for this situation could be offered. His work seems too personal and elusive. The romantic notion of a creative genius operating in a complete vacuum argues against the transferability of design ideas and creates a barrier between the student of architecture and Wright's designs. The discouragement of imitation and the rejection of formal analysis effectively closed off all avenues of access to his work. Finally, on the basis of its particular expression, the judgment that his architecture was inappropriate to the modern age has blocked analysis of his work.

In summary, Wright's impact on architecture seems heavily influenced by his attitudes toward architectural education, namely, that design excellence was more an acquired skill than an intellectual pursuit. On the whole we have inherited an exposure to his architecture rather than an understanding. This inheritance is symptomatic of the profession of architecture that is only now emerging from a craft toward a body of knowledge.

The principal characteristics of Wright's architecture reflect his concern for the central artistic question of the relationships between order and experience, the universal and the particular, or consistencies and variations. He juxtaposed abstract geometry with the special conditions of the building context to achieve consistencies and variety over a range of designs. The consistency of his vocabulary accounts for certain consistencies in the experience of his spaces: stability, security, comfort, relaxation, and familiarity. The vitality of his design invention seems to be related to the degree of limitation he placed on his design palette in terms of geometries, materials, and construction. Although the materials, construction, and sculpting of space and light may imitate nature, the geometries of the work make a direct appeal to the human intellect.

THE IMPLICATIONS OF WRIGHT'S DESIGN PROCESS

Within the extraordinary volume of literature on Wright is an amazing poverty of discourse on his design processes. Even colleagues who worked by his side for thirty years appear incapable of or reluctant to discuss his methods. Yet our studies indicate that a consistency of design process probably played a key role in the linkage he achieved between design principles and formal expression. On the basis of our studies, we offer the following observations regarding Wright's design processes.

The popular notion of Wright as a creative genius operating in a vacuum could be sustained only by a narrow concept of design process that is limited to internal thought and discounts the acquisition of ideas or the processes of visual representation. He was a cultured individual able to absorb, critique, and transform what he saw into a new vision, and the expression of his vision was deeply influenced by the tools and formal concepts he relied on to represent form. Wright had the ability to transcend scales of concern. The design of a vase could be the inspiration for a skyscraper, the design of a dining room table could relate to the plan of a house, and a tile pattern could be enlarged to generate a housing pattern for many acres. Wright was able to learn from design in other media, such as the decorative arts (designs of tile patterns by Owen Jones, ornament by Louis Sullivan) or woven materials. Wright used ornamental design as a basis for his "formal research" throughout his career.

Fundamental ideas about the individual in society and the human's relationship to nature were integrated with his design process through the use of types. Wright's process is a critique of the limits of pure inductive reasoning and an affirmation of the value of deductive reasoning that is framed by standard "type" as useful problem solving.

Wright demonstrated that the knowledge of principle is no limit to form. Form has logic, and the knowledge of structures "formal principles" that can guide and inform meaning without dictating or prescribing results. Wright was a great academic planner and had a highly developed knowledge of traditional compositional principles, including axes, symmetry, hierarchy, scale, and proportion, and he combined Western academic planning principles with Eastern sensibilities (such as the contrast of symmetrical axial composition with a spiraling movement pattern off axis); he looked to non-Western architecture but not in a simplistic or superficial sense. He increased the repertoire of Western architecture.

Wright's achievements in design owe much to his mastery of a design process strongly driven by geometric order. His design approach proceeds from form as well as principle. He gave his design principles a formal expression through the use of the grids that integrated compositional structure and thematic unity. Wright provided an outstanding example of the potential of the building plan to embody basic principles that could guide the total development of the building design. In spite of the genius image that Wright projected, we believe that he struggled with the same problems and doubts as any designer, which he overcame through an extraordinary dedication and sense of purpose. Although judging the appropriateness of Wright's architecture for any era but his own is not necessary, his approach to design should provide lessons for many future generations.

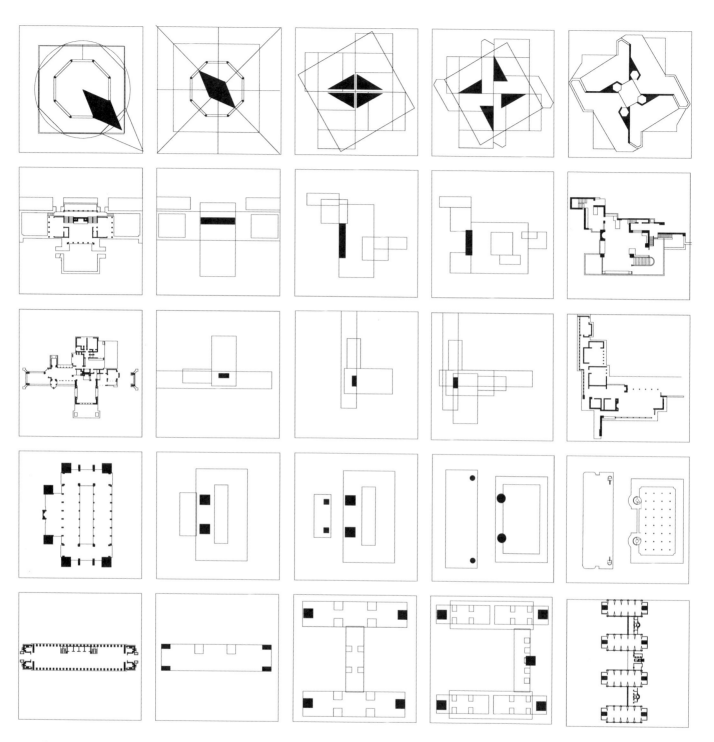

10-2 Comparative diagrams showing hypothetical
transformations between building plans:

Romeo and Juliet Windmill and St. Mark's Tower,
Hardy and Fallingwater houses,
Willitts and Jacobs houses,
Larkin and Johnson administrative buildings,
San Francisco Press and National Life Insurance office buildings

THE IMPLICATIONS FOR ARCHITEC-
TURAL EDUCATION AND RESEARCH

Wright's work underlines the value of instilling a sensitivity to form and space through abstract hands-on means, the Froebel block approach tempered with a knowledge of types and historical precedents and Owen Jones exercises in manipulation and elaboration of form. It also shows the benefits of long-term exploration of form within clear constraints and the value of typology as a guide to creation, with the assumption that the architect is not required to invent out of thin air.

TYPOLOGICAL RESEARCH

The concept of type is in itself open to change insofar as it means a consciousness of actual facts, including, certainly, a recognition of the possibility of change. By looking at architectural objects as groups, as types, susceptible to differentiation in their secondary aspects, the partial obsolescences appearing in them can be appraised, and consequently one can act to change them. The type can thus be thought of as the frame within which change operates, a necessary term to the continuing dialectic required by history. From this point of view, the type, rather than being a "frozen mechanism" to produce architecture, becomes a way of denying the past, as well as a way of looking at the future.[2]

As obvious as it may seem, we cannot overstate the importance of a basic premise of typological research, namely, that insights are to be derived from direct observation of the architectural work. For this reason description is one of the principal tasks of a researcher of types. Description is a process of noting what is immediately observable. The purpose is to identify what is present rather than our reactions or conjectures about the work. In description we are interested in accuracy and completeness appropriate to the features of the architecture being studied. For example, a typological study of building plans need not necessarily include detail drawings of carpentry or ornament. Description is a vital key to the research process because it provides the basic evidence upon which the other operations such as analysis, interpretation, and judgment will depend.

For architecture, description is usually in two forms: graphic and verbal. Graphic description provides the primary visual evidence with which we can interact and explore clues to the underlying principles of form and process. Graphic description helps us to grasp parallels, patterns, tendencies, contradictions, and inconsistencies in the work. Graphic communication promotes simultaneous description of a wide range of features of architecture for comparison. Verbal description has an equally important role of naming and categorizing things we see. Through verbal language we can attach meaning to visual evidence, refine our perceptions, and evoke new concepts. The term hearth, for example, includes concepts of home, heart, core, enclave, identity, communion, warmth, sustenance, and security. The study of architectural types must combine graphic and verbal description to create a framework for research that is accessible and memorable.

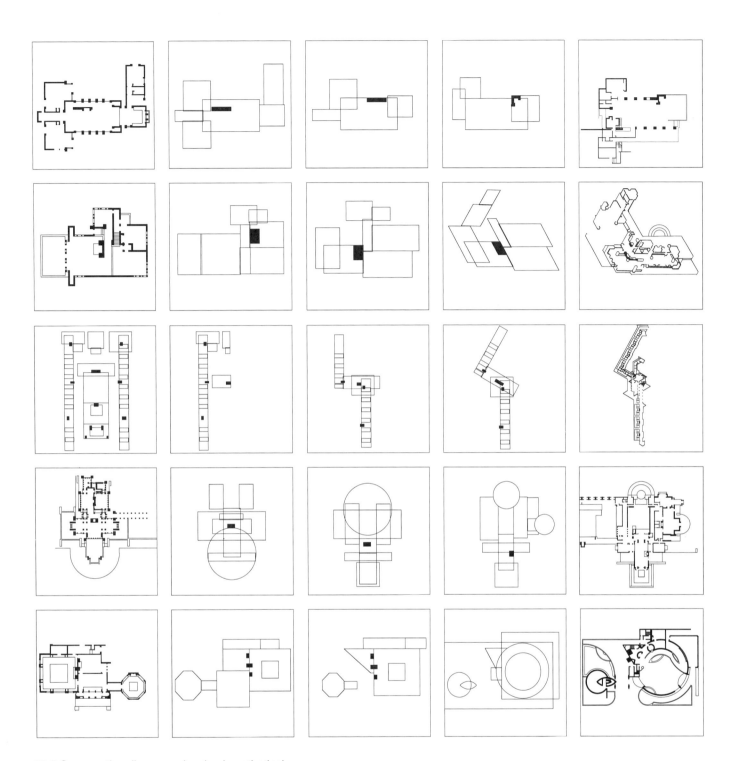

10-3 Comparative diagrams showing hypothetical
transformations between building plans:

Storer and Life houses
Gale and Hanna houses
Imperial and San Marcos in the Desert hotels
Martin and Hollyhock houses
F.L. Wright Studio and house and Guggenheim Museum

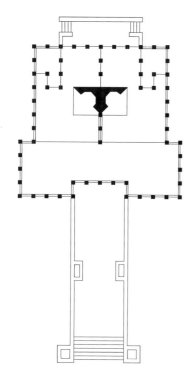 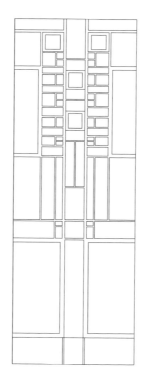 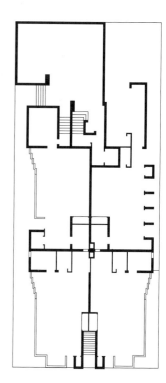

10-4 Comparison of Formal compositional themes:
Gerts summer cottage plan, Coonley house leaded glass doors, Noble Apartment plan

Formal analysis is a necessary comple-ment to description. As we began to identify similarities and distinctions among Wright's building plans, descrip-tive categories emerged: hearth, congregation, tower. Each category, in turn, revealed further variations: compact, aligned, pinwheel, atrium, bi-nuclear. This hierarchical arrangement of description provided a rudimentary map by which we could explore the broad range of Wright's work without getting lost or confused.

The analysis of form highlights the presence and application of known dimensions of form creation: geometry, scale, proportion, balance, symmetry, rhythm, unity. Whereas design is mostly a process of integration of building elements, formal analysis usually

involves the dissection of the building through drawings: plan, elevation, section, and perspective. Studies of different views of buildings can often lead to a range of different insights into the design. Selection of drawing type and dimensions of form to be examined should be carefully made in light of the specific purpose of the analysis. In our study, we focused on Wright's building plans as the most revealing view of the core of his design thinking. The plans can be seen as analogous to the skeletons of animals; they provide many important clues to the basic organization and variations in building designs. Analysis of plans did not address several dimensions of his work, but this limitation of view allowed us to focus on central issues while comparing a broad range of buildings.

Graphic abstraction is an important tool for form analysis. It can be used as a special microscope that not only focuses on specific evidence but also subtracts nonessential information that might obscure our view, much like an x-ray. The plan views of buildings that we used throughout this book incorporate abstraction; the patterns of solid and void are emphasized, whereas descrip-tions of details, materials, and color are purposely subtracted from these views. Even more abstract drawings were used to feature more specialized concerns, such as spatial composition. Graphic abstraction can also be applied at a symbolic level to represent nonphysical patterns such as circulation preferences or priorities of needs.

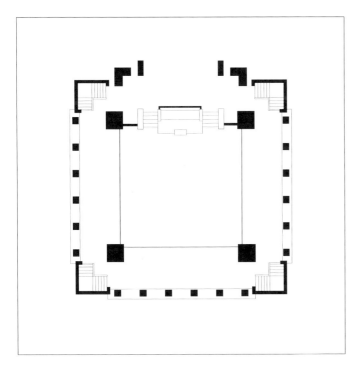

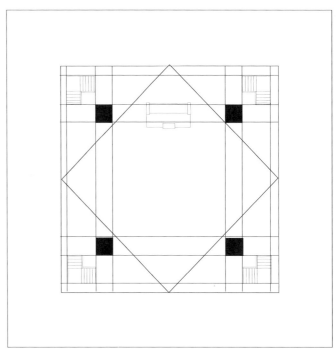

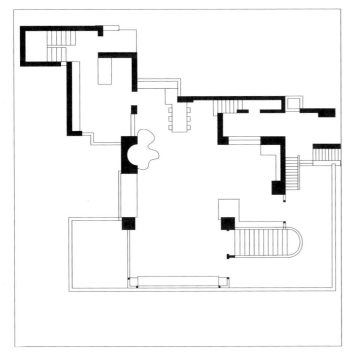

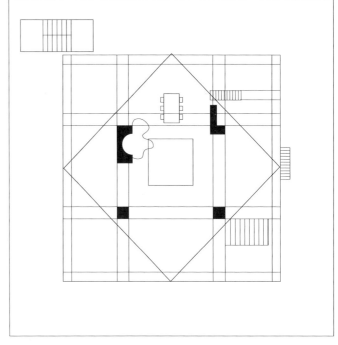

10-5 Comparative plan and analysis of Unity Temple
and Fallingwater showing similar formal order and
focus on the pulpit and dining table

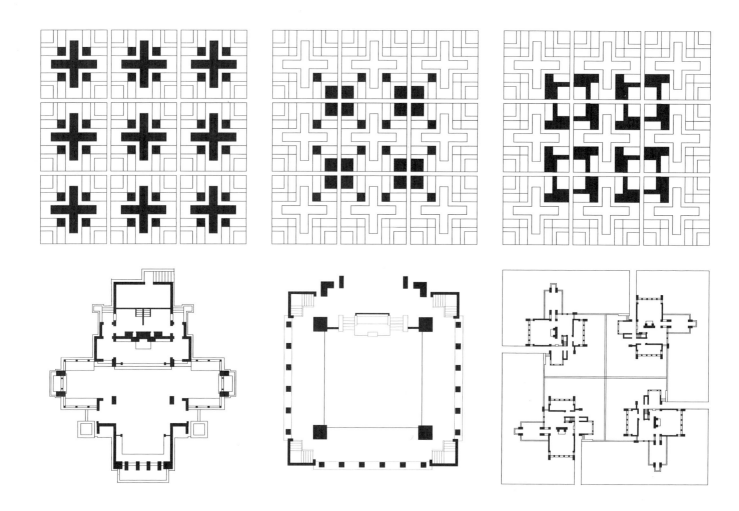

10-6 Interpretations of La Miniatura concrete tile pattern compared
with building plan organizations for the Coonley playhouse,
Unity Temple and Quadruple Block Housing

Any work of architecture is open to
many interpretations; its meaning will
vary somewhat for each person. To
further strain matters, the meaning of a
building will also differ for people in
different historical eras; glass curtain
wall skyscrapers that were once
considered the image of a progressive,
flexible corporate world have become
the symbol of simplistic, impoverished,
and oppressive institutions. In making
our interpretations of Wright's work, we
recognized three criteria: objectivity, that
is, the interpretations had to be reason-
able conclusions that most people could

recognize; candor, that is, our biases
and assumptions should be made as
evident as possible; and relevance, that
is, the interpretations should have
application to contemporary discussions
of architecture.

Although judgment was not a major
focus of our study, it is the component of
critical research that is probably the
least understood. When applied to
design processes, emphasis is placed
on the role of judgment in making
decisions; within research processes the
focus is on the role of judgment as a

path to understanding. An important
part of an articulation of design issues is
embodied in design criteria, which
describe the various relationships to be
sought between architecture and its
value to people. In architectural studies
design criteria are often developed and
refined through the process of making
judgments.

By making comparisons of different
Wright designs, we believe we can point
out relative strengths and weaknesses
and begin to see the work apart from the
architect as part of the body of general

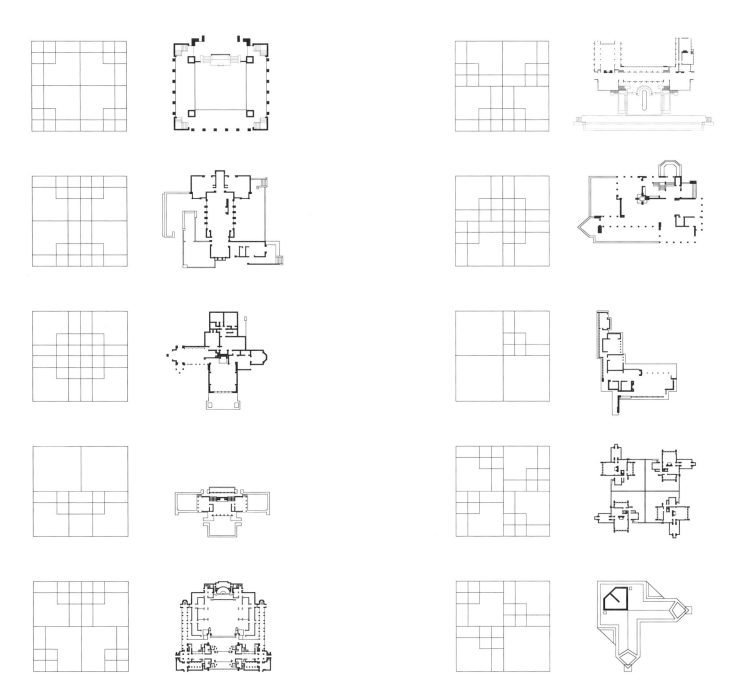

10-7 Diagrams showing permutations of a simple tile pattern arranged in groups of four tiles related to similarly organized building plans:

Unity temple   McCormick house
Storer house   F.L. Wright Studio house
Willitts house   Jacobs house
Hardy house   Quadruple Block Housing
Midway Gardens   Village Service Station

knowledge about design. We can also extend and enrich our repertoire of design criteria, become more sensitive to the formal implications of the design principles that Wright espoused, and recognize Wright's unique contributions to the architecture of this century and the future.

FUTURE IMPLICATIONS

Our experiences in studying the architecture of Frank Lloyd Wright convince us of the utility and potential of typology as a means for analysis of form. Typological studies can help in achieving a grasp of a complex array of forms (such as those produced by Wright), fine-tuning perceptions of formal attributes, and developing a richer vocabulary with which to describe formal concepts. Wright's work provides clear evidence that typology can also be an important tool for design and creativity. He has demonstrated that the adoption of types need not be constraining and can instead focus energy and talent to produce architecture of richness and complexity as well as order and clarity.

In our opinion formal analysis (typological or other) will play an important role in the future development of architectural research and design. Through formal analysis we treat architectural forms as found objects and open our investigations to a range of speculations that lie at the heart of developing theories about architectural design. The development of architectural design theory can play a critical part in meeting the ongoing need for building and sharing a body of knowledge within the profession of architecture. If, finally, the formal analysis of Wright's architecture can promote the cause of architectural knowledge, then we feel it adds an important dimension to his already extraordinary contributions to architecture.

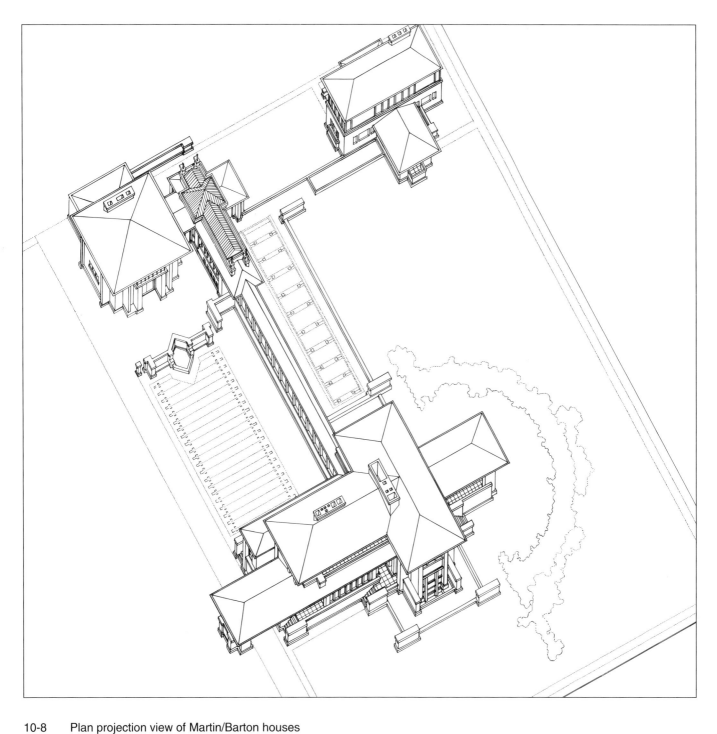

10-8   Plan projection view of Martin/Barton houses

Chronological List of the Designs of Frank Lloyd Wright

The following chronological list of buildings, which includes both constructed and unconstructed designs, is based on several published chronologies including those by: Bruce Brooks Pfeiffer in the *Frank Lloyd Wright Monograph* series; Olgivanna L. Wright in *Frank Lloyd Wright: His Life, His Work, His Words*; and William Allin Storrer in *The Architecture of Frank Lloyd Wright, A Complete Catalog*. Given the continuing disparity in assigned dates for some buildings among authors, this list is offered simply as a general guide for the reader.

Year	Type	Design
1887		Hillside Home School Building for Spring Green, WI (demolished)
1887	Project	Country Residence for Hillside, WI
1887	Project	Unitarian Chapel for Sioux City, IA
1889		House for Wright, F. L. Oak Park, IL
1890		House for Charnley, James Ocean Springs, MS
1890	Project	House for Cooper, Henry N. LaGrange, IL
1890		House for Mac Harg, W. S. Chicago (demolished)
1890		Cottage and Stable for Sullivan, Louis H. Ocean Springs, MS
1891		House for Charnley, James Chicago
1892		House for Blossom, George Chicago
1892	Project	House for Roberts, Charles E. Oak Park, IL
1892		House for Clark, Irving LaGrange, IL
1892		House for Emmond, Robert LaGrange, IL
1892		House for Gale, Thomas Oak Park, IL
1892		House for Harlan, Dr. Allison Chicago (demolished)
1892		House for McArthur, Warren Chicago
1892		House for Parker, Robert Oak Park, IL
1892		House for Sullivan, Albert Chicago (demolished)
1893		Lake Mendota Boathouse for Madison, WI (demolished)
1893	Project	Lake Mendota Boathouse for Madison, WI
1893	Project	Library and Museum Competition for Milwaukee, WI
1893		House for Gale, Walter Oak Park, IL
1893		Cottage for Lamp, Robert Lake Mendota, WI
1893		House and Stables for Winslow, William H. River Forest, IL
1893		House for Wooley, Francis Oak Park, IL
1894	Project	Belknap Apartments for Austin, IL
1894	Project	Monolithic Concrete Bank
1894		House for Bagley, Frederick Hinsdale, IL
1894	Project	House for Goan, Orrin LaGrange, IL
1894		House for Goan, Peter LaGrange, IL
1894	Project	House for McAfee, A. C. Kenilworth, IL
1894		Four Houses for Roloson, Robert Chicago
1895		Edward C. Waller Apartments for Chicago
1895	Project	House for Baldwin, Jesse Oak Park, IL
1895	Project	Office Building for Luxfer Prism Co. Chicago
1895		House for Moore, Nathan G. Oak Park, IL (demolished)
1895		Francis Apartments for Terre Haute Trust Co. Chicago (demolished)
1895		Francisco Terrace Apartments for Waller, Edward C. Chicago (demolished)
1895	Project	Amusement Park for Waller, Edward C. on Wolf Lake near Chicago
1895	Project	Lexington Terrace Apartments for Waller, Edward C. Chicago
1895		House for Williams, Chauncey River Forest, IL
1895		Studio for Wright, F. L. Oak Park, IL
1896	Project	Robert Perkins Apartments for Chicago
1896	Project	House for Devin, Mrs. David Chicago
1896		House for Goodrich, H. C. Oak Park, IL
1896		House for Heller, Isidore Chicago
1896		"Romeo and Juliet" Windmill Tower for Hillside Home School Spring Green, WI
1896	Project	Five Houses for Roberts, Charles Ridgeland, IL
1896	Project	Summer Cottage for Roberts, Charles E.
1897	Project	All Souls Building for All Souls Building Chicago
1897	Project	Factory for Chicago Screw Co. Chicago
1897		House for Furbeck, George Oak Park, IL
1897	Project	Quadruple Block Plan for Roberts, Charles E. Oak Park, IL
1897		Boathouse for Wallis, Henry Lake Delavan, WI (demolished)
1898		River Forest Golf Club for River Forest, IL (demolished)
1898		House for Furbeck, Rollin Oak Park, IL
1898		House for Smith, George W. Oak Park, IL
1898	Project	House for Waller, Edward C. River Forest, IL
1899	Project	House for Eckhart, Robert River Forest, IL
1899		House for Husser, Joseph Chicago (demolished)
1899	Project	Cheltenham Beach Resort for Waller, Edward C. Chicago
1900	Project	Abraham Lincoln Center for Chicago
1900	Project	Residence for Oakland for Oakland, CA
1900	Project	House for Adams, Jesse Longwood, IL
1900		House for Adams, William Chicago
1900		House for Bradley, Harley Kankakee, IL
1900		House for Dana, Susan Lawrence Springfield, IL
1900	Project	Summer Cottage for Foster, Stephen near Chicago, IL
1900		House for Hickox, Warren Kankakee, IL
1900		Boathouse for Jones, Fred B. Lake Delaban, WI (demolished)
1900		Summer Cottage for Pitkin, E. H. Sapper Island Desbarats, Ont., Canada
1900	Project	Summer Cottage for Wallis, Henry Lake Delavan, WI
1901	Project	Village Bank in Cast Concrete
1901		House for Davenport, Arthur River Forest, IL
1901		House for Fricke, William Oak Park, IL
1901		House for Henderson, E. B. Elmhurst, IL
1901		House for Jones, Fred B. Lake Delavan, WI
1901	Project	Studio-residence for Lowell, M. H. Matteawan, NY
1901	Project	House for Metzger, Victor Desbarats, Ontario, Canada
1901		House for Thomas, Frank Oak Park, IL
1901		Exhibition Pavilion for Universal Portland Cement Co. Buffalo, NY (demolished)
1901	Project	Lexington Terrace Apartments for Waller, Edward C. Chicago
1901		House for Willitts, Ward W. Highland Park, IL
1902		Double House for Gerts, George E. Whitehall, MI
1902		House for Gerts, Walter Whitehall, MI
1902		House for Heurtley Oak Park, IL
1902		Building #2 for Misses Lloyd Jones for Hillside Home School Spring Green, WI
1902	Project	Yacht Club for Lake Delavan Lake Delavan, WI
1902		Home (scheme #2) for Little Peoria, IL
1902	Project	House for Metzger Ont., Canada
1902	Project	House for Oak Park, IL for Mosher Oak Park, IL
1902		House for Ross Lake Delavan, WI
1902		House for Spencer Lake Delavan, WI
1902	Project	House (scheme #1) for Waller Charlevoix, MI
1902	Project	Boat Club for Yahara Boat Club Madison, WI
1903		House for Barton Buffalo
1903	Project	Chicago & Northwestern Railway Stations for Suburban Chicago
1903		House for Freeman Hinsdale, IL
1903	Project	House (scheme #1) for Lamp Madison, WI
1903		Administration Building for Larkin Co. Buffalo
1903		House for Martin Oak Park, IL
1903	Project	Quadruple Block Plan (houses) for Roberts Oak Park, IL
1903	Project	House (scheme #2) for Waller Charlevoix, MI
1903		House for Wasler Chicago
1903	Project	Studio-house for Wright, F.L. Oak Park, IL
1904	Project	House (scheme #1) for Baldwin Kenilworth, IL
1904		House for Cheney Oak Park, IL
1904	Project	House for Clarke Peoria
1904		House for Gale Oak Park, IL
1904		House (scheme #2) for Lamp Madison, WI
1904	Project	Workmen's Rowhouses for Larkin Co. Buffalo
1904		House, conservatory for Martin Buffalo
1904	Project	Residence Highland Park, IL
1904	Project	House for Scudder Desbarats, Ont., Canada
1904	Project	Bank Building (scheme #1) for Smith, Frank L. Dwight, IL
1904	Project	House for Ullman Oak Park, IL
1905		House for Adams Highland Park, IL
1905		House (scheme #2) for Baldwin Kenilworth, IL
1905	Project	House for Barnes McCook, NB
1905		House for Brown Evanston, IL
1905		House for Darwin D. Martin for E-Z Polish Factory Chicago
1905		House for Gilpin Oak Park, IL
1905		House for Glasner Glencoe, IL

1905		House for Hardy Racine, IL
1905		House for Heath Buffalo
1905		House for Johnson Lake Delavan, WI
1905	Project	Concrete Apartment Building for McArthur Chicago
1905	Project	Pergola and Pavilion for Moore Oak Park, IL
1905		Bank Building (scheme #2) for Smith Dwight, IL
1905		Church for Unity Temple Oak Park, IL
1906		House for Beachy Oak Park, IL
1906	Project	Studio House for Bock Maywood, IL
1906		House for De Rhodes South Bend, IN
1906	Project	House for Devin Eliot, ME
1906		House for Fuller Glencoe, IL
1906	Project	House for Gerts Glencoe, IL
1906		House for Gridley Batavia, IL
1906		House for Hoyt Geneva, IL
1906	Project	House for Ludington Dwight, IL
1906		House for Millard Highland Park, IL
1906		House for Nicholas Flossmoor, IL
1906		Church for Pettit Mortuary Chapel Belvedere, IL
1906		River Forest Tennis Club for River Forest, IL
1906	Project	House for Shaw Montreal, Que., Canada
1906	Project	House for Stone Glencoe, IL
1907		Larkin Company Exhibition Pavilion for Jamestown, VA (demolished)
1907	Project	Municipal Art Gallery for Booth, Sherman Chicago
1907		House for Coonley, Avery Riverside, IL
1907		Real Estate Office for Cummings River Forest, IL
1907		House for Hunt, Stephen La Grange, IL
1907	Project	House for McCormick, Harold Lake Forest, IL
1907		"Tan-y-deri" House for Porter, Andrew Spring Green, WI
1907		House for Tomek, E. E. Riverside, IL
1907		House for Westcott, Barton Springfield, OH
1908		Browne's Bookstore for Chicago (demolished)
1908		Como Orchards Summer Colony for Darby, MT
1908	Project	Horseshoe Inn for Ashton, Willard Estes Park, CO
1908	Project	House (scheme #1) for Baker, Frank Wilmette, IL
1908		House for Boynton, E. E. Rochester, NY
1908		House for Davidson, Walter Buffalo, NY
1908		House for Evans, Robert Chicago
1908		House for Gilmore, Eugene Madison, WI
1908	Project	House for Guthrie, William Sewanee, TN
1908		House for Horner, L. K. Chicago (demolished)
1908		House for May, Meyer Grand Rapids, MI
1908	Project	House for Melson, J. G. Mason City, IA
1908		House for Roberts, Isabel River Forest, IL
1908		House for Stockman, Dr. G. C. Mason City, IA
1909		City National Bank and Hotel for Mason City, IA
1909		Bitter Root Inn for near Darby, MT (demolished)
1909	Project	City Dwelling with Glass Front
1909		Stohr Arcade and Shops for Arcade Building Chicago (demolished)
1909		House (scheme #2) for Baker, Frank Wilmette, IL
1909		Thurber's Art Gallery for Fine Arts Building Chicago (demolished)
1909		House for Gale, Mrs. Thomas Oak Park, IL
1909	Project	For Sherman Booth for Glencoe Town Hall Glencoe, IL
1909		House for Ingalls, Kibben River Forest, IL
1909	Project	House for Larwill, Mrs. Muskegon, MI
1909	Project	Bitter Root Town for Master Plan near Darby, MT
1909	Project	House for Roberts, Mary River Forest, IL
1909		House for Steffens, Oscar Chicago (demolished)
1909		House for Stewart, George Montecito, CA
1909	Project	Lexington Terrace Apartments (scheme #2) for Waller, Edward Chicago
1909	Project	Bathing Pavilion for Waller, Edward C. Charlevoix, MI
1909	Project	Small Rental Houses (3) for Waller, Edward C. River Forest, IL
1910		House for Amberg, J. H. Grand Rapids, MI
1910		Blythe-Markeley Law Office for City National Bank Bldg. Mason City, IA
1910		Universal Portland Cement Co. for Exhibition Pavilion - Madison Square Gardens New York (demolished)
1910		House for Irving, E. P. Decatur, IL
1910	Project	House-Studio for Wright, Frank Lloyd Viale Verdi, Fiesole, Italy
1910		House for Ziegler, Rev. J. R. Frankfort, KY
1911		Lake Geneva Inn for Lake Geneva, WI (demolished)
1911	Project	Christian Catholic Church for Zion, IL
1911		Taliesin Hydro House for Spring Green, WI (demolished)
1911	Project	Suburban House
1911	Project	House (scheme #1) for Adams Oak Park, IL
1911		House for Angster, Herbert Lake Bluff, IL (demolished)
1911		House for Balch, O. B. Oak Park, IL
1911		Banff Park Pavilion for Banff National Park Banff, Alb., Canada (demolished)
1911		House (scheme #1) for Booth, Sherman Glencoe, IL
1911	Project	Glencoe Park Features for Booth, Sherman Glencoe, IL
1911	Project	Waiting Station - North Shore Electric for Booth, Sherman (scheme #1) Glencoe, IL
1911	Project	Kindergarten for Coonley, Avery Riverside, IL
1911	Project	House for Cutten, Arthur Downer's Grove, IL
1911	Project	House for Esbenshade, E. Milwaukee, WI
1911	Project	American System-Built Houses for First Studies
1911	Project	Summer House (scheme #1) for Porter, Andrew Hillside, Spring Green, WI
1911	Project	House for Schroeder, Edward Milwaukee, WI
1911	Project	Summer Cottage for Wright, Anna Lloyd Spring Green, WI
1911	Project	House - Studio for Wright, F.L. Chicago, IL
1911		"Taliesin" 1 for Wright, Frank Lloyd Spring Green, WI
1912	Project	Kehl Dance Academy for Madison, WI
1912	Project	Press Building for San Francisco, CA
1912	Project	Florida Cottage for Palm Beach, FL
1912	Project	Schoolhouse for LaGrange for LaGrange, IL
1912	Project	Taliesin Cottages for Spring Green, WI
1912	Project	Urban House (ARCS) for Milwaukee, WI
1912	Project	House (scheme #1) for Adams, Harry S. Oak Park, IL
1912		House for Greene, William Aurora, IL
1912		"Northome" House for Little, Francis Wayzana, MN (demolished)
1912	Project	House for Mendelson, Jerome Albany, NY
1913		Midway Gardens for Chicago, IL (demolished)
1913	Project	Double Residence for Ottawa, Canada
1913	Project	Post Office for Ottawa, Canada
1913		House (scheme #2) for Adams, Harry S. Oak Park, IL
1913	Project	Carnegie Library for Carnegie Library Pembroke, Ont., Canada
1913	Project	House for Hilly, M. B. Brookfield, IL
1913	Project	House for Kellog, J. W. Milwaukee, WI
1913	Project	Chinese Restaurant for Richards, Arthur Milwaukee, WI
1913	Project	Office Building and Shops for Richards, Arthur Milwaukee, WI
1914	Project	Farmers and Merchants Bank for Spring Green, WI
1914	Project	United States Embassy for Tokyo, Japan
1914	Project	Vogelsang Dinner Gardens and Hotel for Chicago
1914	Project	State Bank of Spring Green for Spring Green, WI
1914	Project	S. Mori Japanese Print Shop for Fine Arts Building Chicago
1914	Project	Three Houses for Jaxon, Honore
1914	Project	Study for Garden Project for Restaurant and Concert Gardens Chicago
1914	Project	Spring Green Fairgrounds for Women's Building Spring Green, WI
1914		House "Taliesin II" for Wright, F.L. Spring Green, WI (demolished)
1915	Project	Christian Catholic Church for Zion, IL
1915		Imperial Hotel for Tokyo, Japan (demolished)
1915	Project	Lake Shore Residence
1915	Project	Model Quarter Section for Chicago, IL
1915		Ravine Bluffs Bridge for Glencoe, IL
1915		House for Bach, Emil Chicago
1915	Project	Preliminary studies for Theatre Project for Barnsdall, Aline Olive Hill, Los Angeles, CA
1915		Ravin Bluffs Housing for Booth, Sherman Glencoe, IL
1915		House for Brigham, Ed Glencoe, IL
1915		Warehouse for German, A. D. Richland Center, WI
1915	Project	American System - Built Houses for Richards Company Milwaukee, WI
1915	Project	Chinese Hospital for Rockefeller Foundation
1915	Project	House for Wood, M. W. Decatur, IL
1916		Imperial Hotel Annex for Tokyo, Japan (demolished)
1916		House for Allen, Henry Wichita, KS
1916		House for Bagley, Joseph Grand Beach, MI
1916	Project	House for Behn (Voight) Grand Beach, MI
1916		House for Bogk, Frederick Milwaukee, WI
1916		House for Carr, W. S. Grand Beach, MI
1916	Project	Cottage for Converse, Clarence Palisades Park, MI
1916		Duplex Apartments for Munkwitz, Arthur Milwaukee, WI (demolished)
1916		Duplex Apartments for Richards, Arthur Milwaukee, WI
1916		Small House for The Richards Company Milwaukee, WI
1916		House for Vosburgh, Ernest Grand Beach, MI
1917		American Homes (ARCS) for Milwaukee, WI

1939	Project	Usonian House for Kaufmann, Edgar Pittsburgh, PA
1939		House for Lewis, Lloyd Libertyville, IL
1939	Project	House for Lowenstein, Gordon Mason, OH
1939	Project	House for Mauer, Edgar Los Angeles
1939	Project	House for Newman, Sidney Lansing, MI
1939	Project	House for Panshin, Alexis Lansing, MI
1939		House for Pauson, Rose / Gertrude Phoenix, AZ (demolished)
1939		House for Pope, Loren Falls Church, VA
1939	Project	House for Rentz, Frank Madison, WI
1939		House for Rosenbaum, Stanley Florence, AL
1939		House for Schwartz, Bernard Two Rivers, WI
1939	Project	House for Smith, E. A. Piedmont Pines, CA
1939		House for Sondern, Clarence Kansas City, MO
1939	Project	House for Spivey, Dr. Ludd Fort Lauderdale, FL
1939		"Auldbrass" House and Adjuncts for Stevens, Leigh Yemassee, SC
1939		House for Sturges, George Brentwood Heights, Los Angeles, CA
1939	Project	House for Van Dusen, C. R. Lansing, MI
1940		Community Church for Kansas City, MO
1940	Project	Museum of Modern Art - Model House for New York
1940		House (scheme #1) for Affleck, Gregor Bloomfield Hills, MI
1940		House for Baird, Theodore Amherst, MA
1940		House for Christie, James Bernardsville, NJ
1940		Seminar Buildings for Florida Southern College Lakeland, FL
1940	Project	House for Nesbitt, John Carmel Bay, CA
1940	Project	"Eaglefeather" house for Oboler, Arch Malibu, CA
1940	Project	House for Pence, Martin Hilo, HI
1940	Project	Studio for Watkins, Franklin Barnegat City, NJ
1941	Project	Sigma Chi Fraternity House for Hanover, IN
1941	Project	"Oak Shelter" Cottage for Barton, John Pine Bluff, WI
1941	Project	Music Studio for Dayer, Walter Detroit
1941	Project	House for Ellinwood, Alfred Deerfield, IL
1941	Project	House for Field, Parker Peru, IL
1941		Roux Library for Florida Southern College Lakeland, FL
1941	Project	House for Guenther, William East Caldwell, NJ
1941	Project	House for Petersen, Roy West Racine, WI
1941		House for Richardson, Stuart Glenridge, NJ
1941	Project	House for Schevill, Margaret Tuscon, AZ
1941	Project	House for Sundt, Vigo Madison, WI
1941		"Snowflake" house for Wall, Carlton Detroit, MI
1941	Project	Studio-House for Waterstreet, Mary Spring Green, WI
1942	Project	Cloverleaf Quadruple Housing sun top type for Pittsfield, MA
1942	Project	Pittsfield Defense Plant for Pittsfield, MA
1942	Project	"Pottery House" for Burlingham, Lloyd El Paso, TX
1942	Project	Cooperative Homesteads Berm-type for Detroit Auto Workers Detroit
1942	Project	House for Foreman, Clark Washington, DC
1942	Project	Boathouse and Pergola for Schwartz, Bernard Two Rivers, WI
1943		Solomon R. Guggenheim Museum for New York
1943	Project	House for Hein, M. N. Chippewa Falls, WI
1943	Project	House (scheme #2) Hein Type for Jacobs, Herbert Middleton, WI
1944		"Solar Hemicycle" House for Jacobs, Herbert Middleton, WI
1944	Project	"Pergola House" for Loeb, Gerald Redding, CT
1944		Johnson, S. C. & Son, Co. for Research Tower Racine, WI
1944	Project	"Glass House" Opus 497 for The Ladies Home Journal
1945	Project	Adelman Laundry for Adelman, Benjamin Milwaukee, WI
1945	Project	Daphne Funeral Chapels for Daphne, Nicholas San Francisco
1945	Project	Desert Spa for Elizabeth Arden Phoenix, AZ
1945		Administration Building for Florida Southern College Lakeland, FL
1945		House for Friedman, Arnold Pecos, NM
1945	Project	"The Wave" house for Haldorn, Stuart Carmel, CA
1945	Project	House (scheme #1) for Morris, V. C. San Francisco
1945	Project	Boathouse and Summer Cottage for Stamm, John Lake Delavan, WI
1945		House for Walter, Lowell Cedar Rock, Quasqueton, IA
1946	Project	Sarabhi Calico Mills Store for Amedabad, India
1946	Project	House for Adelman, Albert Fox Point, WI
1946		House for Alpaugh, Amy Northport, MI
1946	Project	House for Feenberg, Ben Fox Point, IA
1946		House for Grant, Douglas Cedar Rapids, IA
1946		House for Griggs, Chauncey Tacoma, WA
1946	Project	Rogers Lacy Hotel for Lacy, Rogers Dallas, TX
1946		House for Miller, Dr. Alvin Charles City, IA
1946		House for Mossberg, Herman South Bend, IN
1946	Project	House for Pinkerton, William Fairfax County, VA
1946	Project	House for Rand, Ayn Hollywood, CA
1946		House for Smith, Melvyn Maxwell Bloomfield Hills, MI
1947		Parkwyn Village Dwellings: Master Plan for Kalamazoo, MI
1947		House for Alsop, Carroll Pskaloosa, IA
1947	Project	House for Bell E. St. Louis, IL
1947	Project	House for Black Rochester, MN
1947	Project	House for Boomer Phoenix, AZ
1947		House for Bulbullian Rochester, MN
1947	Project	Butterfly Bridge for Wisconsin River for Spring Green, WI
1947	Project	Deport for San Antonio Transit Co. San Antonio, TX
1947		Meeting house for First Unitarian Society Madison, WI
1947		Galesburg Village Dwellings: Master Plan for Kalamazoo, MI
1947	Project	House for Grieco Andover, MA
1947	Project	House for Hamilton Brookline, VT
1947	Project	House for Hartford Hollywood, CA
1947	Project	House for Houston Schuyler County, IL
1947	Project	Cottage Group Resort Hotel for Huntington Hartford Hollywood, CA
1947	Project	House for Keith Oakland County, MI
1947		House (two schemes, second built) for Keys Rochester, MN
1947		House for Lamberson Oskaloosa, IA
1947	Project	House for Marting Northampton, OH
1947	Project	House for Palmer Phoenix, AZ
1947	Project	House for Pike Los Angeles
1947	Project	Community and Civic Center for Pittsburgh Point Park Pittsburgh, PA
1947	Project	Sports Club for Huntington Hartford Hollywood, CA
1947		Usonia Homes: Master Plan for Pleasantville, NY
1947		Valley National Bank for Tucson, AZ
1947	Project	Auto Display Room and Workshop for Wetmore Detroit
1947	Project	House for Wheeler Hinsdale, IL
1947	Project	House for Wilkie Hennepin County, MN
1948		House for Alsop Oskaloosa, IA
1948		House for Anthony Benton Harbor, MI
1948	Project	Cottage for Barney, Maginel Wright Spring Green, WI
1948	Project	House for Bergman St. Petersburg, FL
1948	Project	Penthouse for Bimson Phoenix, AZ
1948		House for Buehler Orinda, CA
1948	Project	Crater Resort for Meteor Crater, AZ
1948	Project	House for Daphne San Francisco
1948	Project	House for Ellison Bridgewater Township, NJ
1948		House, Galesburg Village for Eppstein Kalamazoo, MI
1948	Project	House for Freenberg Fox Point, WI
1948		House, Parkwyn Village for Greiner Kalamazoo, MI
1948	Project	House for Hageman Peoria, IL
1948		House, Parkwyn Village for Levin Kalamazoo, MI
1948	Project	House for Margolis Kalamazoo, MI
1948	Project	House for McCord N. Arlington, NJ
1948	Project	House for Miller, Sidney Pleasantville, NY
1948		Shop for Morris, V. C. San Francisco
1948	Project	House for Muehlberger E. Lansing, MI
1948	Project	Community and Civic Center (scheme #2) for Pittsburgh Point Park Pittsburgh, PA
1948		House, Galesburg Village for Pratt Kalamazoo, MI
1948	Project	House for Prout Columbus, IN
1948	Project	House for Scully Woodbridge, CT
1948	Project	Hosue for Smith, Talbot Ann Arbor, MI
1948	Project	Valley National Bank and Shopping Center for Sunnyslope, AZ
1948		House for Weltziemer Oberlin, OH
1949	Project	San Francisco Bridge for San Francisco
1949		Usonian Automatics
1949		House for Edwards, James Okemos, MI
1949	Project	Arts, Crafts and Children's Building for Florida Southern College Lakeland, FL
1949		"Fountainhead" House for Hughes, Willis Jackson, MS
1949	Project	House for John, Harry Oconomowoc, WI
1949	Project	Self-Service Garage for Kaufmann, Edgar Pittsburgh, PA
1949	Project	Shops for Kiva, Lloyd Scottsdale, AZ
1949		House for Laurent, Kenneth Rockford, IL
1949		House, Parkwyn Village for McCartney, Ward Kalamazoo, MI
1949	Project	YWCA for Racine Racine, WI
1949		House Usonia II for Serlin, Edward Pleasantville, NY
1949		House for Walker, Mrs. Clinton Carmel, CA
1949	Project	"Crownfield" House for Windfohr, Robert Fort Worth, TX
1950	Project	"How to Live in the Southwest"
1950		House for Berger, Robert San Anselmo, CA

1950	Project	Southwestern Christian Seminary for Canary, Dr. Peyton Glendale, AZ
1950		House for Carlson, Raymond Phoenix, AZ
1950		House for Carr, John Glenview, IL
1950	Project	House (scheme #1) for Chahroudi, A. K. Lake Mahopac, NY
1950	Project	House for Conklin, Tom New Ulm, MN
1950		House for Gillin, John Dallas, TX
1950-	Project	House for Hanson, Richard Corvalis, OR
1950		House for Harper, Dr. Ina St. Joseph, MI
1950	Project	House for Jacobsen, George Montreal, Que., Canada
1950		House for Muirhead, Robert Plato Center, IL
1950		House for Palmer, William Ann Arbor, MI
1950		House for Schaberg, Don Okemos, MI
1950		House, Parkwyn Village for Winn, Robert Kalamazoo, MI
1950		House for Wright, David Phoenix, AZ
1950		House for Zimmerman, Isadore Manchester, NH
1951	Project	"House for GI Couple with Infant"
1951	Project	Gifford Concrete Block Plant for Middleton, WI
1951		House for Adelman, Benjamin Phoenix, AZ
1951		House for Austin, Gabrielle Greenville, SC
1951		Summer Cottage (scheme #2) for Chahroudi, A. K. Lake Mahopac, NY
1951		House for Glore, Charles Lake Forest, IL
1951	Project	"Boulder House" for Kaufmann, Edgar Palm Spring, CA
1951		House for Kinney, Patrick Lancaster, WI
1951		House for Kraus, Russell Kirkwood, MO
1951		House, Usonia II for Reisley, Roland Pleasantville, NY
1952		Anderton Court Shops for Beverly Hills, CA
1952	Project	Zeta Beta Tau Fraternity House for Gainesville, OK
1952	Project	Paradise on Wheels Mobile Home Park for Ackerman, Lee Phoenix, AZ
1952	Project	House for Bailleres, Raul Acapulco, Mexico
1952		House for Blair, Quentin Cody, WY
1952		House for Brandes, Ray Issaquah, WA
1952	Project	House for Clifton, William Oakland, NJ
1952	Project	Point View Residences Apt. Tower (scheme #1) for Kaufmann, Edgar Charitable Trust Pittsburgh, PA
1952		House (scheme #1) for Penfield, Louis Willoughby Hills, OH
1952		House for Pieper, Arthur Paradise Valley, AZ
1952		House for Teater, Archie Bliss, ID
1952		Price Tower for the H. C. Price Co. Bartlesville, OK
1952	Project	Floating Gardens Resort for the U. S. Plywood Co. Leesburg, FL
1953	Project	Masieri Memorial Students Dwelling and Library for Venice, Italy
1953		Exhibition House for New York
1953		Riverview Terrace Restaurant for Spring Green, WI
1953	Project	Hillside Godown for Spring Green, WI
1953	Project	House for Bewer, Joseph E. Fishkill, NY
1953		Cottage for Boomer, Jorgine Phoenix, AZ
1953	Project	House for Cooke, Andrew Virginia Beach, VA
1953		"Sixty Years of Living Architecture" for Exhibition Pavilion New York
1953		"Sixty Years of Living Architecture" for Exhibition Pavilion Los Angeles
1953		House (scheme #2) for Goddard, Lewis Plymouth, MI
1953	Project	Point View Residences Apartment Tower (scheme #2) for Kaufmann Charitable Trust Pittsburgh, PA
1953	Project	Rhododendron Chapel for Kaufmann family Bear Run, PA
1953		House for Price, Harold Bartlesville, OK
1953	Project	FM Radio Station for Proxmire, William Jefferson County, WI
1953		House for Thaxton, William Houston, TX
1953		House (scheme #2) for Wright, Robert Llewellyn Bethesda, MD
1954	Project	Yosemite National Park Restaurant for Yosemite National Park, CA
1954		Beth Sholom Synagogue for Elkins Park, PA
1954	Project	Barnsdall Park Municipal Gallery for Olive Hill, Los Angeles, CA
1954	Project	Christian Science Reading Room for Riverside, IL
1954	Project	Tipshus Medical Clinic for Stockton, CA
1954	Project	Monona Terrace Civic Center (scheme #2) for Madison, WI
1954	Project	House for Adelman, Benjamin Whitefish Bay, WI
1954		House for Bachman and Wilson Millstone, NJ
1954		House for Frederick, Louis Barrington, IL
1954		House for Greenberg, Dr. Maurice Dousman, WI
1954	Project	House for Hoffman, G. M. Winnetka, IL
1954	Project	House for Hoffman, Max Rye, NY
1954		Jaguar Showroom for Hoffman, Max New York
1954	Project	"Continuation" for Oboler, Arch Malibu, CA
1954		"Grandma House" for Price, Harold C. Paradise Valley, AZ
1954	Project	House for Schwenn, Roger Verona, WI
1954	Project	House for Smith, J. L. Kane County, IL
1954		House for Tonkens, Gerald Cincinnati, OH
1954		House for Tracy, W. B. Normandy Park, WA
1955	Project	Lenkurt Electric Co. (scheme #1) for San Mateo, CA
1955	Project	Freund y Cia Department Store for San Salvador, El Salvador
1955		Kundert Medical Clinic for San Luis Obispo, CA
1955		Dallas Theater Center for Baker, Paul Dallas, TX
1955	Project	House for Barton, A. D. Downer's Grove, IL
1955	Project	House for Blumberg, Mel Des Moines, IA
1955	Project	House for Coats, Robert Hillsborough, CA
1955	Project	House (scheme #2) for Cornwell, Gibbons West Goshen, PA
1955	Project	House for Hartman, Stanley Lansing, MI
1955	Project	House for Herberger, Robert Maricopa County, AZ
1955		House for Hoffman, Max Rye, NY
1955		House for Kalil Manchester, NH
1955		House for Lovness, Don Stillwater, MN
1955	Project	House for Miller, Oscar Milford, MI
1955	Project	"Seacliff" house (scheme #2) for Morris, V. C. San Francisco
1955	Project	Guest house for Morris, V. C. San Francisco
1955		House for Pappas, T. A. St. Louis County, MO
1955	Project	House for Roberts, Jay Seattle, WA
1955		House (scheme #2) for Sunday, Robert Marshalltown, IA
1955	Project	House for Sussman, Gerald Rye, NY
1955	Project	House for Trowbridge, Chester Oak Park, IL
1955		House for Turkel, Dr. Dorothy Detroit
1955	Project	"Neuroseum" hospital for Wisconsin Neurological Foundation Madison, WI
1956	Project	Christian Science Church for Bolinas, CA
1956		Annunciation Greek Orthodox Church for Milwaukee, WI
1956	Project	Bramlett Motor Hotel for Memphis, TN
1956	Project	"Mile High" ("The Illinois") Office Building for Chicago
1956	Project	The New Sports Pavilion for Belmont Park, NY
1956	Project	Lenkurt Electric Company for San Mateo, CA
1956		Lindholm Service Station for Cloquet, MN
1956	Project	Post Office for Spring Green, WI
1956		Wyoming Valley Shool for Wyoming Valley near Spring Green, WI
1956		House (scheme #2) for Boswell, William Cincinnati, OH
1956		House for Bott, Frank Kansas City, MO
1956	Project	Motel for Weilands, Daniel Hagerstown, MD
1956	Project	"Alladin" House for Gillin, John Hollywood, CA
1956	Project	"Golden Beacon" Apartment Tower for Glore, Charles Chicago
1956	Project	Gate Lodge and Usonian Automatic Housing for Kaufmann, Edgar Jr. Bear Run, PA
1956		Clinic for Meyers, Dr. Kenneth Dayton, OH
1956	Project	House for Moreland, Robert Austin, TX
1956	Project	"Quietwater" Beach Cottage for Morris, Lillian Stinson Beach, CA
1956	Project	House for Sottil, Helen Cuernavaca, Mexico
1956	Project	House (scheme #2) for Straeke, Victor Appleton, WI
1956	Project	Fiberthin Village for the U. S. Rubber Co. Mishawaka, IN
1956	Project	House (scheme #1) for Wright, Duey Wausau, WI
1957		Marin County Civic Center for San Raphael, CA
1957	Project	Plan for Greater Baghdad for Baghdad, Iraq
1957	Project	Unity Temple for Taliesin Valley, Spring Green, WI
1957	Project	House for Amery Teheran, Iran
1957	Project	"Oasis", Papago Park for Arizona State Capitol Phoenix, AZ
1957	Project	Wedding Chapel for Claremont Hotel Berkeley, CA
1957	Project	Motel for Erdman and Associates Madison, WI
1957		Pre-fab for Erdman and Associates Madison, WI
1957		Clinic for Fasbender, Dr. Herman Hastings, MN
1957	Project	Housing for Negro Families for Fisher, Jesse Whiteville, NC
1957		House for Gordon, C. E. Aurora, OR
1957	Project	House for Hoyer, Carl Maricopa County, AZ
1957	Project	House for Miller, Arthur Roxbury, CT
1957	Project	House (scheme #2) for Mills, Bradford Princeton, NJ
1957		Rayward Playhouse for Rayward, Victoria New Canaan, CT
1957	Project	House for Stillman, Calvin Cornwall-on-Hudson, NY
1957	Project	Loan Office for Tonkens, Gerald Cincinnati, OH
1957		House (scheme #2) for Wright, Duey Wausau, WI
1957	Project	Motel for Zeckendorf New York
1958		Lockridge Medical Clinic for Whitefish, MT
1958		Pilgrim Congregational Church for Redding, CA

1958	Project	Living City
1958	Project	House (scheme #2) for Hennesy Smoke Rise, NJ
1958	Project	Three Cottages for Lovness, Don Stillwater, MN
1958		Cottage for Petersen, Seth Lake Delton, WI
1958		Cottage for Petersen, Seth Stillwater, MN
1958		House for Stromquist, Don Bountiful, UT
1958	Project	Universal Theater for Todd Los Angeles
1958	Project	Jones Chapel ("Trinity Chapel") for University of Oklahoma Norman, OK
1958	Project	Jevenile Cultural Study Center for University of Wichita Wichita, KS
1959	Project	Holy Trinity Greek Orthodox Church for San Francisco, CA
1959	Project	Key Project, Hotels, Apts., Shops and Civic Center for Ellis Island, NY
1959	Project	Fine Arts Center for Arizona State University Tempe, AZ
1959		Lady Gammage Memorial Auditorium for Arizona State University Tempe, AZ
1959	Project	House for Donahoe, Helen Paradise Valley, AZ
1959	Project	Airplane Hangar for Hanley, Pat Benton Harbor, MI
1959		House for Lykes, Norman Phoenix, AZ
1959	Project	House for Mann, John Putnam County, NY
1959	Project	House for Wieland, Gilbert Hagerstown, MD

Illustration Credits

The majority of the illustrations in this book were developed as original drawings on a Macintosh computer using Canvas software. We wish to give credit to a number of sources of reference in constructing these drawings which are included in our bibliography. Among these we particularly appreciate two important resources, the *Frank Lloyd Wright Monograph* series edited by Bruce Brooks Pfeiffer and *In the Nature of Materials* by Henry-Russell Hitchcock. Specific credit should be given to the following sources:

Page 6   1-5   Based on original drawings by D'Arcy Thompson in *On Growth and Form*, ed. J.T. Bonner. Cambridge, Eng.: Cambridge University Press, 1952

Page 6   1-6   Based on original drawings by D'Arcy Thompson in *On Growth and Form*, ed. J.T. Bonner. Cambridge, Eng.: Cambridge University Press, 1952

Page 7   1-8   Based on original drawing by Stephen Tannenbaum

Page 9   1-12   Based on illustrations from Ellis, C. Hamilton in *The Lore of the Train*. New York: Crescent Books, 1987, pp. 80, 91.

Page 16   2-3   Based on original drawing by Grant Manson in *Frank Lloyd Wright to 1910, The First Golden Age.* New York: Van Nostrand Reinhold Company

Page 18   2-7   Based on original rendering by Charles Calvo in "The Concrete Block Designs of Frank LLoyd Wright". *Forum voor architectuur en daarmee verbonden kunsten* 30(4)

Page 20   2-9   Based on illustrations by Thomas Beeby in "*The Grammar of Ornament/ Ornament as Grammar.*" Via III: Ornament. Philadelphia: University of Pennsylvania Graduate School of Fine Arts, 1977, p. 21.

Page 61   4-15   Original drawing by Mike Bartlein

4-16   Original drawing by Mike Bartlein

4-17   Original drawing by Mike Bartlein after Dan Rotner

4-18   Original drawing by Mike Bartlein, based on measured drawings prepared by Ernest Marjoram courtesy of Archiplan Architects, Los Angeles

Page 67   4-24   Original drawing by Mike Bartlein after Massimo Del Medico

4-25   Original drawing by Mike Bartlein after Massimo Del Medico

4-26   Original drawing by Mike Bartlein after Massimo Del Medico

4-27   Original drawing by Mike Bartlein

Pages 72   4-33   Based on original drawings by Massimo Del Medico

Page 78   4-36   Original drawing by Mike Bartlein

Page 79   4-37   Original drawing by Mike Bartlein

4-38   Based on original drawing by Hideaki Haraguchi in *A Comparative Analysis of 20th Century Houses.* New York: Rizzoli

Page 92   5-3   Based on illustration Tetsuro Yoshida in *The Japanese House and Garden,* New York: Praeger Publishers, 1969, p. 84

5-4   Based on illustration from A. G. McKay in Houses, *Villas and Palaces in the Roman World.* Ithaca, New York: Cornell University

5-5   Based on illustration by Tetsuro Yoshida in *The Japanese House and Garden,* New York: Praeger Publishers, 1969, p. 84

Page 93   5-6   Based on original drawing by Steven Price and Dan Mihalyo

Page 103   5-25   Based on original drawing by Chris Reinhart and Leigh Ishida

Page 110   5-29   Based on original drawing by Lionel March and Phillip Steadman in *The geometry of environment.* London: RIBA Publications Ltd.

Page 113   5-32   Based on original drawing by Stephen Tannenbaum

Page 125   6-9   Original drawing by Mike Bartlein

6-10   Original drawing by Mike Bartlein

6-11   Original drawing by Mike Bartlein

6-12   Original drawing by Mike Bartlein

Page 140   7-6   Based on original drawing from F.L. Wright studio reproduced in *Frank Lloyd Wright Drawings* by Bruce Brooks Pfeiffer. New York: Harry N. Abrams, Inc.

Page 141   7-8   Based on original drawing from F.L. Wright studio reproduced in *Frank Lloyd Wright Drawings* by Bruce Brooks Pfeiffer. New York: Harry N. Abrams, Inc.

Page 141   7-10   Based on original drawing from F.L. Wright studio reproduced in *Frank Lloyd Wright Drawings* by Bruce Brooks Pfeiffer. New York: Harry N. Abrams, Inc.

Page 148   7-18   Based on original drawing by Lionel March and Phillip Steadman in *The geometry of environment.* London: RIBA Publications Ltd.

Page 149   7-21   Based on original drawing from F.L. Wright studio reproduced in Frank Lloyd Wright Drawings by Bruce Brooks Pfeiffer. New York: Harry N. Abrams, Inc.

Page 168   9-7   Based on original drawing by Leigh Ishida and Chris Reinhart

Page 171   9-9   Based on original drawing by Lisa Haggerty and Randy Walker

Page 189   10-8   Original drawing by Mike Bartlein

End Notes

Chapter 1

1. Wright, Frank Lloyd. 1936. Recollections. The United States: 1893-1920. *Architect's Journal of London:* July16-August 6, quoted in Kaufmann, Edgar Jr., ed. 1955. *Frank Lloyd Wright: An American Architecture.* Horizon Press; p. 258

2. Storrer, William Allin. 1978. *The Architecture of Frank Lloyd Wright, A Complete Catalog.* Cambridge MA: The MIT Press; Introduction

3. For a discussion of this term and its meaning see Herdeg, Klaus. 1983. *The Decorated Diagram: Harvard Architecture and the Failure of the Bauhaus Legacy.* Cambridge, MA: MIT Press

4. Wright, Frank Lloyd. 1955. Faith in Your Own Individuality. *House Beautiful* November: 270-271

5. Scott, Geoffrey. 1974. *The Architecture of Humanism* . New York: W.W. Norton & Company, Inc.; see especially chapter 6, "The Biological Fallacy"

6. Wright, Frank Lloyd. 1953. *The Future of Architecture.* New York: Horizon Press

7. Wright, Frank Lloyd. 1953. *The Future of Architecture.* New York: Horizon Press

8. Wright, Frank Lloyd. 1953. *The Future of Architecture.* New York: Horizon Press

9. Wright, Frank Lloyd. 1953. *The Future of Architecture.* New York: Horizon Press

10. Wright, Frank Lloyd. 1953. *The Future of Architecture.* New York: Horizon Press, quoted from Sergeant, John. 1976. *Frank Lloyd Wright's Usonian Houses: The Case for Organic Architecture.* New York: Whitney Library of Design, p. 220

11. See Feldman, Edmund B. 1967. *Art as Image and Idea.* Englewood Cliffs, NJ: Prentice-Hall, Inc.

12. Thompson, D'Arcy, *On Growth and Form.* 1952. J.T. Bonner, ed. (abridged edition) Cambridge, England: Cambridge University Press

13. Rittle, Horst. 1970. Some Principles for the Design of an Educational System for Design. Part 1, *DMG Newsletter.* December

14. See Colquhoun, Alan. 1969. Typology and the Design Method. *Perspecta* 12:71-74; and Moneo, Rafael. 1978. On Typology. *Oppositions* 13:23-45

Chapter 2

1. Pfeiffer, Bruce Brooks, and Nordland, G. eds. 1988. *Frank Lloyd Wright: In the Realm of Ideas.* Carbondale, IL: Southern Illinois University Press; p.165

2. For an opposing point of view see Smith, Norris Kelly. 1966. *Frank Lloyd Wright: A Study in Architectural Content.* Englewood Cliffs, N.J.: Prentice Hall, Inc.

3. Wright, Frank Lloyd. 1943. *An Autobiography.* New York: Horizon Press quoted in Broadbent, Geoffrey. 1973. *Design in Architecture.* London: John Wiley & Sons, Ltd. p. 42

4. Scully, Vincent. 1960. *Frank Lloyd Wright.* New York: George Braziller, Inc. p. 13

5. Wright, Frank Lloyd, *A Testament*, Horizon Press, 1957, quoted in Kaufmann, Edgar Jr. and Raeburn, Ben, eds. 1964. *Frank Lloyd Wright: Writings and Buildings.* New York: Meridian Books; pp. 18, 19

6. Wright, Frank Lloyd. 1943. *An Autobiography.* New York: Horizon Press; p. 75

7. Jones, Owen. 1856. *The Grammar of Ornament.* London: Day and Sons; p. 73

8. Beeby, Thomas H. 1977. The Grammar of Ornament/Ornament as Grammar. *Via III Ornament* 3:10-28 p. 20

9. Violllet-le-Duc, Eugene-Emmanuel. 1879. *Discourses on Architecture,* translated by Henry Van Brunt, Boston. Quoted in Hoffmann, Donald. 1969. Frank Lloyd Wright and Viollet-le-Duc. *Journal of the Architectural Historians* 28(3):176, 177

10. Wright, Frank Lloyd. 1908. In the Cause of Architecture. Quoted in Wijdeveld, Henricus T. ed. 1925. *The Life Work of the American Architect, Frank Lloyd Wright*, Santpoort Holland: Wendingen, p.18,19

11. See Hitchcock, Henry-Russell. 1944. Frank Lloyd Wright and the 'Academic Tradition' of the Early Eighteen-Nineties. *Journal of the Warburg and Courtauld Institutes* 7(1-2):46-63.

Chapter 3

1. The following provide an exhaustive chronology of Wright's work: Wright, Olgivanna Lloyd. 1966. *Frank Lloyd Wright: His Life, His Work, His Words.* New York: Horizon Press; Storrer, William Allin. 1978. *The Architecture of Frank Lloyd Wright, A Complete Catalog.* Cambridge MA: MIT Press

2. See Wright, Frank Lloyd. 1928. In the Cause of Architecture: The Logic of the Plan. *The Architectural Record.* February:49-57

3. Eliade, Mircea. 1957. *The Sacred & the Profane: The Nature of Religion.* (translated by Willard R. Trask). San Diego: Harcourt Brace Jovanovich; see especially chapter 1

4. Smith, Norris Kelly. 1966. *Frank Lloyd Wright: A Study in Architectural Content.* Englewood Cliffs, N.J.: Prenctice Hall; p. 77

5. Rowe, Colin. 1978. Character and Composition. In *Mathematics of the Ideal Villa and Other Essays.* Cambridge, MA: MIT Press; pp. 60-87

6. Rowe quotes Wright as saying "composition is dead," p. 78 (above reference)

7. Levine, Neil. 1982. Frank Lloyd Wright's Diagonal Planning. In *In Search of Modern Architecture: A Tribute to Henry-Russell Hitchcock*, Searing, Helen, ed. Cambridge, MA: MIT Press

Chapter 4

1. See Wright, Frank Lloyd. 1901. A Home in a Prairie Town. *Ladies' Home Journal* 18 February:17; and Wright, Frank Lloyd. 1901. A Small House with 'Lots of Room in It'. *Ladies' Home Journal* 18 July:15

2. Wright, Frank Lloyd. 1908. In the Cause of Architecture. *Architectural Record* 23:155-222, quoted in Sergeant, John. 1976. *Frank Lloyd Wright's Usonian Houses: the Case for Organic Architecture.* New York: Whitney Library of Design

3. Wright, Frank Lloyd. 1925. In the Cause of Architecture in *The Life Work of the American Architect, Frank Lloyd Wright*, p.20-21, Wijdeveld, Henricus T. ed. Santpoort Holland: Wendingen

4. From Emerson's essay, Self Reliance, discussed in Smith, Norris Kelly. 1966. *Frank Lloyd Wright: A Study in Architectural Content.* Englewood Cliffs, N.J.: Prenctice Hall, Inc.

5. This term is borrowed from Reyner Banham's article; see Banham, Reyner. 1969. The Wilderness Years of Frank Lloyd Wright. *Journal of the Royal Institute of British Architects* 76:512-519

6. See both Manson, Grant Carpenter. 1958. *Frank Lloyd Wright to 1910, The First Golden Age.* New York: Van Nostrand Reinhold Company, and Nute, K. Horwood. 1990. Frank Lloyd Wright & the Arts of Japan. *Architecture + Urbanism* February:26-33

7. Viollet-le-Duc, Eugene-Emmanuel. 1876, (Facsimile) *The Habitations of Man In All Ages.* translated by Benjamin Bucknall. Ann Arbor, MI: Gryphon Books; pp. 29, 30

8. Scully, Vincent. 1960. *Frank Lloyd Wright.* New York: George Braziller, (See especially pages 17 and 18)

9. Manson, Grant Carpenter. 1958. *Frank Lloyd Wright to 1910, The First Golden Age.* New York: Van Nostrand Reinhold Company; pp. 99-137

10. Wright, Frank Lloyd. 1938.*The Architectural Forum* from Kaufmann, Edgar, Jr. and Raeburn, Ben., eds. 1964. *Frank Lloyd Wright: Writings and Buildings.* New York: Meridian Books; p. 276

11. See Levine, Neil. 1982. Frank Lloyd Wright's Diagonal Planning. in Helen Searing, ed., *In Search of Modern Architecture: A Tribute to Henry-Russell Hitchcock*, Cambridge, MA: MIT Press. The angle was no doubt suggested by the earlier wooden bridge as well.

12. See both Connors, Joseph. 1984. *The Robie House of Frank Lloyd Wright.* Chicago: University of Chicago Press, and Hoffmann, Donald. 1984. *Frank Lloyd Wright's Robie House.* New York:Dover

Chapter 5

1. See Brooks, H. Allen. 1979. Wright and the Destruction of the box. *Journal of the Society of Architectural Historians* 38 (1):7-14

2. See Okakura, Kakuzo. 1964. *The Book of Tea.* New York Dover (originally published 1904, New York:Fos, Duffield & Co.).

3. See Sergeant, John. 1976. *Frank Lloyd Wright's Usonian Houses: The Case for Organic Architecture.* New York: Whitney Library of Design; p. 76

4. Sullivan, Louis H. 1924. *System of Architectural Ornament.* New York: Press of the American Institute of Architects, Inc.; plate 5

5. Wright, Frank Lloyd. 1925. In the Cause of Architecture. The Third Dimension. Quoted in Wijdeveld, Henricus T., ed. 1925. *The Life Work of the American Architect, Frank Lloyd Wright*, Santpoort Holland: Wendingen. p. 57

6. See pivotal essays by MacCormac, Richard C. 1968. The Anatomy of Wright's Aesthetic. *Architectural Review* 143:143-146; and MacCormac, Richard C. 1974. Froebel's Kindergarten Training and the Early Work of Frank Lloyd Wright. *Environment and Planning B*, 1:29-50

7. See Spencer, Herbert. 1864. *Principles of Biology.*

8. Alberti, L. B. 1966. *Ten Books on Architecture.* New York: Transatlantic Arts; and Wittkower, Rudolph. 1952. *Architectural Principles in the Age of Humanism.* London: Tiranti

9. Wright, Frank Lloyd. 1908. In the Cause of Architecture. Quoted in Wijdeveld, Henricus T., ed. 1925. *The Life Work of the American Architect, Frank Lloyd Wright*, Santpoort Holland:Wendingen. pp. 18-19

10. Wright, Frank Lloyd. 1910. *Ausgefuhrte Bauten und Entwurfe von Frank Lloyd Wright.* Berlin: Ernst Wasmuth. There is a partial elevation of the Winslow House.

11. Hitchcock, Henry-Russell. 1942. *In The Nature of Materials. The Buildings of Frank Lloyd Wright, 1887-1941.* New York: Duell, Sloan, and Pearce (the McCormick Residence is figure 139)

Chapter 6

1. For the exception, see Jordy, William. 1972. The Impact of European Modernism in the Mid-Twentieth Century. pp. 279-359, *American Buildings and Their Architects.* New York, Oxford: Oxford University Press

2. See Banham, Reyner. 1960. *Theory and Design in the First Machine Age.* London: The Architectural Press; p. 145, 146

Chapter 7

1. Rowe, Colin. 1978. Chicago Frame, pp. 90-117 In *Mathematics of the Ideal Villa and Other Essays.* Cambridge, MA: MIT Press (see especially pp. 93-98)

2. Mostoller, Michael. 1985. The Towers of Frank Lloyd Wright. *The Journal of Architectural Education* 38(2):13-17

3. Wright, Frank Lloyd. 1943. *An Autobiography.* New York: Horizon Press.

4. Manson, Grant Carpenter. 1958. *Frank Lloyd Wright to 1910, The First Golden Age.* New York: Van Nostrand Reinhold Company; p. 206; see also Wright, Frank Lloyd. 1916. A Non-Competitive Plan. *City Residential Land Development..* Alfred Yeomans, ed., University of Chicago Press. pp. 95-102

Chapter 8

1. Tselos, D. T. 1953. Exotic Influences in the Architecture of Frank Lloyd Wright. *Magazine of Art* 47(4):160-169, 184

2. Banham, Reyner. 1969. The Wilderness Years of Frank Lloyd Wright. *Journal of the Royal Institute of British Architects* 76:512-519

3. See Creese, Walter L. 1985. *The Crowning of the American Landscape: Eight Great Spaces and Their Buildings.* Princeton, NJ: Princeton Univeristy Press; see Jefferson's Charlottesville, pp. 29-42, and Wright's Taliesin and Beyond, pp. 241-165

4. Wright, Frank Lloyd. 1943. *An Autobiography.* New York: Horizon Press; p. 309

5. Hoesli, Bernhard. 1968. *Transparenz.* Basel und Stuttgart: Birkhauser Verlag

6. Banham, Reyner. 1969. The Wilderness Years of Frank Lloyd Wright. *Journal of the Royal Institute of British Architects* 76:512-519

Chapter 9

1. In Wright's "Reply to Mr. Sturgis' Criticism" on the Larkin Building, from In Cause of Architecture (Buffalo, New York, April 1909; cited in Quinan, Jack. 1987. *Frank Lloyd Wright's Larkin Building, Myth and Fact.* Cambridge, MA: The MIT Press; p. 167

2. For similar comparisons see Hanks, David A. 1979. *The Decorative Designs of Frank Loyd Wright,* New York: E.P. Dutton

3. See Menocal, Narciso. 1983-84. Form and Content in Frank Lloyd Wright's 'Tree of Life' Window. *Bulletin of the Elvehjem Museum of Art;* and Castex, Jean. 1985. *Frank Lloyd Wright, le Printemps de la Prarie House.* Pierre Mardaga, editeur.Bruxelles.

4. See Brooks, H. Allen. 1979. Wright and the Destruction of the Box. *Journal of the Society of Architectural Historians* 38 (1):7-14

Chapter 10

1. See Hall, Edward T. 1966. *The Hidden Dimension.* Garden City, NY: Doubleday

2. Moneo, Rafael. 1978. On Typology. *Oppositions* 13:23-45.

References

Alberti, L. B. 1966. *Ten Books on Architecture.* New York: Transatlantic Arts

Banham, Reyner. 1960. *Theory and Design in the First Machine Age.* London: The Architectural Press

Banham, Reyner. 1969. The Wilderness Years of Frank Lloyd Wright. *Journal of the Royal Institute of British Architects* 76:512-519

Banham, Reyner. 1969. *The Architecture of the Well-Tempered Environment.* London: The Architectural Press

Beeby, Thomas H. 1977. The Grammar of Ornament/ Ornament as Grammar. *Via III Ornament* 3:10-28

Beeby, Thomas H. 1980-81. Song of Taliesin. *Modulus* , pp. 3-11

Boelte, M.K. and Drauss, J. 1877. *The Kindergarten Guide, An Illustrated Handbook Designed for the Self-Instruction of Kindergartners, Mothers and Nurses.* New York: E. Steiger

Broadbent, Geoffrey. 1973. *Design in Architecture.* London: John Wiley & Sons, Ltd.

Brooks, H. Allen. 1979. Wright and the Destruction of the Box *Journal of the Society of Architectural Historians* 38 (1):7-14

Brooks, H. Allen. 1981. *Writings on Wright.* Cambridge, MA: MIT Press

Calvo, Charles. 1985-1986. The Concrete Block Designs of Frank LLoyd Wrighf. *Forum voor architectuur en daarmee verbonden kunsten* 30(4):166-175

Castex, Jean. 1985. *Frank Lloyd Wright, le Printemps de la Prarie House.* Bruxelles: Pierre Mardaga editeur

Clark, Roger H. and Pause, Michael. 1985. *Precedents in Architecture.* New York: Van Nostrand Reinhold

Colquhoun, Alan. 1969. Typology and the Design Method. *Perspecta* 12:71-74

Connors, Joseph. 1984. *The Robie House of Frank Lloyd Wright.* Chicago: University of Chicago Press

Creese, Walter L. 1985. The Crowning of the American Landscape: *Eight Great Spaces and Their Buildings.* Princeton, NJ: Princeton Univeristy Press

Drexler, Arthur. ed. 1962. *The Drawings of Frank Lloyd Wright.* New York: Horizon Press

Eliade, Mircea. 1957. *The Sacred & the Profane: The Nature of Religion.* (trans. by Willard R. Trask). San Diego: Harcourt Brace Jovanovich

Froebel, Friedrich. 1898. *Selected Writings.* ed. I.M. Lilley, New York

Feldman, Edmund B. 1967. *Art as Image and Idea.* Englewood Cliffs, NJ: Prentice-Hall, Inc.

Fries, Heinrich de. ed. 1926. *Frank Lloyd Wright; Aus dem Lebenswerke eines Architekten.* Berlin: Wasmuth

Gill, Brendan. 1987. *The Many Masks of Frank Lloyd Wright.* New York: Putnam

Gorlin, Alexander C. 1982. Geometry in the Work of Frank Lloyd Wright. *Architecture + Urbanism* :February:55-62

Graf, Otto. 1983. *Die Kunst des Quadrats*, Vienna: Herman Bohlaus

Gutheim, Frederick. ed. 1941. Frank Lloyd Wright on Architecture. New York: Duell, Slone & Pearce

Hall, Edward T. 1966. *The Hidden Dimension.* Garden City, NY: Doubleday

Hanks, David A. 1979. *The Decorative Designs of Frank Loyd Wright,* New York: E.P. Dutton

Haraguchi, Hideaki. 1983. A Comparative Analysis of 20th-Century Houses. New York: Rizzoli

Herdeg, Klaus. 1983. *The Decorated Diagram: Harvard Architecture and the Failure of the Bauhaus Legacy.* Cambridge, MA: MIT Press

Hitchcock, Henry-Russell. 1942. *In The Nature of Materials. The Buildings of Frank Lloyd Wright, 1887-1941.* New York: Duell, Sloan, and Pearce

Hitchcock, Henry-Russell. 1944. Frank Lloyd Wright and the 'Academic Tradition' of the Early Eighteen-Nineties. *Journal of the Warburg and Courtauld Institutes* 7(1-2):46-63.

Hoesli, Bernhard. 1968. *Transparenz.* Basel und Stuttgart: Birkhauser Verlag

Hoffmann, Donald. 1978. *Frank Lloyd Wright's Fallingwater.* New York: Dover

Hoffmann, Donald. 1984. *Frank Lloyd Wright's Robie House.* New York:Dover

Hoffmann, Donald. 1969. Frank Lloyd Wright and Viollet-le-Duc. *Journal of the Architectural Historians* 28(3):173-183.

Jacobs, Herbert. 1978. *Building with Frank Lloyd Wright.* Carbondale, IL: Southern Illinois Univeristy Press

Jones, Owen. 1856. *The Grammar of Ornament.* London: Day and Sons

Jordy, William. 1972. Chapter V, The Impact of European Modernism in the Mid-Twentieth Century. pp.279-359 *American Buildings and Their Architects.* New York, Oxford: Oxford University Press

Kaufmann, Edgar Jr. 1986. *Fallingwater.* New York: Abbeville

Kaufmann, Edgar Jr. ed. 1955. *Frank Lloyd Wright: An American Architecture.* Horizon Press

Kaufmann, Edgar Jr. and Raeburn, Ben. eds. 1964. *Frank Lloyd Wright: Writings and Buildings.* New York: Meridian Books

Koning, H. and Eizenberg, J. 1981. The Language of the Prairie: Frank Lloyd Wright's Prairie House. *Environment and Planning B* 8:295-323

Lawlor, Robert. 1982 Sacred Geometry, Thames and Hudson

Levine, Neil. 1982. Frank Lloyd Wright's Diagonal Planning. in Helen Searing, ed., *In Search of Modern Architecture: A Tribute to Henry-Russell Hitchcock*, Cambridge, MA: MIT Press

Lipman, Jonathan. 1986. *Frank Loyd Wright and the Johnson Wax Buildings.* New York: Rizzoli

MacCormac, Richard C. 1968. The Anatomy of Wright's Aesthetic. *Architectural Review* 143:143-146

MacCormac, Richard C. 1974. Froebel's Kindergarten Training and the Early Work of Frank Lloyd Wright. *Environment and Planning B,* 1:29-50

Manson, Grant Carpenter. 1958. *Frank Lloyd Wright to 1910, The First Golden Age.* New York: Van Nostrand Reinhold Company

March, Lionel and Steadman, Phillip. 1971. *The geometry of environment.* London: RIBA Publications Ltd.

Menocal, Narciso. 1983-84. Form and Content in Frank Lloyd Wright's 'Tree of Life' Window. *Bulletin of the Elvehjem Museum of Art*

Mitchell, William J. 1990. *The Logic of Architecture.* Cambridge MA: The MIT Press

Mostoller, Michael. 1985. The Towers of Frank Lloyd Wright. *The Journal of Architectural Education* 38(2):13-17,

Moneo, Rafael. 1978. On Typology. *Oppositions* 13:23-45.

Nute, K. Horwood. 1990. Frank Lloyd Wright & the Arts of Japan. *Architecture + Urbanism* February:26-33

O'Gorman, James F. 1969. Henry Hobson Richardson and Frank Lloyd Wright. *The Art Quarterly* 32(3):292-315

Okakura, Kakuzo. 1964. *The Book of Tea.* New York: Fos, Duffield & Co., 1906;

republished 1964 New York: Dover Publications

Pfeiffer, Bruce Brooks1986-88. *Frank Lloyd Wright Monograph* (12 Volumes). Tokyo: A.D.A. Edita

Pfeiffer, Bruce Brooks and Nordland, G. eds. 1988. *Frank Lloyd Wright: In the Realm of Ideas.* Carbondale, IL: Southern Illinois University Press

Quinan, Jack. 1987. *Frank Loyd Wright's Larkin Building, Myth and Fact.* Cambridge, MA: The MIT Press

Rittle, Horst. 1970. Some Principles for the Design of an Educational System for Design. Part 1 *DMG Newsletter.* December:1970.

Rowe, Colin. 1978. *Mathematics of the Ideal Villa and Other Essays.* Cambridge, MA: MIT Press

Scott, Geoffrey. 1974. *The Architecture of Humanism .* New York: W.W. Norton & Company, Inc.

Scully, Vincent. 1960. *Frank Lloyd Wright.* New York: George Braziller, Inc.

Scully, Vincent 1955. *The Shingle Syle: Architectureal Theory and Design from Richardson to the Origins of Wright.* New Haven and London: Yale Univeristy Press

Sergeant, John. 1976. *Frank Lloyd Wright's Usonian Houses: the Case for Organic Architecture.* New York: Whitney Library of Design

Smith, Norris Kelly. 1966. *Frank Lloyd Wright: A Study in Architectural Content.* Englewood Cliffs, N.J.: Prenctice Hall

Spencer, Herbert. 1864 *Principles of Biology*

Storrer, William Allin. 1978. *The Architecture of Frank Lloyd Wright, A Complete Catalog.* Cambridge MA: The MIT Press

Sturgis, Russel. 1905 *A Dictionary of Architecture and Building.* (3 vols.) New York: The Macmillan Co.

Sullivan, Louis H. 1924. *System of Architectural Ornament.* New York: Press of the American Institute of Architects, Inc.

Sweeney, Robert L., and Calvo, Charles M. 1984. Frank Lloyd Wright: Textile Block Houses.*Space Design* 240:63-78

Thompson, D'Arcy, *On Growth and Form.* 1952. J.T. Bonner ed. (abridged edition) Cambridge, England: Cambridge University Press

Tice, James 1981. The Los Angeles Concrete Block Houses of Frank Lloyd Wright. *Architectural Design.* Aug./Sept: 1981

Tice, James. 1989. The Concrete Block Houses of Frank Lloyd Wright: Plastic Idea vs. Pragmatic Fact. *Symposium on Architecture and ACSA Technology Conference '89,* Office of Building research, School of Architecture, Louisiana State University

Tselos, D. T. 1953. Exotic Influences in the Architecture of Frank Lloyd Wright. *Magazine of Art.* 47(4):160-169, 184

Tufte, Edward R. 1990. *Envisioning Information.* Cheshire, Connecticut: Graphics Press,

Tufte, Edward R. 1983. *The Visual Display of Quantitative Information.* Cheshire, Connecticut, Graphics Press

Twombly, Robert C. 1979. *Frank Lloyd Wright: His Life and His Architecture.* New York: John Wiley & Sons

Viollet-le-Duc, Eugene-Emmanuel. 1876 (Fac) *The Habitations of Man In All Ages.* trans by Benjamin Bucknall. Ann Arbor, MI: Gryphon Books

Wijdeveld, Henricus T. ed. 1925. *The Life Work of the American Architect, Frank Lloyd Wright,* Santpoort, Holland

Wittkower, Rudolph. 1952. *Architectural Principles in the Age of Humanism.* London: Tiranti

Wright, Olgivanna Lloyd. 1966. *Frank Lloyd Wright: His Life, His Work, His Words.* New York: Horizon Press

Books and Essays by Frank Lloyd Wright

Wright, Frank Lloyd. 1928. In the Cause of Architecture: The Logic of the Plan. *The Architectural Record.* 49-57 [9 essays from May 1927 to December 1928]

Wright, Frank Lloyd. 1955. Faith in Your Own Individuality. *House Beautiful* November:270-271

Wright, Frank Lloyd, *A Testament,* Horizon Press, 1957

Wright, Frank Lloyd. 1958. *The Living City.* New American Library

Wright, Frank Lloyd. 1953. *The Future of Architecture.* New York: Horizon Press

Wright, Frank Lloyd. 1909. Reply to Mr. Sturgis's Criticism. *In the Cause of Architecture.* April. Buffalo, NY

Wright, Frank Lloyd. 1943. *An Autobiography.* New York: Horizon Press

Wright, Frank Lloyd. 1910. *Ausgefuhrte Bauten und Entwurfe von Frank Lloyd Wright.* Berlin: Ernst Wasmuth

Wright, Frank Lloyd. 1954. *The Natural House,* New York: Horizon Press

Wright, Frank Lloyd. 1967. *Modern Architecture.* Carbondale, IL: Southern Illinois University Press

Wright, Frank Lloyd. 1956. *The Story of the Tower.* New York: Horizon Press

Wright, Frank Lloyd. 1931. *Modern Architecture.* (Kahn Lectures for 1930) Princeton: Princeton University Press 1931

Wright, Frank Lloyd. 1939. *An Organic Architecture: The Architecture of Democracy.* London

Wright, Frank Lloyd. 1916. A Non-Competitive Plan. *City Residential Land Development..* Alfred Yeomans ed. University of Chicago Press. pp.95-102

Index